APPS
THE ACTIVE-PASSIVE PERSONALITY SYNDROME

Why Liberals and Conservatives Believe and Behave the Way They Do

By
Marilyn MacGruder Barnewall

STONEWALL PRESS
PAVING YOUR WAY TO SUCCESS

Copyright © 2018 by Marilyn MacGruder Barnewall.

All rights reserved. No part of this publication may be reproduced, distributed, or transmitted in any form or by any means, including photocopying, recording, or other electronic or mechanical methods, without the prior written permission of the author, except in the case of brief quotations embodied in critical reviews and certain other noncommercial uses permitted by copyright law.

Printed in the United States of America

ISBN: Paperback: 978-1-949362-05-3
ISBN: eBook: 978-1-949362-04-6

Library of Congress Control Number:2018949740

STONEWALL PRESS
PAVING YOUR WAY TO SUCCESS

Stonewall Press
363 Paladium Court
Owings Mills, MD 21117
www.stonewallpress.com
1-888-334-0980

CONTENTS

DEDICATION v
PREFACE vii

CHAPTER 1   What is APPS? What is Wealth? What is Profit?.. 1
CHAPTER 2   Misperceptions of the World........................... 17
CHAPTER 3   FINDING THE APP (ACTIVE-PASSIVE PERSONALITIES) 33
CHAPTER 4   Psychologist/Psychiatrist Evaluate APPS...... 53
CHAPTER 5   Opposing Forces, Unhealthy Extremes 71
CHAPTER 6   THE PURPOSE OF WEALTH 85
CHAPTER 7   APPS, The United States, and Economic Cycles 99
CHAPTER 8   America's Fifty Year Economic Cycles.......... 111
CHAPTER 9   Active Investors: Political Conservatives................................. 125
CHAPTER 10 It's Not Nice to Fool Mother Nature 141
CHAPTER 11 Conservatives: the Media and Social Involvement 157
CHAPTER 12 Observable Passive Liberal Beliefs 177
CHAPTER 13 Passive Security and Power Drives 191
CHAPTER 14 Social Values... 211
CHAPTER 15 Relativism and Our Corporations, Our Courts, Our Churches, Our Families...... 227
CHAPTER 16 Women and Their Place in the World Are Women Passive or Active?.................... 243
CHAPTER 17 Women: A Natural Inclination to... What? 261

DEDICATION

It is with humility and joy that I dedicate this book to my dear friends Bonnie and Harry Talbott. Without their encouragement, I would have continued to sit on this important information at a time when our nation is in dire need of it. There are others to thank... Larry and Jo Pierce who read the original outline and Michelle Smallback, a very talented writer who did a wonderful job of editing. Their faith in this work strengthened my own. Along with a new President in 2016 who rejects the concept of political correctness, I overcame the fear of making the data available to the general public.

PREFACE

Society gets opportunities once in a while to self-correct, to right some wrongs, to change direction.

In the history of the cycles of culture and society, once in a while a revolution can occur. Sometimes an awakening happens, a new trend of thinking, acting or reacting catches on and the momentum is shifted. When such changes pop up on the scenery, it's best to grab hold of them before they dissipate. Sometimes we don't get another chance for positive changes to trend.

Marilyn Barnewall's book, *The Active-Passive Personality Syndrome* (APPS), is such an opportunity.

America has been sailing along in the current societal and political veins since World War II, and we the people really don't know how the course got changed. We just know it changed. Most Americans over age 50 say they no longer recognize their country. The change came so gradually that many people did not think much about it until power abuses became so apparent. For example, according to many politicians who write laws that govern us, illegal aliens are entitled to rights not available to American citizens. Members of one race are pitted against another race by politicians who gain voting blocs by encouraging SUCH hatred and do so because they are impressed with their power of position. Today's behavior suddenly surpasses our views of a society to which we want to belong.

The Active-Passive Personality Syndrome explains why we all have personality traits of which we are unaware – traits that allowed America to go off course and almost destroy herself.

Marilyn entered the scene in America when industries were changing, traditions were shifting, and mindsets were being challenged. She entered a work place where women were practically foreigners and the banking industry was groaning for change. She put herself through college while working as a single mom. She was familiar with hardship and government assistance. She achieved her graduate degree at age 40. She watched, she worked and she learned, eventually landing the prestigious role of Vice-President of United Bank of Denver. Marilyn launched a research initiative that spanned two decades and five thousand participants and her findings were so significant they changed the banking industry and catapulted her to start a consulting business with bank clients around the world. Her findings, published by the American Bankers Association in 1986, in a book that sold for $5000 per copy and her follow-up work was published in a book that sold for $2000. These aren't small accomplishments.

While her findings proved consequential to the banking industry, her insights reverberated to the realm of personality. After retirement, she sifted through the data and findings and was surprised to find the same identifiers that emerged for banking preferences permeated the entire personality and had profound political, economical and social implications. This is why this book is so important. This is why we should read it, study it, study ourselves, and apply it to our own lives. It is the reason an economic turnaround is happening under the Trump administration and it is the reason we should set ourselves to learn and understand the Active-Passive concept. It has everything to do with where we've been, and it has the keys to unlocking a better place of where we can choose to go. It has the potential to turn certain cataclysmic social and political events in our nation away from the ledge; and it has the potential to restore balance in an otherwise out of balance culture.

As the great American industrialist Charles R. Hook once said, "The great need today in every phase of our social, economical and political life is understanding. It has always been so, but today the need is even greater." This book is the tool for greater understanding that can help us personally, socially and nationally. Let's not miss the opportunities it affords us.

Michelle Smallback

CHAPTER 1

WHAT IS APPS? WHAT IS WEALTH? WHAT IS PROFIT?

Control is exercised behind your own nose.
Power is exercised behind the noses of others.

What is the Active-Passive Personality Syndrome (APPS)?
One definition of energy is power and force.
Without control, how energetic or forceful is power?
That is the conundrum with which I fought for twenty years as I interviewed 5,000 participants in focus group research sessions. It is one of the most difficult questions with which I've wrestled in my years as a consultant for the largest (and some of the smallest) companies around the world.

Because the research occurred over a 20-year period, it was possible to structure the interviews in a way that allowed me to place people in one of two groups: Active or Passive. As one personality trait was discovered, it led to further research about a logical trait that seemed likely to follow.

It may surprise you to learn that this research determined and explains the reasons Actives (who are conservatives) and Passives (who are liberals) behave the way they do politically, socially, within the family structure, and in business.

Your personality, like mine, is made up of different percentages of one group or the other: Active or Passive. This book is about you and why you do the things you choose to do. Almost everything in life is a matter of choice.

From 1972 through 1992, these 5,000 people answered my questions about how well their banks were serving their financial needs. What does finding out about peoples' financial interaction with banks have to do with how people behave politically, socially and personally? Why should that interest you?

Whether taking a risk in life involves a loan or getting married or choosing a political party, my research determined that you will either be comfortable with managing risk or you will be uncomfortable with risk and that can be identified by viewing your personal financial statement. Your investments make clear your comfort with risk. It makes clear whether you are an Active or a Passive. Thus by learning how you invest (or would invest if you had the money), it can be determined if you are Active or Passive because your level of risk tolerance is apparent by the investments you make.

That was a major finding.

Interestingly, the two groups define risk differently. Passives view risk as something one takes. Actives view risk as something one manages.

I was a bank consultant who, as a vice president of Denver's largest bank, had discovered a way to use credit to create wealth rather than ongoing debt. This occurred during the Reagan years and the concept I created was partly responsible for the phenomenal growth of independent businesses during those years. For those who want to start new businesses, it is very difficult to gain access to credit. Whether you need money to buy a small, rundown duplex so you can fix it up and re-sell it or whether you want to borrow money to increase the size of your family-owned bakery, credit is hard for independent investors to get. Why? They borrow for business purposes using personal, not business, assets.

Commercial bankers lend to businesses; personal bankers make loans to individuals. Neither knows much about what the other does or how they do it and lending to a business is very different from lending to an individual. Starting a new business requires knowledge of both personal and business lending because both personal and business assets are involved. I merely figured out a way to make bank credit available to independent businesses and entrepreneurs (or those who want to be either) that made it possible for people to create wealth. We called it wealth creation private banking.

The answers given to my questions and the reasons given to explain why the responders felt as they did, however, provided insights far beyond the banking industry and the world of money. They actually provided answers to the questions all of us no matter how wealthy or poor ask about life. Almost all participants earned their affluence in their own lifetimes. Many participants were poor and started their small businesses in a garage or basement. Only a few participants inherited their fortune or were trust fund kids. The research was done during the 1970s and 80s and high-tech home offices had not yet become a reality in America.

The focus group conversations were spirited, sometimes resulting in arguments among participants. These discussions involved differing philosophies of life and it is from them I developed the concept of Active and Passive investors.

The Active-Passive concept was market tested at banks around the world many times during that 20 years and it always succeeded. It was data from those years that I used to write a book for the American Bankers Association (ABA) in 1986. Copies of the book are housed in the libraries of prestigious universities like Oxford and Cambridge in the United Kingdom.

My book sold only to financial institutions for $5,000 a copy ($3,250 to ABA members) and it sold well. Banks and brokerage houses do not spend that much money for research on subjects that have already been analyzed. This was new data and all copies printed were sold. When my two-year ABA contract was completed,

Profitable Private Banking: The Complete Blueprint was picked up by Lafferty Publications (London/Dublin) and the book was very successfully marketed by them throughout the world – again, only within the financial services industry. My contract with Lafferty was renewed for a third year.

The material contained in this book has never before been sold to the public nor was it included in the book about banking. This book applies research responses to personal lifestyle choices rather than financial behavior. The research found that a human being's comfort level in dealing with financial risk accurately predicts our comfort level in dealing with life. That, in turn, predicts personality traits and resultant development and behavior.

Michael Lafferty, President and CEO of Lafferty Publications (London/Dublin) at the time, is one of the brightest and most dynamic men I know. He's an idea guy and understood the concept that was emerging from all of my research interviews. Among other places, he arranged for me to speak about this concept in Toronto, Sydney, London, and Zurich. The book became a topic of conversation within the financial services community and in 1991 I was asked to teach a course about it in Singapore. I also taught wealth creation private banking for the American Bankers Association at the University of Colorado.

It is from the 1972-1992 research data the material for this book is taken. In the first five chapters of this book you will hear the terms "Active Investor" or "Active/Self Investor," and "Passive Investor" or "Passive/Market Investor." The research data for the ABA book was done from 1972-1985.

The purpose of this book is to explain how these two groups were identified, why the names "Active" and "Passive" were chosen to describe each group, why it is important for you to understand it, and what you will gain if you do. Even more important is what society will gain.

The term "investor" is *not* used because my research was done on behalf of the banking industry. It is used because when people allocate personal assets, they invest a broad range of things: Time, energy, creativity, hopes, dreams... and money. Whether large or small, whether financial or personal, whether seeking bank loans or buying a pound of bacon, people invest their assets. We invest when we choose careers. When we vote, we are investors. When we buy a home, we are investors. When we choose a spouse, have children, send them to school, or plan a vacation, we invest our human assets. That is why the word investor is used.

Also in this book the word "wealth" defines intellectual, spiritual, and social, plus monetary substance. Words like "rich" and "affluent" and "profit" reference monetary success. Thus, people whose income places them below the poverty line may be wealthy in ways far beyond those who merely possess money. They may have spiritual wealth or personal wealth gained from a happy marriage. Or they may help the disadvantaged. Though wealth may include monetary success, it also includes character and intellect and social and spiritual values.

Wealth is more than just money. In this book, the words rich, affluence and profits reference money. A person who has learned a job working at it for twenty years has wealth. He or she has gained experience and knowledge. By contrast, a recent college graduate has learned the theory of the job. He has profited from education and has gained future income. He has gained information but has yet to gain knowledge. Education equals profit potential; experience equals wealth accumulation.

This is a key. We have all been indoctrinated to think wealth and money is the same thing. Having wealth and being affluent (or rich or profitable) are different things. The poorest person may have great wealth but no money. The richest person may have a large bank balance but not have wealth, just profit.

I coined the term "Active self investor" to describe the complexities of wealth/job creators. It explains how they achieve wealth ... by investing in themselves and by placing at risk their own assets. The word "wealth" is used to describe Actives because they create companies, risking their own money, to provide jobs for others. When you make it possible for others to enjoy profit, you have created wealth within the total community. Actives start independent businesses that employ people. At least 70 percent of working Americans are employed by independent businesses and are responsible for the vast majority of new jobs each year. It is why that segment of the business community is so important to the economies of our nation.

I coined the term "Passive market investor" to describe the complexities of profit managers and money preservers. It explains how this group achieves affluence ... by investing in publicly traded products available in any market: the stock market, the bond market, the mutual funds market, precious metals, currencies, partnerships, etc. They are most often employed by companies funded by others, not themselves – big companies like airlines, internet companies, energy companies, and other national and international companies funded by stockholders, not by their own personal assets.

Pirelli Tires once said in a great advertisement, "Without control, power is meaningless." If you think about it, power infers force; control implies choice.

What are these differences between power and control?

These two words are misunderstood and yet my research proves beyond a doubt that they are two of the most basic personality traits ingrained in human beings. It is, I found, the reason liberals do not understand conservatives and conservatives do not understand liberals. It is the reason the non-productive do not understand the value of productivity... the reason atheists do not understand the value of faith in God. It is why non-victims do not understand victimizers or the victimized.

Why do I say that?

We often read or hear stories about how someone "tries to control someone else." One does not control others; one exercises power over them, thus "controlling" them. The words "control" and "controlling" are quite different in meaning. The only person over whom you can exercise control is yourself ... your kids, too, sometimes (rarely your spouse).

Think about it for a minute. If a person comes to you and demands you do something you really don't want to do, what might cause you to do it?

If the person making the demand is your boss (power in the workplace) or a family member (the power of love) or someone with the authority to harm you in some way (the power of position), you may do what you really do not want to do. If a person holds no power over you and makes such a demand, you are likely to tell them to go to an unpleasant place or do something to themselves it is impossible to do.

One of the biggest things I learned from interviewing 5,000 people about how they react to specific life circumstances is that personal control occurs behind one's own nose. Power is exercised behind the noses of others and is usually impersonal.

What is power, you may ask, if not the ability to manipulate the behavior of others by controlling them? Power is the ability to control the behavior of others. So, "power" really is an exercise of "control, after all?

"No," I reply. "The word 'controlling' is not synonymous with 'control.' To be controlling is to 'exercise power' and that turns the word 'control' into a verb (controlling) rather than a noun (control). The limits of power, when exercised, can only be extended as far as the controlling person's power base reaches into the controlled person's comfort level.

People in positions of power may be total wimps, personally. All one needs to exercise influence is the power of position. They do not have to be personally strong or influential. Is the Internal Revenue Service agent who audits your tax return personally influential and powerful? It is highly unlikely. Yet, when he or she requests you to spend hours upon hours going through files to identify receipts, you do it. That is the "power of position." That IRS agent is controlling you, manipulating your behavior ... exercising his or her power of position.

I repeat: Power infers force; control implies choice.

Roget's Thesaurus lists synonyms for the word 'control' as: authority, influence, moderation, direction, self-control, restraint, moderate, possess authority, and restrain. There are other words listed, too, but these are the ones that relate most closely with personality.

The synonyms used to describe power are quite different: authoritativeness (as opposed to "authority"), greatness, eloquence, energy, impulse, influence, means, personage, potency, privilege, strength, supremacy.

The difference between the two words sounds like the political environment of the Donald Trump years to date, doesn't it? Actually, it very specifically represents the differences that come close to throwing the total of society into chaos each day.

Looking a little further, my intent with this serious word-play becomes clear. The word "obedience" exemplifies what is meant when the word "power" is applied to human behavior. Going back to my initial example, I refer to how someone "tries to control someone else." In other words, one person forces another into a state of obedience using his or her authority over them. I repeat. This is an exercise of power, not control. It is, however, controlling.

Roget's lists as verbs the following words to describe obedience: obey, mind, heed, keep, observe, listen, comply, conform, stay in line, toe the line, obey the rules, do what one is told, etc.

"You will obey, you will comply, you will acquiesce, you will submit." When one person – or government or employer – uses his or her power to cause another person to modify his or her behavior, it is an exercise of power, not control.

Harvey Weinstein appears to understand the power of position very well, as do numerous other Hollywood personalities – from Oprah Winfrey to Hillary Clinton – who affiliated themselves with him. Many politicians also affiliated with Weinstein.

To understand the differences between conservatives (which my research terms "Actives") and liberals (which my research terms "Passives" whether Republican or Democrat) you must understand the difference between these two words, power and control.

There is far more involved than power and control in these two personality types but these two traits dominate our motivations in life. Here is a basic overview of the traits I identified in all personalities. As Chapter 5 explains, we all have different levels of each group's traits as part of our personalities.

DEFINITION OF A PASSIVE/MARKET INVESTOR: An individual who either inherits or achieves affluence in his or her own lifetime but who *risks the assets of others* – investors, stockholders, partners, taxpayers, family money – to achieve financial objectives. As the term "Market" implies, Passives primarily invest in public offerings... like the stock market, bonds, partnerships, etc.

Passive market investors are risk averse and are motivated by deeply held and hidden fears. It is a primary reason they dislike capitalism which is a risk-management form of economic philosophy. It is also a primary reason they like socialism wherein government theoretically assumes all risk of productivity. The key words to describe Passives are "risk averse." Their hidden fears are often invisible even to the individuals who possess them. All of us harbor fears of which we are consciously unaware.

When you see rioters in the street opposing a politician, public speaker, or other person whose personal philosophies oppose their own, you are observing people motivated by fear who feel they have been pushed into a corner and have no alternative other than violence to be heard. They assume that others, like them, are also motivated by fear and that their violence will frighten these "others" to obey their demands... an exercise of power.

This person's primary drive is to assuage the fears they do not understand... they often are unaware of the fear that causes them to behave as they do. They just know that certain things – like capitalism or Donald Trump or a speaker on a public university campus – make them uncomfortable. Often, they cannot say why.

The Passive personality is developed to support the primary drive... to attain power or access to power so their insecurities can be put to rest. Once a power source is identified, they will either work to attain that power or will support people who have that power to gain access to it. In the view of Passives, the only protection against those who disagree with their need for security is a weapon called "power."

Those who fear managing risk are motivated to gain power because only power can keep the boogie man from under their beds. Those who accept risk management as an interesting challenge are motivated by control which is in direct opposition to those who want to exercise power over them so they will have no control.

Power-motivated profit preservers, asset managers and estate inheritors view the behavior of control-motivated wealth creators as uninformed and naive. They call them extremists and radicals. They use their power base to divide and conquer them. More about that later. The abuses of women by power-driven men (and of men by power-driven women) offer a good example of Passive behavior. I didn't say Democrat behavior, I said Passive behavior. Republicans are part of that ball club too and, as I said, we are all made up of both Active and Passive personality traits. All who are attracted to their positions by the power that flows from the job are Passives. Not all abuse power but the number is higher than a "few."

The products, services, policies and organizational structures at these big companies on which Actives must rely to create wealth are often withheld for no other reason than Passives do not understand what Actives need when managing the risk of creating new wealth. Thus, sometimes for innocent reasons of non-understanding, sometimes for political or ego reasons, Passives stand in the way of Actives who try to do what they are supposed to do: Create the next economy for future generations so ongoing growth can continue.

Few Passives think highly of companies that are small and independent. Why? To Passives, big is good because it is powerful. It is safe and safe means little risk management will be required of them. Big is good because it is compatible with everything from ego need to product and service needs. Big is good because the personalities that dominate big organizations reflect the personalities and lifestyles of Passives. Big organizations are run by Passives for Passives.

DEFINITION OF AN ACTIVE/SELF INVESTOR: An Active individual earns wealth in his or her own lifetime and in the wealth accumulation process *risks his or her personal assets* to achieve financial objectives. Passives do not risk their own assets to achieve affluence; Actives do.

Actives view risk as something to manage rather than a risk to be taken. The entrepreneurs in our focus groups would often say "If I understand the risk..." and would repeat that statement, "... *if I understand it--* and if I decide the risk can be managed, I do it."

Active self investors are good risk managers and have a strong need to control their own destiny.

Wealth creators (conservatives) view profit preserver Passives (liberals) as elitists who believe themselves better equipped than individuals to determine how other people should live and what they should believe. They see the opposing views of Passives as reflective of that group's need for more security and more power (and more and more power) to protect security once it is achieved. They view Passive elitists' relativist philosophies as having no moral value and as being responsible for the moral decline of American culture.

Logically, when your lifestyle is based on risk management it is critical to be able to control the risks you take. This often places Actives in opposition to government, family, church, and other authority figures which are usually motivated by power and want to dictate to them the risks they must take to achieve their objectives. Government, especially, becomes too intrusive in the lives of Actives when they over-regulate the world of business and investment. Or when they over regulate anything, really. When this occurs, job creation within the independent business segment ceases because Actives will not try to manage risks controlled by government. If they cannot control it, Actives won't manage it.

That is what we have witnessed until 2017 when Donald Trump took his Oath of Office as President of the United States. We saw no job growth in the independent business segment under Barack Obama.

Since President Trump has begun the huge process of removing so much regulatory control, job creation within the independent business segment has increased tremendously. Moreover, the unemployment rate for black citizens has dropped to its lowest level in many years. Under the Obama Administration, the black unemployment rate got as high as 16.8 percent. Family income is up for blacks, too. After only 15 months of the Trump presidency, we have the largest employment force in American history. Fewer people receive food stamps than has been true for many years.

The Active person's primary drive is to control their life and their personal destiny. Their personalities require individual freedom because individual control cannot be exercised in an environment driven by group rules and regulations.

Actives are individualists and are usually conservative. Many of them are Libertarians as a result of the move to increase government regulatory controls. Libertarians perceive the new platform of establishment Republicans to be compatible with that of liberal Democrats when it comes to regulating their lives.

Libertarians, however, tend to be the flip side of the liberal Democrat coin. Liberals want all government; Libertarians want none.

An extensive list of personality traits and the jobs to which each group is attracted is provided in Chapter 3.

It will be helpful to read the above definitions several times and become familiar with them before reading further. If you do not familiarize yourself with what the terms mean, you may miss many of the subtle applications of personality traits that were identified by the research which explains why all of us behave as we do.

Few people are totally one or the other – Active or Passive. The personality traits of both groups are explained and why we all have a mixture of both is provided in Chapter 5.

Natural Law accepts that two equally strong but opposing forces result in balance. And, left unfettered, Natural Law is, as usual, correct. Fettered by bank loan policies and government intervention, however, the opposing forces of new wealth must constantly fight – often with the very government they pay to represent them – with the traditionally affluent for their share of access to assets on which all businesses rely for survival. Big companies have a lot more money to spend on lobbyists than do independent business owners.

In his book "Power and Innocence," Dr. Rollo May identifies five different kinds of power. Exploitative power is the most destructive kind and is used to do what the term implies: exploit people. Manipulative power is used to do just that... e.g., use the power of position for the purpose of controlling others. Competitive power can be used negatively in all aspects of life but also applies to one team winning over another. There is nutrient power which is used to help others – like parents lovingly raising their children (but be careful how you define "love" and "help"). And, there is integrative power, where two people (or more) strengthen others by integrating the power each has with another... as in marriage or church or support groups. Power and Innocence" is an excellent book and one I recommend to anyone who questions how the word "power" is used in this book.

In truth, integrative power can be used to change this entire nation. If everyone got up and wrote and read emails about solutions rather than problems and if people thought in terms of good rather than bad outcomes, the corporate, political, family and church environments would change to the positive much faster than most people can imagine. To do that, however, requires an informed public and the mainstream publications in this country see to it that everything that is published about President Donald Trump is distorted -- or outright lies. Please note I did not reference those who publish news as "media." They are not media. They are liars with a purpose.

As the old saying goes, money makes the world go 'round. And the power or control so much a part of money and wealth make the trip enjoyable for those who wield either.

You, in fact, are either a Passive or an Active investor. You may be a stay-at-home Mom or you may be the Chief Executive Officer (CEO) of a multi-national company – or you may be both a Mom and a CEO (I was) – but you possess a personality identifier that makes you either Active or Passive.

I use the word "wealth" in this book to define intellectual, spiritual, social or monetary substance. Words like "rich" and "affluent" reference profits... money. Thus, people with good and loving hearts who seek to do good in the world but who are poor and whose income places them below the poverty line may be wealthy in ways far beyond those people who merely possess more money (profit) than they do.

I coined the term "Active self investor" to describe the complexities of wealth/job creators. It explains how they achieve wealth ... by investing in themselves. The word "wealth" is used to describe Actives because to create a company that provides jobs creates wealth and that's what Actives do. They risk their own assets to start independent businesses that employ people. In other words, a person who creates wealth contributes to the entire community, the total society. Passives create jobs via major corporations but do not risk their own money. They risk the assets of stockholders.

I coined the term "Passive market investor" to describe the complexities of profit managers and money preservers. It explains how this group achieves affluence ... by investing in publicly traded products available on Wall Street and elsewhere: the stock market, the bond market, the mutual funds market, precious metals, currencies, partnerships, etc. Passives invest in products created and controlled by others, not themselves. They rather than Actives suffered high losses in the derivatives scandal, as a result.

Active investor wealth creators? Passive investor market profiteers? Who are they? What makes them powerful and why do they function in opposition to one another? Don't we all have the same objectives?

The information gathered for this research project represented a lot of questions to a great many people. Do the questions have answers? Yes. They are fascinating.

The attitudes of those with the financial wherewithal to make the lives of all citizens, good or bad, indicate that Passive asset managers/preservers and Active wealth/job creators function in opposition to one another. By doing so, they create social and economic chaos. But, it is chaos that results in a kind of balance worthy of a nation of free people.

The ignorance of both groups about the other makes each dangerous not just to one another, but to the ongoing and positive evolvement of societies and economies, worldwide. The problem both groups need to come to grips with is this: Neither is capable of surviving without the tempering force of the positive strengths of the other. Unfortunately, each group can only see the negative strengths of the other.

The negative strengths become particularly damaging when they are used by one group against the other – when one group uses government as a means to gain advantage over the other group – but that is what has happened in Millennial America.

Can the problems be corrected? Yes, they can; but not without understanding the core problem of attitudes in both groups and why they are there.

That's why I decided to go public with this information.

We have wealth and profits... and we have power and control. The Passive group is attracted to profits and wealth management because it is security-driven; that, in turn, motivates them to seek power. Actives must control risk to manage it. They are motivated to control their own self destiny. They seek wealth. They are, after all, risking their own money – their own assets -- not what belongs to investors, stockholders or taxpayers.

Control and power. No two words are more misunderstood than these.

We need to talk more about risk management – and why capitalism is based on the concept of risk management... which is why Passive liberals prefer socialism.

CHAPTER 2

MISPERCEPTIONS OF THE WORLD

If it hadn't been for a serendipitous research session one balmy southern night in Raleigh, NC, 1984, I might never have made the connection between the realities and misperceptions everyone has of the marketplace... retail, political, business, and social, et al.

The realities were quite different from what I expected because what I expected was based on research that was done for the industrial rather than the technology era. When my research project began, the move from industry to technology was still a baby, not yet out of the crib. To this day, I have seen little research that recognizes not only the marketplace has changed (everyone understands that), but people's attitudes changed, too. Anyone who has observed the behavior of Millennials won't argue with that statement. All one needs to do to affirm the comment is look at the television advertisements being put forth to sell products as we near 2020.

Because prior to starting my own company I was a bank vice president and the group I managed specialized in lending to affluent individuals, I knew there was a lot of self-made wealth. However, I had no idea how different attitudes between the traditionally affluent and self-made wealth are. These differences have a major impact on all businesses, from Fortune 500 multi-nationals to independently-owned family businesses. They also have a huge impact on the personal lives of all people who work for either.

It's important to understand that a great deal of research had been done prior to the findings of what I undertook in 1972. I found that time-tested old research to be wrong. As we moved to the new Millennium, as we moved from the economy which had since 1910 been driven by industry to one that began in 1960 to be driven by technology, everything changed.

Perhaps it is more accurate to say that the research others did through the 1960s had application to life before technology began making a huge impact on our lives and our lifestyles. The closer we got to 2000, however, the greater the impact of technology on our society, the less accurate the research about – everything – was. It is because researchers have focused on the marketplace rather than the people who purchase things from the marketplace. Living in a world of dot com companies changed the attitude of consumers and that attitude change impacted the reasons they did things, thought things, and took the actions they did. It was these new attitudes my research picked up and identified.

What's the old saying about being in the right place at the right time? When this story began, that was me. And the biggest breakthrough in my research came one night in Raleigh, North Carolina.

When it comes to how each group functions regarding money and social and political issues, the attitudes go beyond "different." They are opposite. Rather than inherit fortunes, both groups primarily earn their own wealth in their own lifetimes... with each group displaying a significant difference in strategies, beliefs, and behavior, however. A few research participants represented inherited wealth, but they were a very small part of all research participants. About 90 percent of inherited wealth is Passive; the remaining 10 percent is Active.

One group risks its own assets to achieve financial objectives. The other risks the assets of others ... stockholders, taxpayers, partners, investors, etc. Interestingly, each group defines the word "risk" quite differently than the other. Making this determination was a research key to understanding why people behave as they do in all areas of life.

The group that risks its own assets in the wealth accumulation process has opposite personal behavior motivators than the group that risks the assets of others. I didn't understand the significance of this discovery. It took me years to realize just how important it is.

Bankers for whom I consulted for many years thought the majority of people who make up the affluent group inherited wealth or achieved it in the corporate or professional world. As it related to traditional bank customers, that was accurate. But there was a whole new world of technology entrepreneurs emerging in the new economy. The original research objectives I worked out with my bank clients and the means of achieving them supported the old, not the new, thesis. These were reasonable assumptions – at the time.

Unfortunately, our concepts of the marketplace were based on a distortion. It was an accurate distortion, but resulted in research design error.

How can this be? How can anyone make an accurate mistake? Isn't the coupling of these two words oxymoronic... an impossible combination? In a way it is.

Let's say you run a vegetarian restaurant -- in California, of course. Every day, your customers come in and order veggie burgers or avocado salads. While they are sitting in your establishment, they discuss with you their attitudes about food and restaurants. They like your food and bring their friends. You define your marketplace, in this instance, as people who eat in restaurants. After fifty or a hundred years, you might begin to believe you understand the attitudes of the restaurant "marketplace." Right?

Wrong!

In this example, you have insight into the attitude towards food in which vegetarians find delightful repasts.

What does this tell you about meat-eater attitudes?

Nothing!

In other words, bankers over the years created trust departments in which the banking needs of the traditionally rich were served. Trust customers referred their friends to their trust bankers. Because the old saying about birds of a feather flocking together is accurate, they, too, had vegetarian attitudes toward money and banking.

It was only natural for trust bankers to think the rich people they met over many years represented the entire marketplace (or, at least, most of it). Because the vegetarians of affluence were happy with their banks and the services provided, it was assumed bankers were doing a good job of handling the needs of all wealthy clients. Everyone thought they understood their lifestyles and attitudes, especially towards money.

This same analogy can be drawn about the 2016 presidential race. Voters had become apathetic. They were too disgusted with those they had elected to office to publicly denounce them and the political corruption that had become apparent via Donald Trump's political campaign for President. That is why pollsters sent incorrect information to candidates' campaign managers. The guy who understood that people had lost their trust in government and the media – and pollsters – won that political race.

This same pattern is true about every product manufactured and sold. Big companies are run and staffed by Passive vegetarians, just as banks are. How do I know that? I know it because research told me that Passives are attracted to positions of power (big offers more power than small), are motivated to find security (big offers a more secure environment than does an independent business), they work well with others and are team players and they are willing to make the compromises required to thrive in a corporate environment. In return, their need for a secure feeling that comes from working at a large company and the benefits provided (better than benefits offered by independent businesses) makes them feel valued and safe... and important.

It is very tempting for anyone to assume their world represents the views of everyone else – at least everyone in the intelligent world. That is not the case. One need only look at college campuses and students' sometimes violent rejection of factual, truthful opinions from those whose views of life oppose what their Passive professors tell them. They are not yet well enough educated to realize that information they have been given does not equate to knowledge. It is just opinion. And just as information is only information, not knowledge, knowledge is just knowledge, not wisdom. To find knowledge requires experience and to acquire wisdom requires wins and losses in life that develop character and teach unforgettable lessons.

Because Passives are attracted by the security offered by employment at multi-national corporations and government, marketing offices at the world's giants of industry, manufacturing, and technology are staffed almost exclusively by Passives. Because they are Passives, because they work for large employers, they believe their attitude toward things is the dominant and best one. Perhaps they do not look at statistical data that shows 70 percent of new jobs created come from the independent, not the multi-national, world of business.

Sanctuary cities are good examples of assuming that people (like Mayor Bill Deblasio of New York and Governor Jerry Brown of California) think they have the right to put the preferences of illegal aliens above the needs of taxpaying American citizens. Americans have paid for the benefits illegal aliens demand which Deblasio and Brown give them for nothing – for which the illegals have paid nothing.

Everyone should pay higher taxes to support their views. Neither Brown nor de Blasio has a clue that American citizens whom they slap in the face in favor of illegal aliens disagree with them… and rightfully so.

American citizens want to put Americans first. Americans want elected officials to obey the law, not pick and choose which laws they will obey. If they don't like the laws, they should get them changed through the legitimate process put in place by State and Federal Constitutions. These same elected officials have no problem forcing average citizens to obey laws on the books but view themselves as exempt from them.

Thus, elected officials – like we bankers of the 1980s – are like the California vegetarian restaurant owner who, after 100 years, thinks he or she understands the world of fine foods when, in reality, they only understand how to create epicurean temptations for vegetarians. Like the vegetarian restaurant owner who thought he knew the business of restaurants, politicians are out of touch with the total picture.

What we found is that we knew a great deal about the attitudes of people who are traditionally affluent because bankers have compatible personalities with them. Bankers, however, knew and know almost nothing about the attitudes of non-traditional wealth.

Thus, bankers were accurate in their perceptions about traditionally affluent customers and their attitudes toward financial services. They were inaccurate in their perceptions that traditional customers represented all affluent customers in the community – or, even the largest, most profitable segment of that market.

Regardless that our views of the affluent marketplace were distorted, they were based on experience. The research project represented that with which we, as bankers, had experience, knowledge, and with which we were familiar. The implementation of this project expanded our horizons to the unfamiliar.

Why is banker experience – limited, but experience nonetheless, with a large portion of the affluent marketplace – distorted? Bank loan policies and organizational structure are pitted in opposition to the needs of meat-eating non-traditional Active bank customers. It sounds like a conspiracy theory. It's a bit more complicated.

Business policies have been created for traditionalists by traditionalists. People tend to think the word "conservative" means traditionalist and with regard to social issues that assumption is largely accurate. Yet, the traditionalists in the world of business are Passives.

"Conservative means traditionalist" is not accurate when applied to business. Tradition is safe when it comes to jobs and money. Passives are motivated by security and Actives are not. Passives embrace fiscal conservatism *where someone else's money is at risk running the business. They seek security where none of their money is placed at risk.* It is for this reason Passives work for others. Since Passives are largely liberal progressives, not conservatives, the concept that "fiscal conservatism means traditionalist" does not apply when it comes to business and money management. Interestingly, 80 percent of corporate executives are Passive. They are fiscal conservatives but are political and social liberal progressives.

All large corporations are mostly staffed by Passives who are attracted to the security offered by big companies and whose Passive attitudes are reflected in all products, advertising, corporate policies, organizational structure, etc., of those big organizations. As I said, the personalities of these two groups are opposite so the regulated environment of big business doesn't work for Actives whose primary motivation is control. Actives do not function well in environments where they lack control of self destiny.

People today complain about universities and colleges that are staffed with professors who teach socialism rather than capitalism. These "educators" do not look at the people of Venezuela whose government recently became socialist. They ignore people in that country (which was a wealthy nation until recently) who are starving and overlook cities that cannot afford to make light available at night. Why? Because becoming a professor at the university level represents power – the key Passive motivator – over the minds of the young and attracts Passives like moths to a light. Passive professors love the "risk free" environment socialism says it offers (and largely does if people do not mind becoming slaves to government) and so they promote it. Sir Winston Churchill was correct when he said "...the inherent virtue of socialism is the equal sharing of misery." That has proven to be true wherever it has been tried.

People today complain about all of the regulations being dumped on the heads of new start-up companies. People can't afford to start new businesses. Welcome to the world of Passives (politically liberal) who use regulation to protect everything... except the economy that pays their salaries. Passives will not understand the meaning of what I just said. Of course they believe they protect the economy! And they believe that statement. No new business start ups doesn't signify anything to them because they simply do not understand the risk management process. In their minds, the success of big companies is the economy, not their policies that harm small businesses which provide 70 percent of America's jobs. Many liberals truly do not see that their policies are what cause the sick economy.

The point is, almost all of the assumptions bankers made about affluent people and their buyer behavior turned out to be incorrect. As I watch the advertising of the new millennium, all industries appear to make the same mistakes bank marketers did in the old days (and, still do).

To say research results surprised my traditional banker expectations is the understatement of the year. The truth is, I thought I was open to any message. I must have been a little open, or the message would never have gotten through ... but I was a partial product of a large corporate environment. Fortunately for me, I ran my own small business before becoming a banker. Only now, by looking back, can I shake my head in wonder at how large organizations function in such boxed-in parameters. How can people who can't open their ears to hear what customers really mean when they pragmatically discuss concepts of customer service provide good customer service to customers whose words are not really heard and understood?

In reality, bankers – particularly at large banks and management at large corporations and bureaucrats working for the government – hear what they want. They hear it because it validates important things like existing policies and organizational and production line structures. Mostly, it agrees with the pre-conceived security-motivated ideas and attitudes of Passives who are the large majority employed by all large companies.

One big lesson I learned from this career-long research project is this: To identify what you do right (whether a multi-billion dollar company or an entrepreneur) ask those who approve of and do business with you. To find out what you might do better, ask those who do not list you on their Top Ten and who do not do business with you.

Until I became disabled in 1993 and stopped consulting, I was not in any way a political person. Nor was I very involved with social issues of the day ... consultants live in airplanes and hotel rooms. It does not leave time for such things (often, I was lucky to get home for weekends). My objective was to maintain my cutting edge status in private banking. Many people were trying to imitate my creation. I didn't have time to worry about how deficit spending might affect my future and that of my family or how lobbyists were corrupting the system intended to represent me and my better interests. In other words, I was an average American.

Even now, after retirement, I'm not what you could call "politically involved" or a "party" person. But I did begin reading more than the business pages. I suddenly had time to read books or listen to them on tape. I began to educate myself about social and political issues. I even went monthly to Republican lunches and began corresponding with a liberal Democrat about politics and political philosophies. The letters were eye-openers. They proved to me that no matter how hard either of us tried, we simply could not understand one another's positions. We wrote pages and pages to each other in an attempt to explain our views. We were opposites ... he a Passive, me an Active. As the old saying goes, "never the twain shall meet." It never did. I doubt it ever will.

I was amazed to find heavyweights run things in the political and social arenas using personality styles almost identical to those of affluent individuals who achieve business objectives at big companies. The behavior unfolding before me in the political and social arenas made me feel I was seeing, as Yogi Berra would say: "Déjà vu, all over again."

Looking back, it probably shouldn't have been such a huge surprise. The affluent are the primary players not only in business but also in politics and societal standards. Their attitudes toward money are merely an extension of what motivates their attitudes toward politics and social issues – towards power and control. And guess what? The attitudes of those who earn their own fortunes in their own lifetimes while risking their own assets are not very different from anyone else, regardless of their monetary status. Many of them started at the bottom of the income ladder. People who fall into this category have taken some hard hits over the years and have learned some important lessons. They achieved wealth through hard work and dedication. They are the American Dream.

Perhaps the most important questions deal with subconscious drives. For example, do you think people *take* risks? Or, do people *manage* risk? Passives view risk as something one takes. Actives see it as something one manages. It's one of the subtle things which, when you know it, tells you if someone is likely a Passive or an Active. What causes the Passive low-risk tolerance and a resultant distaste for risk – viewing it as something one takes rather than manages?

A MacGruder Axiom: *The difference between dreams and reality creates a risk environment. To achieve your dreams, you must risk your current reality to create a new one.*

As my research showed beyond a reasonable doubt, people's tolerance for risk – their very definition of risk... whether it is "taken" or "managed" – is one of the most basic drives inherent to human personality development. It determines whether we fight or run when challenged. It determines for whom we will work. It determines whether we will stay in an unhappy circumstance or go start new lives for ourselves. It determines what elements are required by us to be confident people. It determines who we choose as friends and why we buy consumer goods and what advertising and sales promotion messages cause us to buy one product over another.

It could be argued that Dr. Freud's finding that sex is the core drive of human personality development is wrong because, in and of its self, sex is an endeavor that involves risk management in numerous ways. Surely whether one views risk as something to manage or take impacts one's approach to sharing one's body with another... fear of embarrassment, fear of non-performance, fear of disease, fear of pregnancy, fear of... many things.

People motivated by risk aversion usually find a way to allow the end to justify the means because they often lack moral certainty. Passives subscribe to a philosophy that all things are relative.

To Actives, nothing is relative. Things are black, or they are white. There is little gray in their lives. That does not mean they do not have open minds and will not change their opinions. It merely means the opinions they hold at any given time are not based on relativism or, as it is called today, post modernism. Those who manage risk with confidence often refuse to compromise – even when it is the best thing to do – because they are so morally certain. They need to learn that too much moral certainty can be as destructive as too little, especially when dealing with a total population.

Like the mare who instinctively nurses a newborn foal, our human instinct motivates us to develop either Active traits or Passive traits. We either thrive on risk management, or find ways to spread risk around so no one person will take much of a loss and face will be saved when failure occurs. Saving face, by the way, is a very Chinese trait. That should tell you why they choose a communist form of government: They are Passives by nature and communism is a Passive form of government designed to remove risk from people's lives by removing their freedom to make decisions about their careers and education, how many children they should have, etc.

Capitalism is an economic system that requires risk management to succeed. That should explain why individualist Actives love it and group-dominant, risk management-averse Passives dislike it; they are frightened by it. It is why Passives are attracted to positions of power as politicians. Passives are fear motivated and the best way to deal with fear is to gain power that can protect you from future mishaps in your life. Chapter Three lists specific personality traits of each group. Read the list and see if you can find yourself.

This list should make clear to you why this research and its findings offer significant answers to the problems of today's chaotic world. If you understand Passives, you will understand liberals and progressives. If you understand Actives, you will understand conservatives. Hopefully this understanding will make it possible for voters to discern the difference between the two... no more Passives posing as conservatives to get elected to office and then voting as liberals. You will be able to ask them questions the answers to which will tell you what any candidate really represents. You will recognize personality traits of Passive school board candidates and stop destructive policies in that realm (and every other political candidate for whom you cast a vote).

The traits people develop determine career path choices. We were able to identify to which occupations and professions Actives are attracted and which appeal to Passives.

If your strongest personal motivator is the need to seek the right to self-determination your lifestyle will require an ability to manage risk. You are an Active. You may be a plumber or a multi-billionaire techie, but you will control your work environment.

When one's lifestyle is based on risk-management, one's lifestyle is also based on the need to control – or, manage – risk. Only a fool takes risks the outcome of which are controlled by another. That's like saying, "I'll risk my future and that of my family by wagering I can beat you in a game ... any game you name and you get to make up the rules as we go along." It's the shortest road to failure... and until Donald Trump began doing away with regulations that were destroying independent business, failure in job growth was precisely what we got.

Government wants to control the risks independents view as something to be managed by business owners, and business owners are not fools. They are not going to try to manage risks that are controlled by an entity like government with no skill in business management and no capital invested in the outcome. Government makes decisions on the basis of political popularity not business experience and common sense. Or necessity.

Until Trump, government used regulation to achieve this objective. It made starting new businesses all but impossible for the past 20 years.

Actives instinctively know that risk management must be in the hands of the person whose capital is at risk. It is inherent to business growth. That is why under regulation-writer President Barack Obama independent businesses did not grow. Sure. He inherited a broken economy, but had he or members of his liberal administration understood what independent business needed for recovery to occur, we could have actually seen some economic growth during his eight years in office. It is why given the opportunity, Donald J. Trump, who does understand this process because he has lived it, is healing our economy. To do so, he needs to fend off all of the Passive liberals who think his election to office to be illegitimate and he needs to assuage the hurt feelings of the "Never Trump" Republicans who, in reality, are liberals. His personality type tends to achieve the opposite.

All socialist nations today face this same problem. They do not understand the most basic human and economic need for risk managers: Control of risks to be managed. They do not understand it because Passives, not Actives, are attracted to secure career positions with big government -- and no government is bigger or more powerful than a socialist government except a communist government. Thus, bureaucrats and politicians have no insight about the needs of independent businesses and how to make them grow – and that's why no new jobs were being created until Trump took office. It's why governments worldwide continue to make wrong decisions that will not motivate individuals to manage the risk of new business start-ups – because government defines and controls the risks the individuals must manage. Personal risks can only be managed personally.

This is a significant element for governments like China. It is a nation almost totally dependent upon selling its goods to foreign nations. Why? There is no middle class because in socialist and communist countries salaries are so low it is impossible to create a middle class. Communism and socialism are two-class systems:

labor and elite. Only capitalism requires a middle class to succeed. A middle class enables a country to sell its own goods to its own people and is, thus, not dependent upon international trade to survive economically.

That is why China, under a communist form of government, will never become the dominant world economic power. You cannot be a world power without a middle class because you are too dependent upon foreign nations to buy your goods (the nation's poverty class consumers cannot afford to buy them) so you can increase productivity on an ongoing basis (as the population and its wealth increases). All the world needs to do is turn off the spigot of its international trade with China to gain equality with them. The world can thus manipulate socialist economies which are dependent on international trade. Please note I did not say China will not be a potential tyrannical power in the world. If their economy disintegrates, they will become a bigger and bigger danger to the world.

You may want to give some thought about the war against America's middle class and the reasons for it. The two paragraphs preceding this one should explain it to you. That war was begun in 1988 under the administration of "No New Taxes" and "New World Order" George H.W. Bush. The political objective for both political parties in America has been socialism since the early 1900s. Ronald Reagan, like Donald Trump, was an unexpected bump in that road.

Socialism and communism dictate that government rules, it does not govern. The dictates of government directly discourage Actives from new business start-ups and expansion of existing companies because communist and socialist governments tell business owners which risks they must manage and that discourages the desire to be productive. Why would a government in a capitalist economy discourage new business start-ups? Because it destroys the middle class and paves the road for a socialist government... and the power that goes with it. In other words, the destruction of our middle class is the result of a long-term power play.

In capitalist nations, usually the smaller the company, the more independence employees have when exercising authority on the job and more personal accountability for decisions made. There is not an "old boy's" or "old girl's" or "old elitist's" club to cover errors as there is in all large companies. Corporate political cultures dictate that executive management and certain select others must be protected from perceived errors and that is what these clubs were created to do. It was conceived in the womb of political correctness. Hollywood's Harvey Weinstein is a perfect example of that statement.

The kind of personnel attracted to big companies versus independent ones reflects personalities that either like or dislike personal accountability. The less people like taking individual responsibility for their actions (which is a risk), the more they prefer to function as members of a large team. Each person within a corporate team may have individual responsibility and be held accountable for it, but no one team member is responsible for the total risk of success or failure of a project. This is a primary reason certain people are attracted as employees to reduced risk-management environments at big companies. Too, they are often attracted by power that accompanies a climb up the corporate ladder.

Independent business owners or professionals who own their own medical or dental or accounting, legal or handyman or home improvement businesses must manage all risk. They are totally accountable financially for the success or failure of their ventures. People who thrive on risk management and the opportunity to seek self-destiny are attracted to the independence of self-employment.

The more independent an individual's personality, the more likely it is he or she will seek a work environment that encourages individual responsibility. Thus, the very personalities of people who work for small, independent companies are usually more compatible with Actives who own the business and share the same individualist traits. Or, they start their own companies (when the economic environment makes it possible).

How do these two personality types affect the news we read or hear each day?

Have you heard the term "the power of the press"? Who do you think is attracted to these positions of power: Actives or Passives? That's why you read so much "fake news" today.

What is the purpose of wealth? Why do Passives appear to feel guilty about it? Do they think because they have a boat someone else is doing without one? Because one person earns a huge annual income, someone else must earn less? People usually earn that for which they prepare themselves.

Why do Actives appear to Passives to be so cold-hearted about social issues? Have they no compassion?

Actives are compassionate. They, however, define the word "compassion" quite differently than do Passives. You will find this to be true in almost every endeavor... especially between men and women. It's not that men are from Mars and women from Venus. It's that men are more likely to be Actives and most women are, by nature, security-driven Passives. It is a hangover from the days women considered their primary responsibility in life to provide a secure, safe environment for the babies they bear. To understand why women tend to be Passives, a chapter on that topic is included in this book. I encourage you to read it.

Perhaps various misperceptions of the world could be alleviated if those in positions of power better understood the forces that drive it. Just like the banking industry or vegetarian restaurant owner that thought they had the beat on the whole picture, we make the same mistakes. If we understood that those who seek power do so to assuage fears, or that managing risks is required to create and manage a thriving economy, we could make changes that actually benefit more than this or that group. Maybe positive changes could be made for humanity... or, at least within our own nation.

CHAPTER 3

"We must love them both – those whose opinions we share and those whose opinions we reject. For both have labored in the search for truth, and helped us in the finding of it." --St. Thomas Aquinas

FINDING THE APP (ACTIVE-PASSIVE PERSONALITIES)

PASSIVE LIBERAL PSYCHOGRAPHIC CHART

SECURITY DRIVE

The Passive group, at all socioeconomic levels, comes by assets passively. Passives risk the money of others (stockholders, taxpayers, investors, etc.), inherit money, or save via retirement funds with major corporations. Because of security needs, they seldom place their own assets at risk if such an investment places consumer lifestyle at risk. Passives seldom start their own companies though will buy them after someone else has successfully managed the start-up risk. Passive investors view risk as something one takes, not something one manages. They are reactive people, socially and politically.

POWER DRIVE

Big equals powerful which equals safe. Big and Passive/market investors go together like water and rain. Passives prefer big institutions: public schools (and teachers' unions), colleges, government, businesses, banks, media, airlines, etc. as employers. Big is good. The dominant behavioral motive of Passives is power ... or, access to it. Power provides security and security removes the need for managing risk. This group is risk management averse.

Affluent Passive/Liberal Occupations:
... Journalism/Media/Publishers
... Politicians
... Major corporations (including big banks)
... Educators/Professors
... Entertainers
... CPAs/Lawyers (big firms, many partners)
... Non-surgeons (excluding some specialties)
... Inherited Wealth
... Arts and Humanities

WEALTH PRESERVERS, MANAGERS
Middle Class Occupations:
... Bureaucrats, government, major corporations
... Social Workers
... Health Care Workers
... Firemen, Policemen, Teachers, EMTs
... Non-professional staff at big companies and professional firms
... Administrative and labor/union
... Airlines/transportation/travel
... Media – editing, writers, etc.

PASSIVE/MARKET INVESTORS
... "Passive" refers only to how these people manage risk to come by money, social and professional status, and it explains their security-based consumer behavior. It does not refer to personalities. They are often strong and dynamic people.

- ... Invest in passive assets controlled by others (e.g., stocks, bonds, etc.); significantly, they support the current economy and the wealth and jobs resulting from it.
- ... When they achieve a 30 percent risk tolerance level (or, once their wealth is sufficiently large so whatever loss is taken is no threat to lifestyle), Passives are big consumer spenders and market investors in gold, silver and other more aggressive publicly-controlled products.
- ... Passively rely on third parties -- trust officers/bankers, brokers, lawyers, CPAs, and other advisors.
- ... They passively achieve wealth by risking the financial assets of others (stockholders, partners, taxpayers, and investors).
- ... Invest in traditional public market products.
- ... Utilize power or their access to it (for which they often work very hard in political campaigns and community activities) to help them preserve existing affluence, their perceived status, and existing possessions.
- ... Strategies used to maintain current wealth often thwart new wealth creation. The primary purpose of Passives *is to expand the existing economy.* To achieve this, they utilize power to gain abnormal favor from the marketplace. For example, they work to get government regulations passed that protect the status quo. They resisted the change from manufacturing and industry as the primary drive of the economy to that of service and technology. Or, they use access to power to gain bureaucratic or political protection to oppose new businesses over which they exercise no power.
- ... Power-based regulations that manipulate the marketplace have a detrimental effect on wealth creators and the new jobs they create.

EXTERNALISTS/COMPASSIONATES
- ... Group achievement favored over individual achievement
- ... Natural team players
- ... Team ego/Politically correct
- ... Joiner (country/social clubs, political activist, etc.)

... Like to impress others positively
... More easily see the obvious (external) rather than the subtle (internal)
... Capable of delegating authority
... Use (externalize) personal power
... Empower other people (to prove you have power, it must be exercised to the benefit – or detriment – of others)
... People-oriented
... Externally nice, social people
... Tend to take more responsibility for others than for self (everything is external, not internal... everything outside of the event is at fault rather than the "thing" that caused the event to occur. For example, guns not people kill people).
... Advocates of social (group) rights and diversity; compassion for underdogs
... Good communicators/public speakers
... On the darker side, manipulative
... External (not internal) factors always determine outcomes, personally/socially ("I, you, he, she, it had a bad childhood; I have – they have -- been abused; I am/they are a victim...").
... Define compassion by how many people come to them for help
... Too much emphasis on the Passive/liberal group results in a booming short-term economy, loss of future expansion into a new economy designed to serve tomorrow's achievers and expected population growth.
... Tolerant until you disagree with them

APPARENT OBJECTIVES
... Government or its agencies empower people
... Government removes risk from people's lives
... Pro-public dependency on big companies and government for survival (energy, food, transportation, etc.) and productivity
... Government should reward all people equally, regardless of individual contribution to society/self
... Federal government runs education system
... Federal government runs health care

... Support the rights of groups over the rights of individuals. For example, Passives strongly support multiculturalism (Passives view groups of people as "individuals" and support them in that context, socially and politically – DACA is a good example).
... Gain support through fear. This is a natural trait for risk-averse people. People judge the behavior and reactions of others through the personal motivators of their own eyes. Thus, Passives tend to believe all people are motivated to act if they are made insecure and/or fearful.

POLITICAL AFFILIATION
... Mostly Democrats because they are fiscally and socially liberal; corporate executives are often social Passives, fiscal Republicans (less than half are conservative Actives).
... Some are communists; many are socialists
... They are mostly social liberals who have a greater innate understanding of socialism than of capitalism
... They generally consider themselves to be progressive

ACTIVE/SELF INVESTOR PSYCHOGRAPHICS

HIGH RISK MANAGEMENT SKILL
... As long as Actives control/manage the risk environment. Risk tolerance drops in direct proportion to lost control. *If they do not control the risks taken (in whatever endeavor)*, Active risk tolerance may be *lower* than the Passive group at equal socioeconomic levels. This drive results in the need for self-determination and strong individualism (both of which motivate the need for control). Actives view risk as something that needs to be managed – and can be. They are pro-active people.

CONTROL DRIVE
... Small is beautiful (big equates to power you cannot control)
... Control/manage risk rather than eliminate it. It is the basis of free enterprise.

... Control government, not citizens
... Control the emotional; utilize logic to deal with problems
... Commitment to control of self-destiny

Affluent Occupations:
... Independent business owners (some of these businesses are quite large)
... Medical/dental surgeons, radiologists, anesthesiologists, (some non-surgeon specialists)
... CPAs/Lawyers (independent, small firms)
... Self-made wealth
... Builders, real estate developers
... Oil and gas – independents and corporate and numerous support jobs and businesses
... Entrepreneurs, Inventors
... Contractors
... Scientists unaffiliated with universities and government-sponsored projects, high tech inventors and programmers

Middle Class Occupations:
... Same occupations as Passives while young; often depart corporate work environments to start businesses using expertise gained at corporate employer.

ACTIVE/SELF INVESTORS
... Advocates of individual rights as defined by the Constitution
... Advocates of the rule of law as stated by the Constitution
... Consider the purpose of the Constitution is to limit the power of government, not the people
... Invest in assets controlled by themselves (real estate, new start-up businesses -- their own and those of others, provided they control the outcome); significantly, they support the coming economy and all wealth that results from it.
... Actively control personal investments and use but are not dependent on third parties

- ...Actively achieve wealth in their own lifetime; risk their own financial, social, personal and professional assets
- ...Actively control investment risk and oppose regulatory controls that make managing risk impossible
- ...Primary investment product is self -- "I trust me; I control me."
- ...Heavily into real estate development, in one form or another
- ...Do not invest *primarily* in gold or silver coins or bullion (controlled by the marketplace), but will buy a gold mine, oil well, etc. which they do control.

INTERNALS/LOGIC-DOMINANT
- ...Pro individual achievement
- ...Primary concern is opinion of self; they function from a perspective of moral conscience, popular or not
- ...Individual, not team, ego
- ...Politically incorrect; creative drive prevents moral compromise with standards set by others if they violate personal beliefs
- ...Delegation must be learned
- ...Logical rather than emotional
- ...Good negotiators
- ...Pro-victim rights
- ...Define compassion by how many people they can motivate to become productive and self-sustaining.

NEW WEALTH (JOB CREATORS)
- ...Utilizes control to manage risk in a way that creates new wealth, new jobs (non-traditional, independent by nature)
- ...Creates and supports the new economy for future generations
- ...Understands that free enterprise (and the personalities that support it) requires risk management, not risk elimination.
- ...Risks personal assets to achieve wealth
- ...Too much emphasis on the Active segment results in a detrimental effect on the existing financial, economic, social and political order.
- ...Provide tomorrow's wealth/jobs; are not today's major political contributors.

- ... Actives are involved in personal projects and objectives resulting in too little community and political involvement.
- ... Actives are under-represented in such professions as education (all grades, including college), politics, social services, and other positions which hold little interest for them. They often pay taxes for representation they do not get in the political and social realms.

APPARENT OBJECTIVES
- ... Self-determination, self-reliance; individuals are responsible for providing health care, retirement, etc. Taxpayer help to those without financial resources and no way to gain access to them (disabled, elderly).
- ... Task, rather than people, oriented
- ... Advocates of social responsibility
- ... Without responsible accountability, Actives say there are no rights, just license
- ... Self-reliance, self-dependence, self-destiny
- ... Unless trained, usually not good public speakers or communicators
- ... Pro-American sovereignty; no taxpayer assistance to non-citizens, anti-immigration unless strategy-based and well-controlled, anti-illegal immigration, American soldiers in the American, not the United Nations military, etc.
- ... Smaller government and less bureaucracy
- ... Anti-small business regulations that oppose or deter from the creation of new wealth, jobs
- ... Return power to the states so they control welfare, education, and health care
- ... Tax policy that does not discourage new wealth and new jobs (smaller government, less taxes)
- ... Pro U.S. Constitution and Bill of Rights
- ... Fiscally and socially conservative
- ... Government should not intrude in people's rights to seek lawful self-determination
- ... People empower government; government does not empower people

...Value not compassion-driven society; Actives believe good, moral social values are the ultimate compassion.

...Strongly supportive of societal laws based on the laws of nature, common sense, and/or a Supreme Being.

POLITICAL AFFILIATION:
Republican (less than half of Republicans are conservative Actives), slightly over half of Independents are Actives. The majority of Libertarians have more in common with liberal Passives than with Actives – the flip side of the coin (liberals want all government, libertarians want none).

ACTIVE WEALTH CREATORS
PASSIVE MONEY MANAGERS
WHO ARE THEY?

The research project made me realize that just as Passives place their investments in the safest possible vehicles with the greatest profit potential and in products that spreads risk to the greatest possible degree, Actives invest in themselves. I changed the name "Passive" to "Passive/market investor" and the name "Active" to "Active/self investor. Quite simply, Passives invest in the markets; Actives invest in themselves (or in deals they control).

The terms are not pejorative... the word "Passive" does not mean "wimp." It merely explains how this person comes by wealth: by passively risking the assets of others and with as little personal risk as possible. For example, corporate executives put up corporate, not personal, assets as collateral when borrowing for their companies – just as Lee Iacocca did when he borrowed from the government to pay the bills at Chrysler Corporation when that company almost went belly-up in the late 1970s.

Lee Iacocca is a dynamic man and a likely Passive/market investor because he earned his riches via a major corporation; he achieved affluence by risking the assets of others (stock-holders and taxpayers).

Donald Trump is a dynamic man --- a man who, when he borrows, he usually risks his own assets, not those of partners or investors or taxpayers. Trump is an Active.

When Chrysler Corp had severe financial problems in the late 1970s, Iacocca borrowed from the federal government to prevent his company's failure. Had the loans not been repaid, no foreclosure notice on Iacocca's personal assets would have been issued. His stockholders would have been royally screwed – but American taxpayers would have been left holding the bag. When Donald Trump borrows, his personal assets are at risk. The assets he puts up as loan collateral may be part of the Trump Corporation, but they belong to him, not to stockholders who invest in his company via the stock market because his is a privately-owned company.

> *A MacGruder Axiom: When you seek information, ask people with practical, positive knowledge on the subject. Never ask a duck how a dog barks.*

If it hadn't been for the serendipitous research session I mentioned in the previous chapter, I might never have made the connection between the realities and misperceptions regarding affluent people... that they were not one homogeneous group. And had that experience not moved the research forward in an unexpected direction, the risk management and risk-averse personality traits might not have been found... and the power/control opposite personalities would not have been identified. So Raleigh was very important.

We always did focus group research with people having similar backgrounds and/or professions... we interviewed CPAs as a group, lawyers as a group, independent business owners as a group, physicians (surgeons and non-surgeons) as a group, etc.

The Raleigh experience involved the medical profession. Surgeons and non-surgeons are important because their answers to questions were later expanded to include all other professions and careers. It made clear that all people have a place in the Active/Passive Personality Syndrome.

> **A MacGruder Axiom: We prepare ourselves to handle big things by successfully handling little things ... we must crawl before we walk and walk before we run.**

On this night all of the surgeons scheduled for a focus group session could not attend. There were evidently a lot of emergencies in Raleigh. We had a sufficient number of successful non-surgeons with whom to hold the session so we continued.

The answers we got from Raleigh's non-surgeons totally conflicted with results obtained from previous sessions held all over the country where both surgeons and non-surgeons were present.

For example, Raleigh non-surgeons were adamant they would never leverage their personal residences to borrow for business investment opportunities. There were other pro-Passive non-Active statements made that night, too. This one stands out, though. The home is the core of consumer lifestyle and we knew Passives did not put their homes up as collateral for a loan. It was a risk they disliked. Consumer lifestyle is important to them. In the other research sessions, non-surgeons did not indicate that giving a second deed of trust on their personal residence bothered them. Until this night, non-surgeons and surgeons were both viewed as Actives. My initial reaction to the glitch was, "Well, this is the conservative South, after all." But it troubled me. I recalled that we had done similar research in other North Carolina cities ... and in South Carolina, Texas, Florida and a lot of other places. We had asked the same question of members of the same professions.

The only difference between this group and previous ones was that no surgeons were present. In general, surgeons do tend to be more assertive and verbally dominant in focus group sessions. As I thought back over other sessions, I realized that non-surgeons never really said they would not leverage their personal residences. They did not say they would, either. Surgeons were the ones who did not hesitate to say a house is an asset to be used in the achievement of financial objectives. Non-surgeons did not contradict them, but they never really made the same statement.

> ***A MacGruder Axiom: There's nothing wrong with not knowing something. What is wrong is to not know and think you do.***

Because of this obvious glitch in research assumptions, more focus group sessions were scheduled to include non-surgeons only and surgeons only.

We found the Raleigh experience to be the norm, not the exception. At the very least, Raleigh non-surgeons had stated risk must be "spread" to make it acceptable and so did most other non-surgeons in other cities across the country. Access to credit should in no way threaten a family's lifestyle and social life.

The knowledge learned in Raleigh that night: People's reactions to risk management also determine political and social attitudes on the basis of perceived risks involved in each situation.

> ***A MacGruder Axiom: Chance is a friend, not an enemy, to those with self-confidence and the knowledge to manage it.***

A lot of analysis and numerous focus group sessions occurred after Raleigh. I found that most surgeons and non-surgeons have basic personality differences. Most prominent among the differences is an attitude toward risk. By keeping the two groups apart, we were able to get an entirely new set of research materials with which to work.

In analyzing the difference between the two groups, it became obvious that risk for a surgeon in his or her day-to-day work was much higher than for non-surgeons. Both dealt with life and death issues, but surgeons more aggressively than non-surgeons. Since I had already determined that the risk management factor defined the difference between Actives and Passives, it was too coincidental to ignore. When you think about it, it makes complete sense. Surgeons have a higher tolerance for managing risk or they wouldn't be surgeons. The idea of a surgeon standing over me with shaking hands caused by risk management intolerance is not reassuring.

Thus, an evaluation of which research participants controlled (managed) risks to achieve affluence was undertaken. Were they active risks? Or, was risk management passively assigned to outside third party experts? Was risk passively spread among many, or did one person control it?

Next, we looked at the data to see if we could tell which people behaved what way ... could any specific group of people be identified as Active or Passive risk-managers or avoiders? If so, what was the pivot point?

Also, in the aftermath of the research, I wanted to use the definitions of risk management and security to determine if Actives or Passives are more likely to be politically conservative or liberal. I found the original results about risk management capabilities being the core issue that determines whether people were Active or Passive were absolutely accurate and as I compared that definition to legislation and public support or opposition by political figures for social issues it became apparent that Actives were conservative and Passives were liberal.

The research that divided surgeons and non-surgeons into different groups was expanded to include lawyers, CPAs, independent business owners, entrepreneurs, oil (independent and major corporations like Exxon) and others.

The non-surgeon group in Raleigh ended up providing a beacon of light to this very important finding about risk management skills being the core from which human behavior evolves. It was not difficult to apply the same definitions to social issues and the world of politics. All you need to know about someone to determine whether they are more likely to be conservative than liberal is their occupation. It is not 100 percent accurate, but it is pretty close.

Whether you are poor or rich has little to do with whether you are a social liberal or conservative. Whether you are homosexual or heterosexual, whether you are black, white, yellow, brown, black or any other color... none impact this finding. Your tolerance for risk management will determine whether you are a conservative or a liberal. It determines whether children born into poverty will spend years in jail or become a Dr. Ben Carson or a Herman Cain.

For some, their tolerance for and ability to manage risk results in the need to control risk... to manage it. These traits are clearly seen in poverty stricken areas where gangs thrive and compete with others for dominance. Money has little to do with Active/Passive energy; how people use money, however, tells us a great deal about them.

For others, their distaste for managing risk and resultant need to exercise power over outside forces to ensure a risk-free environment dominates. These traits, too, are seen in poverty stricken areas where gang life dominates the existence of youth.

Because of this power drive, Passives have to work hard to achieve a risk-free environment. Because of that, Passive liberals are much more susceptible to the Lorelei-like appeals of socialism. Passives tend to overlook the tyranny that has accompanied socialism wherever it has been tried... and wherever it has been tried, it has failed. The risk management factor determines whether you will end up an entrepreneur or be employed by a corporate giant and it will also determine whether you love capitalism or fear it.

Here are the results of the findings of the research by occupation and profession:

Active Investors' Occupations and Professions

Corporate executives	20 percent (Almost all are fiscally conservative)
Small business owners	70 percent
Surgical physicians	90 percent
Non-surgical physicians	20 percent
Surgical dentists	90 percent
Non-surgical dentists	20 percent
CPAs (independent)	90 percent
CPAs (Big Eight)	20 percent
Lawyers (independent)	90 percent
Lawyers (large firms)	20 percent
Entrepreneurs	100 percent

Passive Investors' Occupations and Professions (omitted inherited wealth)

Corporate executives	80 percent
Small business owners	30 percent
Surgical physicians	10 percent
Non-surgical physicians	80 percent
Surgical Dentists	10 percent
Non-surgical dentists	80 percent
CPAs (independent)	10 percent
CPAs (Major Firms)	80 percent
Lawyers (independent)	10 percent
Lawyers (large firms)	80 percent

You will note that 20 percent of corporate executives are Active and 80 percent are Passive and, thus, 100 percent of corporate executives have been placed into one group or the other. Corporate executives were a particularly interesting group to analyze because we have been brain washed by the media to view them as Actives (as Republican conservatives). The media took this position because corporate executives are held out to the public to be fiscally conservative (Actives). That is true. Most are fiscally conservative, but 80 percent of them are social liberals.

The individuals who took part in the research from 1972 through 1986 came from various backgrounds and occupations and professions.

600+ surgeons
550 non-surgeons
750 corporate executives
650 independent business owners
300 entrepreneurs (with no other occupation)
250 inherited wealth
350 CPAs with major firms
400 independent CPAs
450 lawyers at major firms

500 lawyers who owned their own firms (largely courtroom lawyers)
250 dental practitioners
200 dental surgeons

Note: Numbers quoted are approximate and rounded.

The same guidelines for determining whether a person is Active or Passive can be used in a broader sense with the non-affluent or non-professional. Re-read the personality traits listed at the start of this chapter. After reading the above explanations of the research project, they should make far more sense to you now than they did when you first read them.

Threats to security occur socially, politically, in career choices, and in all areas of human endeavor. All change is a threat to security. Thus, all change is a threat to Passives. And that takes us back to the risk/reward concept. If Passives perceive the reward is worth the risk which must be taken to achieve the objective, they may take the risk – the belief that risks must be taken rather than managed makes handling risk more difficult (nerve-wracking) for Passives. As a result, they are more likely to compromise. Perhaps that is why so many Passives are attracted to politics and are good at it. Politics requires compromise. It also requires common sense and a lack of fear to know when to avoid compromise.

Children look to parents as moats that protect childhood castles. Security needs are very involved in our choice of marital partners. All lifestyle choices involve an analysis of our personal ability to manage risk. They require decisions by each individual: "Do I want my dream badly enough to manage the risk required to get it?" And, "Can I sufficiently manage this risk?"

Those questions exemplify how the Active/Passive Personality Syndrome (APPS) has equal application to all areas of life.

People who are uncomfortable with risk management are motivated by high security needs. Access to power so they can achieve and maintain security is very important to their sense of well being. This explains why you see so many liberal progressives acting like children at the loss of a presidential election. They have lost their access to the power grid that has supported all liberal causes. Thus their protection is gone. It frightens them and they react like frightened people. When any animal is cornered and becomes frightened, it fights.

People who manage risk well are motivated to control the risks they must manage to achieve a stated objective. The need to control their destiny is ranked critical/high in importance to this group's sense of well being. *In fact, the Active group's willingness to manage risk goes down in direct proportion to the amount of control taken from their hands. If they cannot control and manage risk, they become unwilling to manage the risk of entrepreneurism.* Donald Trump needs to pay attention to this factor because it is on this trait his support base transports into a movement. Without it, he merely has political support, like any other politician.

I relate my epiphany of understanding this concept to that serendipitous research session that balmy southern night in Raleigh, N.C. Without it, the research would have continued down the traditional road and the extreme value of the next phase of research would have gone unnoticed.

A MacGruder Axiom: It matters not at what you succeed ... provided the result harms no one and helps you and others live better lives (better means better, not easier).

A human being's tolerance for risk – the ability to manage risk – tells us a great deal about them. It tells us how secure they are in their ability to manage change because change is always defined as risk. Change means giving up that with which one is familiar for the unknown. Risk management skills define whether you prefer a form of government that gives you as much freedom as possible in return for your agreement to manage the risk of being productively responsible for yourself, or whether you are willing to give up freedom to have government fulfill your inability to manage risk... your security needs.

Understanding the importance of risk management skills versus a lack of them are the keys to understanding why some people support capitalism which gives people the maximum amount of freedom possible and others support socialism or communism which remove freedom in direct proportion to the amount of security it promises its citizens.

The Active group is driven to control its own destiny and willingly manages the risks required to achieve that objective. They do not need government to give them a college education or a job or health insurance. They will provide it for themselves – provided they are free to manage the risks involved with any endeavor.

The Passive group is driven to gain and exercise power over the destinies of others. They seek to gain sufficient power (or access to power) to ensure their own lives are safe and secure. They do so by involvement with government, by positioning government programs to build safety nets for any eventuality should a mistake be made. They are the bureaucrats who really run the government. It is an attitude that borders on (sometimes is) socialism or communism. Passive politicians then involve their brother and sister Passives within the media who seek their power base by holding themselves out to the public as one who keeps the electorate informed. The problem is they do not cover news. They indoctrinate the public with their own opinions and views of what the news should be. That's how they make sure the public hears what needs to be heard to attain needed public support for Passive objectives and do not hear about conservative alternatives.

Interestingly, watching the 2015-16 political campaigns for President of the United States, my findings regarding Passive liberals and Active conservatives was totally reaffirmed. Liberal progressives have for years pushed freedom-loving Americans too close to socialism and the average Joe and Jane America just wasn't (and isn't) ready for it. The Republican Party had, under both Bush neo-conservative presidencies, moved too far to the Passive liberal position and the people registered with that political party rejected it.

It was the risk management skills of Donald J. Trump that won the presidential race.

> **A MacGruder Axiom: What I see is my truth. What you see is yours. Facts are always facts. Research requires all facts (not just familiar or preferred ones) be included.**

Everything we do in life is an investment of something we own and are willing to barter for something else. Once that is understood, it is easily seen that the next logical question is: How much is someone willing to risk to get what he or she wants and what does it have to do with achievement?

The answer to the last question makes it clear that everything we do in life is impacted by our tolerance for risk – our ability to manage it -- or lack thereof. To get from where we are to where we want to be requires us to risk what we currently have to get what we want.

The research identified two affluent markets. Additional research into the middle markets (done mostly in Colorado, Massachusetts, Pennsylvania, California, Tennessee and Ohio) indicates these personality drives span all levels of wealth and are not at all unique to affluents.

This is an important finding. We now know for sure that the Active/Passive Personality Syndrome equally impacts both the affluent and the middle class market segments. Each Active and Passive group functions from a totally different philosophy base. More will be said about these differing philosophies, but for now the discussion focuses on an overview.

No one is totally Active and no one is totally Passive. Each individual has different levels of energy from one group or the other. Chapter 5 explains this statement more fully.

Actives are responsible for short-term momentum in the world of economic progress. They create the products and ideas that evolve into economic base change... from agriculture to manufacturing, from manufacturing to technology, and from technology to... what? Perhaps to a world of quantum physics...

a world where we speak to one another mentally rather than verbally? The economies they create are long-term, but it takes time to build momentum.

Passives are responsible for long-term stability in the world of economic progress. After Actives have created the technology revolution, Passives are responsible for expanding it – making it bigger and safer, more stable.

If the power drive of Passives could be contained to achieve Nature's life purpose for giving them this drive, life would be much easier. The insecurity that requires them to seek power in the first place, however, appears to force them to seek more and more power. They seek ways – lawful and unlawful – to exercise more and more power over Actives in an effort to prevent these wealth creators from fulfilling their destinies. In what unlawful ways? Every time they pass regulations that violate the Constitution they are abusing power in an unlawful way.

Since Actives seek only control of self destiny, there is no temptation to manipulate other people to gain their objective. They mostly want to be left alone by powerful others.

And that's what the rest of this book is about.

CHAPTER 4

PSYCHOLOGIST/PSYCHIATRIST EVALUATE APPS

The following information comes from a chapter in the book I wrote which was published by the American Bankers Association, *Profitable Private Banking: the Complete Blueprint (1986)*, a book written for bankers.

Dr. Douglas Fancher, an industrial psychologist based in Denver, Colorado, wrote a chapter for that book and I have quoted from it here. I have not included the entire chapter because that book dealt exclusively with banking and some of the data has no application to this material.

The following also includes comments made by industrial psychiatrist, Dr. E. David Beaty, Jr., who, in 1986, was employed by my former employer, United Bank of Denver, prior to the time I started my bank financial and economic analysis company.

This material by Dr. Fancher was written to explain my research done for the banking industry from 1972 through 1985. The research continued until 1992, seven years after publication of the *Blueprint*. Thus Drs. Fancher and Beaty did not have access to the research contained in this book and so it is not reflected in their comments herein. This material updates the data available to Drs. Fancher and Beaty and applies the later research results through 1992 to *people's personalities* rather than to banking.

This chapter is provided more for the benefit of those who may harbor doubts about the validity of the determinations made as to how research data targeting financial interests could be accurately applied to social and political personality sketches or to basic issues of philosophy of life. How could financial information gathered for my bank clients create a psychographic picture of your and my -- of everyone's -- personality?

Remember, we learned from the early research that comfort with risk management or discomfort with it separated Actives from Passives. Thus, by looking at a person's financial statement and perusing their investments, it is possible to identify Actives and Passives. How this is done is explained in Chapter 5. How heavily is a person invested in products controlled by the marketplace rather than the individual? What is the level of investment risk? By who is the person employed? These questions (and others) when applied to identifying personality traits can very accurately create a political psychographic overview.

I laugh as I write this because all day the television news has been telling me how Facebook provided Cambridge Analytica and Strategic Communication Laboratory in Great Britain with information about millions of people. From the information people put on their Facebook accounts, it has enabled Cambridge Analytica, a firm that does political, government and military work worldwide, to draw a psychographic picture of prospective voters. It appears they have used it to identify personality traits that can be used to entice someone into voting for one person or another. Who knows for what else?

The material contained in this book is far more accurate in achieving that objective. You do, however, need to know what you are doing. Therein is the problem.

The thing this chapter makes clear is how, by evaluating bank client financial statements, it is possible to determine that two personality types emerge, whether they are called Active and Passive or Tom Sawyer and Huckleberry Finn.

If you have no concerns or curiosity as to how the research was done and how it has been applied in this book, you may find this chapter less than interesting. It is important information in its own right, but is not important to the psychographic personalities that have been generated by the research done for this book. It has nothing to do with the behavior of liberals and conservatives or husbands and wives. It, however, validates the research done.

COMMENTS FROM DR. DOUGLAS FANCHER AND DR. E. DAVID BEATY, JR.

"The MacGruder concept, with which you are about to become familiar, represents over a decade of work and research by Marilyn MacGruder Barnewall. Before starting her own consulting firm, the MacGruder Agency, Inc., 6 years ago, Ms. Barnewall was employed by United Bank of Denver and was for several years vice president of their executive banking department, the first 'private banking' group in the country. She left that position in 1979 to start her own consulting company and make available to bank clients a program on how to implement private banking successfully. Her bank clients—and, thus, Ms. Barnewall—have been very successful in developing cost-efficient private banking programs. By using creative credit as a point of leverage to generate low-cost bank deposits, these programs tend to break into the black within 5 to 9 months after implementation. The reason she is so well known in the banking industry on this topic is that her client banks have realized substantial profits from her private banking concept."

Dr. Fancher pointed out that the MacGruder concept is a total program for implementing private banking. It covered structure, philosophy, marketing, loan policies, personnel policies and job descriptions, training, space planning and design recommendations, product development, research methodologies, and customer communications.

The program was explained thoroughly to Dr. Fancher and after speaking with some of my client banks he understood that "central to this concept is the idea of segmenting the affluent market in order to offer products that have strong appeal to individuals with certain common personality traits."

This was especially meaningful in the 1980s marketplace, which is when the market changed to consumer need-driven. It was no longer product-driven. Segmentation of affluent customers is achieved by the extensive use of psychography, which is the technique of writing a biographical sketch or character description based on input from a group of people and completing a psychological analysis of the people and their motivations from that input.

In the chapter Dr. Fancher wrote, he pointed out that the data from the marketplace "...allows bankers to segment affluent people into homogeneous groups with greater precision than ever possible before."

The data I gathered produced a psychographic profile that covered attitudes, goals, personality characteristics, and psychological traits. The psychological traits, which are persistent and consistent behavior patterns manifested in a wide range of circumstances, provide some of the most useful information. "These traits develop from the interactive effects of childrearing practices, childhood experiences, and environmental pressures. To a large degree, they determine the type of coping behavior the person will manifest; that is, whether the person is likely to be proactive or reactive in dealing with any environment, financial or otherwise," Dr. Fancher said.

In the recent past (and, for some corporate marketers in the immediate present), all affluent people were seen as one homogeneous group. They were alike in that they possessed money. All one had to do to capture this market was to continue to provide and advertise traditional services, positioning them through the advertising message to have special appeal to rich people. In the view of some advertising agencies, that meant using $30 words, or descriptive phrases about how this product "is truly for the person who has everything." This logic is flawless as far as it goes but it does not go far enough to uncover numerous basic facts.

"The facts that are startling indicate that affluent customers differ from each other in some fundamental ways. For example, their attitudes toward investing and the risks involved, short- and long-term goals, and a variety of personal psychological characteristics are quite different. These differences are as dramatic as night and day. In fact, they are so extreme that one affluent segment may have difficulty communicating with another segment, because they simply do not understand each other," Dr. Fancher said.

Passive and Active Investors

The affluent market can be divided into several segments, but the two most critical divisions have been labeled "active investors" and "passive investors." These two terms are not intended to have a pejorative meaning and the reason for their selection can be found in earlier chapters. (Note: Chapter 5 is also important to these research findings.)

Passive investors are traditional bank customers and, as such, bankers have viewed the entire marketplace as reflecting their values. As Dr. Fancher says in concurring with research data: "The dynamics of their personalities relative to money revolve around the need for security of capital, the production of income, and social acceptance in achieving those two objectives."

Dr. Fancher and I discussed both the social and personal levels and he found it of great interest that what I had termed "Passive investors" are concerned with things that enhance their quality of life: personal possessions, travel, high quality education for their children, and, in general, "la dolce vita," define the quality of life to affluent Passive investors. They tend to invest in money market accounts, blue chip stocks, certificates of deposit, and Treasury bills. They want the highest rate of return on their deposits so that interest (passive) income can help support their lifestyles. As a result, just before the deregulation of Regulation Q, when non-bank money market accounts were paying substantially more than banks were allowed to pay (still, at that point in time, being tied by law to the 5 percent maximum rate on transaction savings accounts), the desire for higher interest income motivated these people to move their money into the accounts on which they could receive a much higher rate of return. Merrill Lynch's money market account was paying 21 percent. For the first time, affluent Passive investors, who like and respect their bankers and who trust the banking industry, were lured from commercial banks.

Before deregulation, many bankers felt they "owned" these traditional bank customers. They had always been the 20 percent of the retail market who maintained 80 percent of banks' retail deposits, and bankers thought as long as they provided high quality service along with the traditional products that appeal to rich people they would retain that 20 percent. Given their experience, bankers' misperceptions that passive investors comprised the entire affluent market is understandable. However, there definitely is another perspective.

"The MacGruder concept is essentially a socio-personality approach to marketing and, as such, offers a provocative hypothesis about how people behave. In the final analysis, this material is actually a personality theory. It attempts to predict behavior in some very specific situations. All theories that attempt to account for human behavior must be seen as highly tentative. They are not judged right or wrong but rather are evaluated on (1) how well they explain the behavior that is seen and (2) how much of the behavior they can really explain. Based on the profits achieved by banks using the MacGruder concept, it can be said that this particular hypothesis is useful," Dr. Fancher wrote in the Introduction of the book published by the American Bankers Association.

Social Learning Theory

In psychological literature, there is a social learning theory created by clinical psychologist Julian Rotter that deals with how people make choices. At the heart of this theory is the belief that people exhibit certain behavior in order to achieve some needed or valued goal. E. David Beaty, Jr., Ph.D., director of market research at United Bank of Denver in 1986, combines his expertise on Rotter's theory with his banking experience to give us the following insights on how this theory affects the MacGruder concept.

"Technically speaking, the potential of any behavior occurring in a given situation is the function of (1) the expectation that behavior in that situation will lead to a particular goal, and (2) the value of that goal in the situation. Behavior then always involves a process of selection or choice. The particular behavior chosen is the one with the highest potential for satisfaction. Three parts of the theory play an important role in understanding the personality dynamics of the active and passive investor: the perceived opportunity structure, the personal belief structure, and the personal control structure."

Perceived Opportunity Structure

Dr. Beaty further stated: "The principal concern of the perceived opportunity structure is with the values or goals an individual is striving toward and the expectations he or she holds of attaining them. Psychologically speaking, if the importance attached to the goals is high and the chance of obtaining it is low, a 'psychological gap' exists. One way to characterize this psychological gap is to define it as 'risk.'

"The attainment of wealth is a goal that, in one form or another, most members of the society share. However, three important distinctions in Rotter's theories have not been mentioned. First, values refer to an individual's personal preference for certain goals. While these goals may be ones that the society shares, the reference point is the individual, not society. Second, values are motivational states, such as the values for independence, control, power, or recognition. Third, since the relevant point is the individual and not society the achievement of the goals or satisfactions is psychologically defined. All three of these distinctions help segregate active from passive investors in terms of their perception of risks. For example, passive investors tend to be security oriented and evaluate risk as anything that would jeopardize their financial security. Active investors are concerned about security but tend to evaluate risk in terms of their knowledge of the investment."

Personal Belief Structure

Dr. Fancher points out that the second main feature of Rotter's social learning theory is the personal belief structure. "At the core of this structure is the concept, "locus of control" (LOC). Using a locus-of-control questionnaire, people may be labeled 'external' or 'internal.' People who score in the external range believe that rewards in life come from outside forces: luck, chance, fate, or powerful 'others' who control rewards. Those who score in the internal range feel they can influence events in the world. They seek to exert active control over their environment and feel rewards in life are directly related to their efforts and skills.

"By merging the two concepts, active and passive investors and internality and externality as a locus of control, we develop a potentially useful conceptualization. The usefulness of these two concepts, active-passive and internal-external, would be enhanced if it could be shown they do, in fact, lend themselves to quantification. Putting the LOC scale and MacGruder psychographic research together, quantification becomes possible. By comparing the hypotheses of the two concepts, the 'external' in the LOC theory is analogous to the MacGruder concept of 'passive' and the 'internal' in the LOC theory equates to the MacGruder concept of 'active.' "

Thus, Dr. Fancher explains below how I arrived at the concept of "active-internal" and the "passive-external."

"Research data using the LOC scale and MacGruder fieldwork," says Dr. Fancher, "suggest how the active-internal person approaches the world. For example, this person wants to control his or her environment. To exercise control over the environment, it is necessary to have considerable information about it. The active-internal person appears to seek greater amounts of relevant information and use it more effectively to control the environment than the passive-external person. The rationale of the active-internal person is that if the reward of being able to control the environment is contingent upon specific behavior and action, then he or she will seek all pertinent information about that behavior and action. This results in the enhancement of personal effectiveness and self-approval. Active-internal individuals indicate that they see themselves as more active and effective than others. They feel they have more autonomy and independence and they actually strive to achieve control and success more assertively than passive-external people."

This active seeking of information for environmental control is also seen in the area of risk taking or management. The more information gained about any situation, the more it is possible to control the outcome. In focus group research, an active-internal individual will frequently say, "If I understand the investment (frequently, the person will repeat that phrase to emphasize its importance — *'if I understand the investment'*), it is not a risk. For example, the more information I have about an investment into raw land development and the more I understand and have control over it, the less of a risk and the more of an investment it is." Thus, when an active-internal person understands investments that appear risky to passive-external people, they appear only as investments, not risks, to that person.... provided he or she controls the investment

"Risk, like beauty, is in the eye of the beholder," says Dr. Beaty. With sufficient information, the perception of risk has decreased. As a result, active-internal people engage in investments that others perceive as having greater risk, because with superior information they are more likely to circumvent the odds. Risk then depends on perception and a level of inner comfort. The active-internal person becomes more comfortable with risk as information increases.

The data indicates that the largest groupings of active-internal investors can be found among small business owners, surgeons, dentists, certified public accountants, lawyers, and entrepreneurs. However, only a particular percentage of each occupational or professional group is labeled active-internal. For example, 90 percent of all surgeons are active-internal but 80 percent of all non-surgical physicians are passive-external. In addition, about 80 percent of corporate executives are passive-external. However, because of the number of corporate executives who economically qualify for private banking, the 20 percent of corporate executives who are active-internal represent a sizable market. Again, the risk a person is willing to take, or the ability to perceive diminishing risk as information, knowledge, and experience are gained, is at the heart of such statistics. How many risk-averse people are attracted to careers as brain surgeons? How much more security does a corporate executive really have than does an independent business owner?

Active-internal investors all have one thing in common: they want to acquire wealth and will manage calculated risks to do so. Or perhaps it would be more accurate to say that they want to acquire wealth and, because of their personality types, they perceive risk associated with its acquisition decreasing as their knowledge increases. By gaining all available knowledge regarding specific investments, they do not take what appears to them to be risks but invest in financial opportunities.

Personal Control Structure

Active-internal people resemble one another in other ways. This brings us to the third important part of Rotter's theory, the personal control structure. According to Dr. Beaty, "Central to this structure is the person's perspective on time and ability to delay gratification. A large percentage of active-internal people have advanced degrees; this is important in the identification process. This suggests that considerable self discipline is available for goal achievement and striving." Data also indicates that the active-internal person has a greater capacity than the passive-external person to delay gratification and, thus, not dissipate energy on immediate needs.

It is interesting to note that active-internals tend to either be highly educated, or, at the other end of the spectrum, do not seek a higher education. Rather, in their younger years they worked for large companies and learned a trade that they could carry into a new business start-up. You will find far more college educated people seeking lifelong careers with major corporations in the middle of the marketplace who are passive-externals than you will find active-internals who may choose to work for major corporations long enough to learn a trade before leaving the major corporation to start his or her own business.

Active-internal people have strong ego control needs that they bring to investment situations. They are able to sustain this persistent, focused attention for considerable periods of time. Active-internal people also have a high level of ego strength that is seen as available psychic energy. This energy is a major factor in determining whether the personality will deteriorate or, in fact, break down when and if the environmental factors become unfavorable and adverse.

The focus group data further suggest that active-internal people are driven to acquire profit that is then reinvested in other profit generating enterprises. This may not sound different from the behavior of affluent passive-external individuals. However, profit is not as important to passive-external people as income. For example, we found that passives often keep large deposits in high interest bearing accounts in order to receive secure, passive, insured income from those deposits, even though their tax liability may be substantial. Taxes paid substantially reduce profit. Thus, passive-external people are more motivated by income and the reduced risk that accompanies such financial behavior, than they are by investing in speculative ventures that require a high tolerance for risk management, result in higher returns, and have substantially greater tax advantages. (Please note: This material was written during the time banks by regulation had to pay consumers 5 percent or 5.25 percent on savings accounts and more on Certificates of Deposit; banks' cost of funds was much higher than it is today.)

Active-internal people, on the other hand, behave in precisely the opposite way. They make investments that result in tax shelters as one way to maximize investment profits which they then reinvest. Because they invest in what they personally control, it results in an ongoing creation of jobs which then can be termed "wealth." As mentioned earlier, they tend to take a calculated risk when they have sufficient information to reduce or minimize it. Their perception of risk will consistently be less than that perceived by passive-external people.

Active-internal people tend to be very sophisticated about their investment strategies and think that bankers are rather less informed than themselves. They do not want a banker to be an adviser, but rather a facilitator who helps them achieve their goals. Active-internal investors operate on the premise that the only way people without money make it is through speculative investments. They are convinced that the outcome of their actions is under their control and it is this active, personal control they demand.

One guideline bankers can use to evaluate the degree to which a customer is active-internal or passive-external from a personal financial statement is to look at how much control the customer has over the investments listed. The lower the level of control and risk, the lower is the customer's rating on the active-internal scale. Thus, although bankers might believe a person who invests in real estate syndications is necessarily an active-internal investor, unless the rest of the financial statement justifies that belief, the lack of control the person has over a real estate syndication deal might indicate the opposite is true. Active-internal people want total control over their own financial and personal destinies.

Dr. Fancher makes clear in his writings that "The active-internal investor is the surprise that MacGruder research has uncovered. As a rule, many active investors do not have anything to do with commercial banks. They find bankers "good at banking but not at the business of making money," so they feel they do not have much in common with them. Instead, they bank with brokers, venture capitalists, or investment bankers. As their cardinal characteristics, these people are risk management-oriented and profit motivated and do not believe that paying taxes is a moral imperative.

Forces That Shape Active Investors

What are some of the forces that have shaped active investors and their attitudes? There is a revolution going on. It has been gathering steam for some time and will most likely continue into the next century. This is the much heralded entrepreneurial shift in the U.S. economy as it moves from an industrial base to one dominated by the forces of high technology, service, and information enterprises. When a major shift occurs in the economic base, entrepreneurial activity flourishes. It is a period of rapid change, considerable societal turbulence, and a high rate of technological innovation.

Some of the factors that have caused this shift include the knowledge explosion that followed World War II and gained speed after the Russians launched the first satellite. Following these events, the number of people who had access to advanced education and specialty degrees dramatically increased. Along with this went prosperity and a new generation that had different attitudes, values, and aspirations. The advent of the entrepreneurial movement is based on demographic factors, cultural changes, psychological outlook, and technological innovation.

High technology companies have received a major share of the newsprint devoted to the entrepreneur, but many others participate in enterprises that are less glamorous but nevertheless major forces in the economy. One only needs to consider the physician who uses income to convert apartments into condominiums or the lawyer who explores the advantages of owning a fast food franchise to see the major contribution they make to the economy. Most of these professionals are active-internal investors. They may be conservative in their primary occupation, but they have to act and think like entrepreneurs if they are to preserve their incomes after retirement.

Motivations of Entrepreneurs

A number of attempts have been made to understand the motivation of the person who seeks entrepreneurial activity. Dr. Fancher points out that: "Karen Homey, an American psychoanalyst, and Alfred Adler, an Austrian psychiatrist, have offered a view of the personal dynamics that drive such a person. They feel that feelings of insecurity and inferiority are the motive force for high achievement.

"According to their studies, childhood feelings of weakness and helplessness lead to feelings of inferiority. Such feelings may be greatly accentuated in a poor family situation, for example, where parents were rejecting or emotionally aloof. These accentuated feelings of inferiority lead to compensatory activity and a lifestyle characterized by active striving. The goal is to overcome the feelings of being inferior by replacing them with feelings of being superior. Such behavior is often seen as over compensation for the perceived deficit. Once again, it is the perception of the situation rather than the objective facts that carry great weight.

"A psychograph of the family dynamics for the person who displays entrepreneurial behavior would include some of the following facts and perceptions of the individual. Of course, this is a composite so a perfect fit with any one person is very unlikely.

"A study by Kets De Vries points to the importance the father has on the formation of attitudes that facilitate high achievement in children. Many entrepreneurs seem to come from a family where one or both parents were self-employed. The ups and downs and turmoil of self employment became well known to the child and had a profound effect. The facts indicate that the familiarity with these vicissitudes and other turbulence in the environment paved the way for an attitude that obstacles can be overcome," states Dr. Fancher.

Life histories of entrepreneurs indicate that childhood for many of them was seen as a very disturbing experience. Themes of desertion, neglect, and poverty are frequent. Again, as far as the dynamics of the personality are concerned, it is the perception rather than the reality that is important, because it is the memory that motivates a person.

In these memories, the father seems to be the main villain. He is often pictured as deserting the family either physically or emotionally and this remote or absent father provides a poor role model for the growing child. As a result, the child may reach maturity with problems that center on low self esteem, lack of confidence, and insecurity. Dr. Fancher points to Kets de Vries who makes the point that, in "conversations with entrepreneurs, their mothers usually come across as strong, decisive, controlling women who give the family some sense of direction and cohesiveness."

Conclusion

We now have the picture of an individual who has experienced rejection, insecurity, and helplessness along with confusion and frustration. United Bank of Denver's Dr. Beaty says, "Learning to cope with these kinds of experiences tends to drive the individual to either end of a continuum that has risk aversion and security at one end and risk management and entrepreneurship at the other. Both ends of the continuum address the strong need to contradict these feelings. For example, the person the MacGruder concept labels the active investor becomes a psychological risk taker. The original feelings covered by a proactive behavioral style become the dominant force."

"One of the most interesting aspects of the MacGruder concept is the attention paid to the establishment of a personal relationship with active-internal customers. That they respond positively to such relationships and that they are actually valuable is a universally accepted fact," stated Dr. Fancher.

The problem is that in today's rapidly growing, complex world, people are often depersonalized in the name of "efficiency." Of course, banks must not lose sight of profit opportunities due to structural and attitudinal efficiency, but much can be gained from developing personal relationships with these customers.

As my research points out and as I explain many times in this material, any program that seeks to dichotomize people according to psychological traits and personality characteristics has a ready-made arena for conflict. When a banker is a passive-external person and a potential customer is an active-internal person, they may have difficulty communicating with each other. This conflict may be increased if the banker has a moralistic attitude about "the right way" to manage one's personal financial affairs.

A banker's non-judgmental attitude toward the speculative plan of an active-internal investor can help develop an ongoing positive relationship. This is further enhanced when the banker takes the time and energy to learn the vocabulary, plans, and strategies of active-internal investors. These people respond readily to private bankers whose banking knowledge includes specialization by occupation and profession. Dealing with customers on this personal level will help promote high trust and credibility.

In summary, attention to the "human equation," the prolific basic research data, and the identification of active-internal investors poses an interesting challenge for the implementation of a private banking program as well as the rest of our social order.

Dr. Fancher's comments were made before the research done after 1986-87, when *Profitable Private Banking: The Complete Blueprint* was published. The above text was written before the application of much of the later research data to the social and political worlds and before the realization that security motivated people are motivated by fear and that is why they seek power and before finding that individualists do not just manage risk, they manage risk they can control. We knew Actives were risk managers... in the *Blueprint* it was assumed that Actives were the ones who invested in precious metals because the risk factor is greater than placing assets in the stock market or with mutual funds.

It was finding that Actives do purchase precious metals but do not view them as an investment but as a hedge against a failed government or currency that turned on a light which shined on Active needs to invest in themselves rather than the publicly-traded markets. Why?

Actives are control motivated and cannot control publicly-traded products. What can they control? Themselves! And it is in themselves they invest.

When we look at the numerous multi-million dollar fines heaped on the heads of investment and commercial banks in the U.S. and Europe for manipulating gold and silver in this new millennium, it seems Active instincts are based on sound thinking. When you look at the TARP government funds spent bailing out Wall Street which was found to be telling some clients to invest in mortgage-based derivatives while telling others that product line was about to explode into nothingness and to stay away from them, Active/self investors seem to be a step ahead of Passives.

In this later research, we also found that Passives do invest in precious metals and other higher risk management products... but they never put at risk assets that if lost will have a negative impact on consumer lifestyle. They wait until they have sufficient financial resources to afford a loss should one occur.

Thus the name change from Active and Passive Investors to Active/self and Passive/market investors was made.

These two findings did little to change the application of the earlier research data as it relates to banking, monetary investments and asset accumulation. It did, however, make the application of the data to the worlds of politics and society much more logical and made it much easier to begin seeking the basic personality traits of both Actives and Passives.

But wait a minute.

The next step in understanding how this applies to you and your choices in life – at least the choices with which you will be most comfortable – is to realize that no one is totally Active and no one is totally Passive. We all have a mixture of both personalities housed in our hearts, minds and spirits.

See if you can identify yourself in the next chapter which explains this phenomenon.

CHAPTER 5

OPPOSING FORCES, UNHEALTHY EXTREMES

Risk Tolerance Level: 0% 10% 20% 30% 40% 50% 60% 70% 80% 90% 100%

Security Need Level 100% 90% 80% 70% 60% 50% 40% 30% 20% 10% 0%

No physically, mentally and emotionally healthy human being is 100 percent motivated by security. None is totally motivated by managing risk, either. Let me correct those statements. No healthy, stable individual is totally Active. Neither is such a person totally Passive. Healthy people are a mixture of both risk management Active and low-risk management Passive traits.

Look at the Security Need Level on the above chart (lower line): One group of Passives has a 60 percent security need and a risk tolerance level of 40 percent (upper line). They are the opposites of Actives with a 60 percent risk tolerance level and a 40 percent security need. Passives with a 60 percent security need with risk tolerance at 40 percent are opposites of Actives with a 60 percent risk tolerance and a 40 percent security need. These Passives have a 60 percent need for power and are comfortable with 40 percent risk management. Actives with a 60 percent control drive have a 40 percent need for security/power.

Interestingly, it is at the 60/40 security need to control drive you will find most politicians, both Democrat and Republican, those who both say they are liberal and conservative. I once evaluated George Herbert Walker Bush as being a 50/50 security/control politician. His son, George W., is not far behind him... probably a 55 security 45 control level. Neither is conservative. Why are politicians at this level of security versus control need drawn to politics?

People at these levels have no real anchor in either world. Real conservatives (at 70 percent control and 30 percent security) live in a black and white world and real liberals live at 70 percent security and 30 percent control... in a world of grey.

Why do I say Passives live in a world of grey when they are at the 70 percent security 30 percent risk management/control level but do not say Actives with a 70 percent risk management/ control level and a 30 percent security need also live in a grey world? Because to gain security requires compromise which requires a relativist (or grey) attitude towards making decisions and living life as a result of decisions made.

At the 60/40 and 50/50 levels in either world (security need/control drive), there is no strong anchor in either the Active or the Passive side. They believe one thing today and another, opposite thing tomorrow. If that doesn't explain politicians, I don't know what does. I also believe that is the major reason the public worldwide has less respect for politicians than for just about any other social class (except members of the media).

In other words, the world as shown in the above chart of Active and Passive personality traits is made up of various opposing groups, not just one giant group of Actives in opposition to one huge group of Passives. Rather, opposition between groups exists in direct percentages of the opposition that exists. An 80 percent risk tolerance 20 percent security need person is not in total opposition to a 60 percent security need 40 percent risk tolerance person. They are in total opposition to the 80 percent security need and 20 percent risk tolerance group. That same comparative applies across the entire scale of Actives and Passives.

Personality traits listed at the start of Chapter 3 are compatible with these percentile categories. For example, in 30 percent risk and 70 percent security drive personalities (the largest Passive group), individuals place 70 percent of investment assets into the most secure vehicles possible. The other 30 percent are available for higher risk ventures – e.g., to purchase a small business (usually for a security-driven reason – like providing retirement income). Looking at other personality traits, each person is a 70 percent joiner, 30 percent individualist; each communicates well 70 percent of the time and is an uncomfortable communicator who sends poor messages 30 percent of the time. This information makes the list of personality traits in Chapters 1 and 3 even more meaningful to readers who seek to identify themselves in those pages.

Actives with a 30 percent security drive and a 70 percent risk tolerance level (the largest group of Actives) embody 70 percent of the personality traits described under the Active Personality Traits category and 30 percent of the traits listed in Chapters 1 and 3, as belonging to Passives.

An explanation follows of the various percentage mixes relative to financial and investment behavior. *Remember, risk management levels regarding money also extend to other personality traits... e.g., political beliefs, marriage, faith, careers, etc.*

0% Risk/100% Security: These are people who bury their money (or gold coins) under a tree on a moonless night after midnight (then place a large, killer guard dog in the yard close to the tree). People with no tolerance for risk are psychologically unhealthy; few, if any, are affluent. Those that are usually inherit money rather than earn it. They often suffered mental, physical or emotional abuse as children.

10% Risk/90% Security: This risk tolerance group invests in insured accounts ... certificates of deposit (CDs), whole life insurance policies, etc. Highly affluent people from this category do loosen up a bit more to invest in T-bills, quality municipal bonds, gold coins, and other higher-risk (from their perspective) products. At this level of security, the need for access to power is very strong for protective reasons. When affluent, these people are very strong political contributors and social activists. This group loves the idea of socialism and communism. The affluent from this group overlook the fact that neither economic philosophy would allow them to maintain their money – it would become part of the collective – and the non-affluent overlook the fact that either socialism or communism would require them to work to have access to government funds. Both the poor and the affluent in this group live in a world of selective ignorant non-reality.

20% Risk/80% Security: People with this level of risk tolerance invest in products that have insured returns ... e.g., CDs, money market accounts, life insurance products. Up to 20 percent of their portfolios are comfortably invested in blue chip stocks, another 20 percent in T-bills/bonds, municipal bonds, and other government-backed investment vehicles. These people also consider their primary residence as family/lifestyle investments. Homes are rarely leveraged (and only when absolutely required) for credit dollars to fund any kind of speculative deal ... homes are the basis for Passive quality of life and are put at risk as collateral only when absolutely necessary. As people in this group gain affluence, their investments include mutual funds and a larger percentage of blue chip stocks. Because insecurities at this level are still fairly strong, this group is hesitant about displaying its wealth in the form of luxury automobiles and other conspicuous consumer goods. When they become highly affluent, they are more likely to go from a Buick to a limousine with a driver/body guard than to a Cadillac, Mercedes, or Lexus. These people are strong political contributors and social activists. Those individuals who are not part of the upper or middle class segments are politically defensive and their security needs focus more on survival than saving. Lower incomes usually result from lower educational achievement and place almost unchangeable limitations on this group which tends to increase their stress/security (and social resentment) levels.

30% Risk/70% Security: The greatest numbers of successful Passive affluents reside in this category of risk tolerance and security need. For affluents, this is the primary niche for Passive (money management, trust based) private banking clients. The higher their levels of affluence, the greater the likelihood they are affiliated with trust bankers. As this group's affluence increases, they rely more and more on outside third parties, from tax accountants and attorneys to brokers and financial planners. The very rich employ others to do nothing but keep them wisely invested. They are volume investors in blue chip stocks; some make the leap to NASDAQ. Until tax laws erased benefits, these individuals were heavy investors in limited partnerships and real estate syndications. Their other investments include commercial paper, mutual funds, and municipal bonds. They will leverage about 30 percent of their assets for access to credit used for investment purposes. The 30 percent they are willing to leverage will not include items needed to enhance consumer lifestyles. Even at this higher level of risk, homes are an investment in family and are not part of the asset base to be risked. Consumer lifestyle is of primary importance and will not be leveraged, short of an emergency. These people are the primary targeted niches for luxury cars and homes and just about anything else that falls under the category of "conspicuous consumption." They are the strongest Passive political contributors, the strongest community activists. They are more income-driven than profit-motivated/tax sensitive. The more affluent they become, the more they contribute. Access to power becomes very important to Passives at this level of profit and risk tolerance. They happily put at risk 30 percent of liquid assets to invest in aggressive products like calls, puts, precious metals, etc., considered higher risk. *But they risk only that 30 percent compatible with their risk management level and assets uninvolved in lifestyle/security.*

40% Risk/60% Security: The total portfolio for people with this level of risk tolerance will strongly resemble the 30 percent customer, described above. The major difference is that 40 percent instead of 30 percent of the asset base not associated with lifestyle security is comfortably put at risk. Historically, the 40 percent risk tolerance group has invested more heavily in real estate than the 30 percent group. Passive real estate investment is done via outside third party experts and is not personally managed by the investor. Acceptable replacements for traditional real estate investments managed by outside third parties include more aggressive mutual funds (international funds, for example ... new company start-up funds, etc.), most stocks including calls, puts, options and commodities, and new high-quality over-the-counter stock issues, cryptocurrencies, etc. The latter, more aggressive investment products listed will represent a minority portion of the investment portfolio. However, 10 percent of a high six- or seven-figure net worth represents a sizeable investment... some of them show up as contenders for the highest offices in their nations – and they sometimes win. This is where you will find political game players whose moral compass may bounce as easily from the moral to the immoral (more likely amoral) depending upon their mood and needs of the moment. They have a foot in both camps and their decisions may go one way today and in an opposite direction tomorrow. A lot of intelligence officers in all nations fall into this and the 50/50 categories because of the moral flexibilities required of them in their area of expertise.

50% Risk/50% Security: This group, more than any other, relies on outside third party advisors. They are difficult clients for financial planners and advisors because they go one way today, another tomorrow. One might think that the higher the risk management capabilities, the more aggressive people would become in making personal investment decisions. Individuals in this group can be torn between one-half of their personalities saying "take a chance," and the other half warning against it. All of the groups that come before this one generally allow their security dominance to rule. Those that come after, risk tolerance.

This one is half-and-half. This group's solution is investment advisors – and, worry. For half of the people with this level of risk tolerance, their portfolios resemble that of individuals at the 30 percent risk tolerance level. Again, the major differences are that 50 percent instead of 30 percent of the asset base not associated with lifestyle security is comfortably put at risk. With the help of financial advisors, Passives invest in some pretty interesting things: agriculture investments such as water rights and wineries, oil and gas limited partnerships, hopper cars, and other more aggressive investments like cryptocurrencies, cable television, equipment leasing, and all forms of stock with some percentage in calls, puts, options and commodities. I emphasize: with the assistance of advisors. The more affluent the individual, the more investment funds available for higher- risk stock market products. At this level, the biggest behavioral change is investor need for personal involvement in the product. As risk tolerance levels and investment risk increase, investors gather more information and become more personally involved in controlling the outcome. The non-risk portion of the portfolio will resemble that of other Passive investors with higher security needs. As for the moral compass question, I would categorize George Soros as a 50/50 personality. He, a Jew, spent his youth showing Nazis where the Jews of his village lived and sending them to their deaths. If that is not bad enough, in interviews Soros recalls this as one of the most fulfilling times of his life. People who have committed treason against their country and helped murder their neighbors are most likely to be found in this group. They can be internalists or externalists; they can be emotional or logical. They are fabulous liars but can just as easily tell the truth. This person's personality is a conundrum and is not easily solved in any area of life – the risk management of monetary decisions, social issues, and particularly in the world of politics. There are probably more intelligence operative James Bonds in this category than any other -- but the greater the risk involved in an intelligence operation, the more likely they are 60/40, the next category.

60% Risk/40% Security: At least 40 percent of the investment portfolio for people with this level of risk tolerance will be in products offering a high level of security but the individual will be more personally involved and will exercise more control. Self-owned real estate investments and businesses will dominate the 60 percent risk portion of the portfolio – remember, this group invests in themselves with 60 percent of their assets and 40 percent in more secure market products. The biggest behavioral change comes in the form of control. Outside third-party advisors are relied on less. Real estate deals are self-directed, for example, rather than turned over to outside third parties for management. The purchase of an apartment building and control of its conversion into condominiums is a highly favored investment for this group. Though not yet at a risk level that makes it comfortable for total and personal control of investments, this group takes a step in that direction. Like their Passive counterparts, however, the 60/40 Active plays political games and their moral compass may bounce as easily from the moral to the immoral (more likely amoral) depending upon their mood and needs of the moment. They have a foot in both camps and 40 percent of their decisions may go one way today and an opposite direction tomorrow. A lot of intelligence officers in all nations fall into this category because of the moral flexibilities required of them in the political arena, especially in the arena of black operations. These people represent the Deep State.

70% Risk/30% Security: The largest number of Active investors reside at this address. The group is made up of independent business owners, CPAs and lawyers who partner small, independent firms, surgeons, anesthesiologists, radiologists (80 percent of non-surgeons are Passive), dental surgeons, and entrepreneurs. Fifteen percent of non-Passive corporate executives reside here, too. The group's primary behavior motivator is control of investment risks managed. Thirty percent of the investment portfolio will reflect security needs ... blue chip stocks, CDs (though they place less money in banks since the Dodd Frank Bill passed), mutual funds, commercial paper, etc. The 70 percent available for risk-based investments will not be in publicly controlled products, regardless of the level of risk or security. The type of investment is as diverse as the group – from water rights deals to thoroughbreds and small but profitable oil deals -- but is usually in a business about which a great deal is known and where a modicum of control can be maintained by the investor(s). Surgeons, for example, may start a medical billing computer service or a home nursing or medical supply service. Or, they may buy a small apartment building close to the hospital to condo convert into medical office space. Information is important to them. This is the primary niche market at banks wanting to implement credit-driven private banking. These people are extremely tax sensitive and profit (as opposed to income) motivated but the projects they launch tend to result in wealth... community growth and jobs. Non-medical group members also love real estate. Bankers can be of tremendous help to those just starting out with real estate investments by serving as advisors ... "be sure to get Workmen's Liens signed before making payment to a contractor," etc. New practice start-up lending for physicians, attorneys, dentists, accounts, etc., is of great significance to members of this group and attracts them to financial institutions like a magnet.

80% Risk/20% Security: People with this level of risk tolerance and resultant control needs can be disruptive employees at large companies. They have non-team egos and behavior modes not usually welcomed at major corporations (including banks). They have an abundance of energy, and are usually very creative and internalized. They may have been viewed as "Nerds" in school. Their primary investments are self-controlled small and large companies ... cryptocurrencies, shipping, robotics, Internet businesses (e.g., Amazon.com, Yahoo, independent banks, factoring companies, etc). The businesses they own are as diverse as the individuals that make up this group. There are fewer professionals (medical, accounting, legal) in this group versus the 70% risk/30% security group, and more entrepreneurs and independent business owners. Contractors are heavily represented here. Little is said about which investment products they prefer because their products are themselves. Still, 20 percent of the security need is reflected in the portfolio ... stocks, bonds, municipal funds, etc. On the publicly-controlled investment security-based products, this Active group's risk tolerance is lower than its counterpart group on the Passive side because risk tolerance goes down in direct proportion to the inability to control the investment. These people are strong individualists.

90% Risk/10% Security: At 90 percent, the customer's risk tolerance becomes too risky for bank borrowing unless the bank has special expertise in tracking tax-sheltered income that is difficult to find and monitor (for example, thoroughbred depreciation). The personal financial statements of these customers are often highly leveraged. It has a negative credit implication. Like people with an 80 percent risk tolerance, these people usually invest in/start businesses that they own and may have aggressive purposes (which can make them candidates for litigation ... another credit risk). They are very egocentric, control dominant, and profit motivated. Think Howard Hughes. A lot of them started now defunct dot com companies. They like working in home office settings. This is the smallest group of functional Active/self investors (with the exception of the 100%/0% group that follows ... many of which are not socially functional).

100% Risk/0% Security: Like their counterparts at the other end of the spectrum, these people are not mentally or emotionally healthy. The higher a person's tolerance for risk, the greater is the potential for gambling problems, for example. These are very control-dominant people with very large egos. They have difficulty establishing strong personal and family relationships. They will not invest in anything they do not control. Their very attitude sometimes stifles their ability to achieve success. People in this group were often child victims of abuse.

NON-INVESTMENT PERSONALITIES AND HABITS

Actives are from Pluto. Passives are from Mars. The point is they live on different planets. They speak different languages and have opposite belief systems. Their investment strategies and life choices, from careers to investment preferences, reflect their state as opposites.

If you say the word "compassionate" to Actives, they literally see different pictures in their minds than do Passives.

The purpose of this material is to explain Actives and Passives as consumers of products in any industry with emphasis on banking and financial services. It also looks outside of their consumer personalities and asks: What are they like as human beings with opposite philosophies to guide their daily behavior?

Total Active/self investors, for example, are those with a 100 percent tolerance for risk and a zero need for security. They live at the right end of the above chart. These people spend their lives gathering knowledge, often having insufficient time or energy at the end of the day to do anything with it. Because their risk/security drives are so extreme, they often lack the discipline required to apply themselves to any single objective for long periods. The same is true of Passives at the left side of the chart. "Any single objective" means marriage, politics, careers, and all of the social and psychological elements of life.

People whose security needs are zero and who can tolerate risk at 100 percent are driven to control everything that touches closely on their lives. They are compulsive about everything they do. These people are fearless (which can make them targets for flipping from supporting America to terrorism). Harboring strong opinions, they allow their social and political beliefs to carry them to an abortion clinic with a gun in their hands. Or, they go to a federal building in Oklahoma with a bomb in the back of a truck... or they manipulate someone to drive a truck filled with explosives to a building while they plot to set off explosives already placed in the building, leaving the driver to suffer the total consequence of the devastation.

People at the opposite end of the scale -- those who have a 100 percent need for security and a zero tolerance for risk -- are also like wagons running on three wheels. In reality all Passive lives are driven by fear. They think they seek power – sometimes at any cost. In reality, they are seeking security which only power can provide.

As total fearlessness makes 100 percent Actives targets for groups like ISIS, so does the total fear of the 100 percent Passive group. They perceive that power will provide the security they need. Power protects them psychologically if not physically from their fears. They often have addictive personalities and their addictions have a wide range of application. For example, people whose lives are motivated by insecurity are often lured by drugs or alcohol as a means of escape from real life.

People who live at the far end of the risk or security spectrum can be sociopaths. They are so driven by their own fear or by the total lack of it that it can lead to compulsive behavior and a little item like conscience can be seen as missing from the personality. Both Actives and Passives at this level can be abusers of children, wives or husbands, employees, etc.

As Passives gain access to power, their fears become subconscious. Politically, Passives support the philosophies of socialism or communism. They much prefer the State take the risk of home and property ownership. They are more comfortable when "powerful others" make important decisions about their lives. They are willing to impose their fear-driven philosophies on others. Like healthy people, the unhealthy often assume that others see the world the way they do ... and, if they do not, they should.

People at the 100 percent end of the security spectrum are often institutionalized. They may never leave home ... or, like Howard Hughes, may lock themselves in a hotel room with bodyguards because of perceived threats and dangers.

When you look at the two extremes, an Active may blow up a building and kill innocent men, women and children. Actives with no need for security become hermits and seldom get politically involved -- or, become a Unabomber or join with terrorist groups.

Randy Weaver lived in isolation on a mountain in Idaho. He exhibited a high tolerance for risk. He could easily be categorized by the standards set forth herein as a far right Active conservative. That is not to suggest that government had the right to invade his personal life and begin shooting his family, especially an innocent wife standing in the doorway of her home holding her baby. In fact, the government's reaction in the Randy Weaver invasion of property suggests those in government power at the time had 90 to 100 percent Passive (abuse of power) personalities.

Passives with no tolerance for risk can become political zealots, too. Fearful people become so enamored with the power they gather and the protection it offers, they abuse it. They may be so fearful of the future, they decide nothing can save them and seek to "end it now" rather than sit around waiting for whatever they think is going to happen and they make it happen.

They are so certain their causes are right they believe the end justifies the means. Thus, they are capable of spying on and attacking American citizens, killing women and children in Waco, Texas or killing Randy Weaver's wife in Idaho, a woman who did and was doing nothing more wrong than holding a baby. This type of person kills the Weaver's child who is playing on his own property with his dog on a lonely mountain. Sociopaths with power almost always abuse it. It is how they exhibit having power: by abusing it. Policemen and child care workers who abuse their power fall into this category. Nurses and teachers – and university professors -- are in the same category.

Two percentile groups among Passives and Actives hold the greatest population for each group. The typically healthy and successful – or, upscale – Active is at the 70/30 level ... 70 percent risk tolerance, 30 percent security need. The typically healthy and successful Passive is at the 30/70 level ... 30 percent risk tolerance, 70 percent security need.

The second area where the largest number of successful people will be found is on the above scale is at 45/55 or 55/45 levels. These are "middle-of-the-roaders." Politically, they call themselves moderates. Corporately, they rise to the top because they are malleable people with few strong convictions. Thus, they are flexible to the point of sometimes being chameleons. They are usually very charming, social beings. Many politicians from both parties fall into this group. So, too, do many of those who inherit wealth.

Applying the traits explained in Chapter 3 to financial services behavior, it is only logical to conclude that Actives are credit-driven wealth creators. Passives oppose credit for other than necessaries until their resources are sufficient to warrant there will be no costly losses resulting in lifestyle threats. They are asset preservers and managers. Each plays an important part in a healthy capitalist society.

The Introduction and first five chapters of this book are devoted to explaining who -- and what – Active and Passive people are. It is now time to apply the research data to specific subjects. It explains how the personalities of people who reflect the Active Passive Personality Syndrome impact society.

CHAPTER 6

THE PURPOSE OF WEALTH
New Wealth and New Jobs vs. Old Money: Socialism vs. Free Enterprise

"To everything there is a season. A time for every purpose under heaven: A time to be born, And a time to die; A time to plant, And a time to pluck what is planted; A time to kill. And a time to heal; A time to break down, And a time to build up... A time to gain, And a time to lose..." Ecclesiastes 3:1

"Wealth has two purposes. The first is to create new jobs and new wealth. The second supports wealth once it has been created. Balance between wealth creation and preservation must be achieved and maintained for healthy economic growth that benefits all people." M. Barnewall, Chapter 6, Verse 1.

DOES WEALTH HAVE A PURPOSE?

There is a purpose for everything -- even wealth. It is a natural purpose. And, like every other thing on this earth, when we do not learn from the mistakes recorded by history, we are bound to repeat them. Nowhere does this old adage apply more aptly than to money.

A MacGruder Axiom: We learn from our mistakes, but please remember: they teach us what does not work. They teach us little of what does work.

Contrary to what a lot of people think, wealth is an impersonal thing. It may not seem that way to parents whose child needs medical care the family cannot afford, but wealth, in and of itself, is impersonal. It is societal structure that causes the problem, not the concept of wealth.

In America, wealth is accessible to any person willing to properly prepare himself, or herself who will work like the dickens to achieve it.

That said, achieving affluence is more difficult for some than for others. Those who have money to buy advantages like education at private schools and top universities are likely to have an easier time becoming rich than those without money. I didn't say getting rich was easy. I said wealth is accessible and impersonal. Remember, for the purpose of this book, wealth is defined as how much personal and spiritual character a person has. Money is a by-product of the things that create positive personalities who contribute much to society.

I know. I started my young adult life with a husband in prison and two babies ... on welfare for several months because of an automobile accident. I know how difficult it is to become successful without social advantage. I also know it can be done.

Wealth cares not who joins the millionaires' (or billionaires') club. Certain people may care -- snobs, we call them -- but wealth does not. Like Old Man River, it just keeps movin' along, in tune with the Laws of Nature that govern it.

Some people term money "success." Others understand wealth is a *byproduct* of success. They realize success is a state of mind, not dollars in a bank account. True wealth embraces the human heart and spirit as surely as it embraces money. True wealth leaves a legacy... hospitals, companies, jobs, family, churches, etc. Many people poor of pocket are far wealthier physically, spiritually, and mentally than those with big bank accounts.

A MacGruder Axiom: Success is a creative person with discipline. All are creative; all are not disciplined.

The primary drive of Passives is to gain security. Their primary motivator is power ... enough power (or access to it) to provide personal security. More often than not, they are liberal progressives.

Actives are, more often than not, political conservatives. They and their risk management skills bring to the technology age what Eli Whitney, Alexander Graham Bell, Henry Ford and Nikola Tesla brought to the industrial age: innovation and opportunity. Their creative energies and high-risk management capabilities drive the heartbeat of a new economy and the future jobs that come with it.

No economy can survive without giving balanced support to both groups. Economies do not thrive in the short-term if only Active philosophies are in place because Actives are the economically far-sighted. They see tomorrow.

They certainly do not survive in the long-term when Passive philosophies control the marketplace. Passives are economically shortsighted. They see today.

A MacGruder Axiom: Short-term goals provide momentum; long-term goals provide direction. Passives provide short-term objectives and Actives provide long-term direction.

There is a wealth cycle. Like most cycles, if part of it gets left out the rest of the cycle is broken. It takes a total cycle to feed a total economy.

If you look at America's business history, you find two elements of significant importance: big business and its healthy expansion; and, independent business and its healthy expansion. The two feed positively off of one another when government allows the marketplace to function independently and an entire list of things occurs. Big businesses support small businesses -- not just by buying products from them, but by hiring and training young people who, once trained, leave the big company to start their own small ones. Small businesses support big businesses, too.

Large corporations must periodically reduce their labor force. They fire people in other words. Small businesses hire them and put them back to work. If they did not, a recession would occur and people would not have sufficient funds to purchase the products of the big companies. No business, big or small, thrives during economic recessions.

The upsy-downsy curve of the stock market results from the inability of small businesses to meet promises made to big businesses. The failure of over-priced, over-funded and under-productive dot.com companies of the late 1990s and early 2000s spilled over into big business and an imbalance in the markets grew. Too much emphasis was placed on traditional versus new business concepts which caused the imbalance. That, in turn, causes lost jobs, reduced productivity, and a loss of consumer confidence in the markets.

In 2007-08, the implosion of Lehman Brothers and Bear Stearns bared the ignorance of investment bankers regarding the total world of business; it bared the corrupt practices of the entire financial services market... from investment banks to commercial banks. Stock brokers at investment banks had purchased small mortgage companies which created what became popularly known as liar loans. The Mortgage Electronic Registration System (MERS) almost succeeded in replacing county clerks in registering real estate... especially consumer homes – those belonging to the middle class. MERS was found to be an unlawful trust – not a trust at all – but it did great damage during the long process of getting the courts to find it misrepresented its power to perform functions it simply assumed it could do and which it did... unlawfully.

Millions of unlawful foreclosures occurred as people went into court with bankers who provided a copy of the loan papers the about-to-be foreclosed defendants signed when financing their new homes. The bank could not lawfully foreclose without a copy of the Deed to the property, but they could not provide one. Why? Because the investment banks that had purchased the mortgage (from the foreclosing bank) to place it in mortgage-backed derivatives had the Deed and once the property went into a derivative, the Deed went with it. The foreclosed properties had Deeds owned by Wall Street brokers which put them into derivatives which were heavily sold in the international marketplace – putting not just America's financial system in jeopardy, but the world's as well.

The more important question was never asked: "Your Honor, the law states that to foreclose on my property the bank must prove to the Court that it has standing to foreclose. To do that, the bank must provide proof of ownership to the Court via a Deed showing that it owns the property. Why are you not requiring the bank to provide a Deed to prove ownership, as required by law, because without one they have no standing with this Court to foreclose on my property!

"The loan papers accurately state that I willingly gave my home as collateral for my mortgage loan, but it does not say the bank has the right to foreclose on my home without proving ownership to the Court and it can only do that by providing the Court with a Deed to the property."

Ignorance of the law causes errors in judgment and many homes were lost to foreclosure unnecessarily because people (and often their lawyers) were ignorant of how the system works. Had more home owners asked this question of the courts, more of them would have avoided unlawful foreclosures.

Nature will always find a way to replace a loss of balance because to nature balance represents the normal, the healthy. Millions of Americans who went through the trauma of foreclosure paid a huge price as they watched their dreams destroyed by the unlawful legal system largely caused by MERS. It was an unnecessary price paid to the god of greed. I would point out – strongly – that greed and profit are two different things.

The above should explain to you why as we moved into the new Millennium a stock brokerage house, Lehman Brothers, was one of the largest mortgage brokers in the country. Lehman was very, very dependent upon the income from mortgage-backed derivatives. They purchased small mortgage companies and those companies aggressively made liar loans to buyers who were economically unqualified for the homes they purchased.

A liar loan is one in which the loan applicant is told ahead of time that there will be no verification of the borrower's employment and salary history placed on their mortgage application... so loan applicants lie. They put on their loan applications whatever was required to qualify for the loan and totally avoided the truth.

Consumers had not gotten over their mistrust of the dot com stock market losses of 2000-2001. In 2007-2008, they had their eyes opened even wider and began to realize that the corruption went deeper than just Wall Street. It penetrated government at all levels. I wrote many editorials about how difficult it is to regain the trust of the people once it is lost.

Judges should have known better than to accept signed loan papers as justification for foreclosure on a property – I'm sure many of them did and overlooked it. My guess is, many of them were paid handsomely for their corruption. Consumers realized the entire system was corrupt.

The point is, without one group fulfilling its role in the cycle, the other group loses financial stability. Each has a purpose in a capitalist environment that is equally important to the ongoing health of the other.

To achieve their objectives, each group must be able to exercise the personal motivators supportive of its particular role in the social order. In America today, there is much animosity between the two groups. One only needs to look at the damage being caused to our nation by Democrat resistance to President Donald Trump to understand the literal hatred by Democrats for Conservatives. It appears they would rather lose their nation -- or perhaps that was always part of their world government socialist plan -- than to approve members of the Trump Cabinet or his appointees to our federal courts. If true, this is not just sick. It is stupid and borders on sedition.

Neither group understands the other. Neither understands the necessity for the other's existence. Each views the other as radical or extreme or elitist. In some cases, the actions of some members from both groups are radical, extreme and elitist.

Anything that distracts wealth from its two primary purposes – asset management/preservation and wealth/job creation -- deviates from Natural Law.

Perhaps the first reference to the purpose of wealth appears in the parable of the talents in the Holy Bible, Matthew 26:26.

The parable of the talents is a story about a man who goes on a journey. He calls his servants to him, and gives one five talents, another two talents, and another one talent. A talent is equivalent to an ounce of gold or, in today's world, close to $1,500.00.

Upon the man's return, he calls his servants to him to ask for the return of his money. The first has invested wisely and returns his five talents plus five more. The second has also invested wisely, returning the original two with two more. The third, however, tells his master, "And I was afraid and went and hid your talent in the ground. Look, there you have what is yours."

In verse 28, the wealthy man says, "...take the talent from him and give it to him who has ten talents. For to everyone who has, more will be given, and he will have abundance; but from him who does not have, even what he has will be taken away." The one-talent servant was cast into the outer darkness with much weeping and gnashing of teeth.

The idea that wealth has a purpose, then, is not a new one. Whether the "talent" is in the hands of an Active or a Passive, it is a Law of Nature that we put the assets granted to us to work. If we hide them under a rock because we are insecure and afraid, we will lose them. This Natural Law was observed in our history as long ago as the days of Moses.

> **A MacGruder Axiom: If it's better to give than to receive, why do people who have much get more? Because the more you have, the more you are able to give.**

Nowhere is a Law of Nature more abused than the one pertaining to wealth. Passives pay too little attention to economic progress for future generations. Actives pay too little attention to what needs to occur to support the traditional, existing economy.

With money comes power ... that for which tyrants have fought since the beginning of time. What does each of these groups need to help it work with – rather than against – Nature's Laws so its objectives can be fulfilled?

Passives require a secure investment environment and a strong current economy to encourage them to invest in the stock market. This is one way Passives are supposed to support today's economic needs. When the market becomes unstable and begins a downward trend, it is natural for a climate of fear to result. The natural security drive of Passives causes them to remove their investment dollars... or do things like sell stocks short – which can cause an overall lowering of the total stock market. It causes politicians to pass protective regulations intended to keep investors safe but because they do not understand the risk management strategies required by capitalism, end up damaging business growth which ends up making things worse.

Affluent Passive senior and executive corporate managers need careers with large, safe companies. They need a professional environment that encourages ever-increasing knowledge, responsibilities and personal challenge. Personal as well as professional growth must occur. And it must be remembered that corporate growth represents access to ever-increasing power.

Middle class Passives require a secure, stable job environment. They seek career opportunities, appropriate rewards for labor and loyalty, and a means to progress and grow within large organizations. They require good work and retirement benefits that meet security needs. When labor demands more in wages than the market will bear (when products cannot be sold for an amount sufficient to cover the costs of labor demands), jobs are lost. Labor union leaders need to learn that the Laws of Nature are more powerful than their organizations.

Actives require a business environment that gives them control of the risks they are asked to manage. No one provides independent business owners with good work and retirement benefits and sick leave. No one provides independent business owners a secure, stable job environment. No one hands them a paycheck for showing up for work. If they do not produce each day, they lose money. If they lose too much money because they do not make a profit on too many days, their company closes. Jobs are lost.

What the two groups need exemplifies opposite natures. Passives upgrade their personal residences and continually improve family lifestyles. Actives place a second trust deed on their homes to buy old properties in run down areas. They rehab them and provide low-cost housing for the poor. At least, they do if they control the risks inherent to the process. And, they profit from their investment of time, labor, and risk management.

How does buying an old property and rehabbing it relate to wealth?

The person who buys it and fixes it up will profit. The workmen... the tilers, roofers, carpeters, carpenters, masons, plumbers... will profit. The retail outlets where products to make repairs are purchased will profit. The poor person who can only afford to pay minimum rent will benefit.

And, the profits from this deal will be invested in another, possibly bigger improvement project next time (and it will provide more jobs, more rental opportunities, etc.). Wealth is thus created.

A MacGruder Axiom: Every problem holds an opportunity.
It is also true that each opportunity holds a problem.

A few pages ago, I said that no economy survives without giving balanced support to both Passive and Active groups. I also mentioned when Passive philosophies dominate the marketplace,

Passive short sightedness can be economically damaging to the long-term. They see today, rather than tomorrow.

At the end of the first eight-year term (for many years) of a Passive liberal Democrat, President Clinton, we also ended eight years of Passive control of the marketplace. By September of 2000, the stock market was taking periodic downward dives because of investor fear.

Some people blame Federal Reserve Chairman Alan Greenspan for not dropping borrowing rates more quickly. After his inauguration, others blamed George W. Bush for pointing out the obvious... we are headed for a recession.

Passives, in their usual "if people avoid the issue it will go away" mode suggest that when President Bush talked about a recession (to add momentum to the passage of his tax bill), he caused the recession to occur. They are partially right. It is no secret that the Bush family supports neo-conservatism which has very little to do with conservative philosophy and is far closer to liberal ideology. Neo-conservatism is a philosophy largely created by Irving Kristol, father of Bill Kristol, founder and Editor-at-large at the "Weekly Standard" (the magazine which calls itself conservative but was among the first to take a "Never Trump" stance).

The truth is, after eight years of a Democrat president placing too much emphasis on big business, entrepreneurs and independent businesses felt the pinch. I know. I know. Republicans are the political party that supports big business. At least, that's the Democrat line. To test the truth of that concept, look at the anti-small business legislation that, through either Executive Orders or the regulatory route, was disadvantageous to small business from 1988 through 2016... from Presidents George Bush Sr., through Barack Obama.

Remember the "Read my lips: No new taxes" statement made by neo-conservative George H.W. Bush to secure his 1988 nomination by the Republican Party as its candidate for President of the United States? He made the statement just before raising taxes. You also probably remember him being the first President to say the words "New World Order" – hardly conservative (Active) philosophy.

The tax increase that passed while there was still a Democrat majority in Congress is certainly small business unfriendly. Environmental regulations that increased the cost of starting new businesses were anti-independent business. So, too, are OSHA requirements ... and family-leave bills and dozens of others. The demand that employers take responsibility for worker health care plays a large role. These do not come from Active/conservative ideology. They come straight from the hearts of Passive/liberals (Republican and Democrat).

Too much emphasis placed on Passive philosophies (which are compatible with socialism) by Passive bureaucrats for too many years caused the economic downturn at the end of 2000 and the beginning of 2001. It was detrimental to Active business survival. That, in turn, causes supply and demand problems from the small business sector that eventually impact big business.

The same thing happened at the end of the Reagan administration. For eight years, the Gipper placed too much focus on independent business. It resulted in a kinder, gentler recession during the George Herbert Walker Bush presidency immediately following the Reagan years. Bush Sr. had adjusted the economy nicely and the recovery was credited to Bill Clinton. Stopping the recession of the late '80s and early '90s must be credited to then-President George H.W. Bush, not the guy who took credit for it, Bill Clinton. I don't say so. Statistics do.

The cause of the recession of 2001 is part of the cyclic effect that results from partisan political views that place too much emphasis on either independent or big corporate business needs.

Until politicians understand the need for a balanced approach to both Active and Passive economic contributions and resultant needs, we will continue to have economic swings.

When there is too much regulation, only a handful of new business start-ups succeed ... and they do so in spite of government regulatory agencies and banks, not because of them.

This was proven true again in 2007-2008 and this time the corruption of the Washington swamp became apparent to voters. The election campaign of 2016 made the corruption a fact in voters' minds and the man who promised to clean out the swamp was elected to the Presidency. It is no secret that Passive liberal progressives are doing everything they can to bring down the Presidency of Donald J. Trump... even at the cost of the security of their nation.

Government regulation is the tool Passives use to deter rapid change from an old to a new economic base. In this case, the change was from an economy driven by industry and manufacturing to one driven by information, service and technology.

If it were up to Passives, we might still have stables with horses rather than garages with cars. The advent of the combustion engine was as much of a threat to the Passives of the late 1800s as the advent of technology is to that group in the late 1900s. Passive resistance to the move from an economy driven by agriculture to one driven by industry and manufacturing was one factor that caused the Great Depression and gave us the Federal Reserve System.

Both groups, Active and Passive, are necessary parts of a free enterprise economy. Neither understands the importance of the other's role. In fact, neither group recognizes the significance of the role the other plays. Even worse, government does not understand the specific responsibilities of each group.

Polar opposites seldom do.

Remember Nature's Law: two opposing forces, left unfettered, create balance by fighting for their positions. Government intervention via regulatory controls does not leave the marketplace "unfettered."

POLITICAL CONFLICTS

Politicians and bureaucrats simply ignore the fact that wealth has a dual purpose. A quick look at failed efforts to assist nations whose governments function under economic policies other than free enterprise exemplifies the importance of recognizing the significance of the Active Passive Personality Syndrome.

Third world countries can prosper under a system of free enterprise, but the Passives in control of the New World Order must achieve something they, as a group, have never been able to do. They must learn the significance of contributions made by people they call "radicals" and "extremists." Some even call them "deplorable."

Without them, their efforts to create a world economy will continue to fail.

New business start-up risks are understood and taken by Actives, not Passives. It is the largest stumbling block to the success of the New World Order. It is an invisible stumbling block to Passive energies. They do not see differences (or the economic, social or political values inherent to those differences) between Passive and Active attitudes.

How do I know Passives control the move to the new world order?

Passives are the ones attracted to bureaucratic career positions of power. They love to micromanage government. It is the ultimate exercise of power. How will anyone know someone holds power if someone doesn't exercise it? The more powerful the government the more enticing is the exercise... and what is more powerful than world government?

And, I know Passives control the move to a new world order because the people moving it forward have failed to motivate the kind of risk management behavior required for new wealth/job development to occur (which is why Passives keep failing in these efforts). This is a basic requirement when implementing economic conversion to free enterprise. The fingerprints of Passives are all over these failures. The lack of considering the important role small business plays in the success of big business is one big clue. It is a Passive trademark.

A MacGruder Axiom: When developing the economies of third world nations, it's not the economy, stupid! It's the attitude!

Passive investors think all it takes is money. They have no insights into wealth creation risk-management. They think they do, but they do not. Just as it required Active attitudes to found a new nation called America, the same is required in Haiti, Iraq, Libya, Iran, China, Russia and any other non-capitalist nation that wants to convert. When a wealth base needs to be created rather than managed, Active risk and individual achievement attitudes are required.

CHAPTER 7

APPS, THE UNITED STATES, AND ECONOMIC CYCLES

When we offer to help poor nations move from socialism to capitalism, we need to remember that America did not spring from the womb complete with multi-national companies. It is an acquired, not an inherited skill.

Our system of free enterprise evolved over time... as did the personalities capable of creating, managing and running it. Passives in positions to assist poor nations who want to establish a system of free enterprise appear to have forgotten that capitalism is based on risk management, not risk elimination. Since most people who work for government are Passives, it is a significant finding. It is especially significant when examining problems at the FBI, e.g.

Too, multi-national corporate executives need to admit their vested self-interest in attaining cheap labor when they build factories in poor nations like Mexico, Brazil, China and elsewhere which, contrary to their claims, does nothing to motivate or prepare nations to adopt a system of free enterprise and capitalism to drive their economies.

In truth, had the objective of the United States been to move nations – whether they be called Iraq or Libya – to capitalism, we would have educated both the people and the governments with the philosophy of the concept, helped people start their own small companies, helped governments understand the need for risk management skills, and helped them build small companies and grow them into big ones. It would have been relatively inexpensive and it would have required no American blood to achieve. It makes me question if capitalism was the objective... or was it to establish a central banking system? Or was it to get cheap labor for General Motors, et al?

What becomes apparent when history is analyzed is that American multi-national corporations were (and are) seeking cheap labor and providing jobs for the locals (while taking jobs from Americans) where they built the factories once housed on U.S. shores.

Free enterprise is about profits so there is nothing wrong with corporations seeking ways to increase their cash flow. However, when the process of increasing profits involves the tearing down of the nation that made their success possible, it becomes a different issue. Moreover, when the seeking of profits involves the military of the nation they are tearing down and loss of life it becomes a very big different issue. Our military's purpose does not involve nation building or meals on wheels. The military is to be used to protect the nation from dangers, inside or outside of America.

NAFTA and other trade agreements, the take-down of Libya's Moamar Kaddafi and Iraq's Saddam Hussein, were all intended to gain a profit result. That is what President Trump is trying to put a stop to – and it is apparent he will have to fight Passives weeping, rioting, breaking windows and theft every step of the way. Passives do not want to lose their power bases, including the drugs being brought across the border to sell to American young people, ruining lives – regardless of the dangerous loss of life of so many young Americans to OPIOIDs.

They will fight President Donald Trump to their own ruin – or his.

In other words, Passives are not living up to the responsibilities with which nature blessed them; they are not playing their required role because they are not taking from Active hands the small, independent companies created during the economic base change from industry and manufacturing to technology and making them bigger and more stable through Passive, low-risk growth. This is to be done within America, not on foreign ground.

Rather, Passive greed for more and more power provides them with a realistic motto: "We did it in the United States, let's do it everywhere in the world and use the economies of other nations to make us richer and more powerful. We'll call it a 'New World Order'."

They have failed everywhere they have tried to re-invent America's economy. They have failed because they are mostly Passives, politicians and corporate executives who do not understand what makes America great!

The point is, risk tolerance sufficiently strong to build a capitalist republic in any nation results from attitude. To create broad-based wealth from which a middle class emerges requires risk management skills which result from attitudes that make people desire the freedom to control their own destinies. Both capitalistic attitude and skills start small and grow big, just as they did in America.

We have been trying to build capitalist economies in other nations with no recognition of the things that made America great: an attitude by one group of people that develops risk management skills and the need to control their own destinies which motivates them to start small companies.

A second attitude by another group of people who like the safety of big companies takes over the reins of small companies started by Active risk managers. Passives, motivated by security, grow those companies and employ people while Actives go out and create a new economic base and start more new businesses.

The skill required to manage profits and turn them into wealth – to use profits to build schools, churches, hospitals, companies, jobs -- once profits are created is an important part of the capitalist puzzle. Otherwise, you end up with emirs and sheiks and politicians worldwide who, not understanding the real value of wealth, seek only money/profits. They become power-seeking and greedy... open to pay or receive bribes – and that's what we have in the international elitist group.

All socialist and communist systems are oligarchic in nature. They have an elitist class and a labor/poverty class. They have no middle class. That makes them unable to sell their own products to those who live in poverty in their own country. It is the reason communism does not work anywhere it has been tried.

If America goes the way of socialism, it will make America's economy totally dependent on international trade... just as China's economy is today. It is a weakness; not a strength. It is tyranny attempting to replace freedom. People seem to forget that almost all innovative ideas that positively impact economies come from the middle class... Bill Gates and Steven Jobs did not come from the elitist class.

The attitudes of the people who live under a free enterprise system are at least as important as building a Fortune 100 office in a third world nation and then hiring and training locals. That is the Passive view of free enterprise and capitalism. This is especially true when the Passives who are trying to teach free enterprise have little insight about the key role independent business plays in healthy economic cycles... an economy that produces a middle class. Passives have no insight into entrepreneurs' attitudes, the heart of a free enterprise economy. It is from the small business that big business attitudes evolve. It is part of a process.

It takes time to develop the confidence required of free people who make risk-based decisions daily. It takes a lot of time when the people who live in the nation being converted to free enterprise have no risk-management skills. Those entrepreneurial skills that foreigners think come so naturally to Americans are carefully honed by a competitive marketplace, not by oligarchs and dictators.

A MacGruder Axiom: Capitalism is dependent for success on risk management. Socialism is based on risk-elimination and that's why it appeals to Liberal Passives.

The idea that establishing branch offices of major corporations in poor countries will somehow evolve into free enterprise shows a total lack of appreciation for the complex underpinnings of capitalism. Or, it shows greed for more and more power, more and more of an elitist class and less and less appreciation of a middle class.

In the next chapter, I explain how and why fifty-year economic cycles occur in capitalist economies. Each cycle is dominated by either Active or Passive philosophies.

I was not the first person to identify fifty-year wave cycles as they impact the natural laws of capitalism and force political change. That change allows tired economies to recover from political delusions of grandeur suffered by so many of those who enter politics to "serve."

A little over a hundred years ago, a Russian economist by the name of Nikolai Kondratieff identified fifty-year cycles that proved capitalism recoups from its economic downturns. Kondratieff's writings helped me connect the dots and identify a more verifiable cause of cyclical change every fifty years.

As history teaches us, Kondratieff was right in seeing that capitalist economies have fifty-year cycles. Each downturn is corrected by the marketplace in a natural way. His discovery did not sit well with the Russian power elite. Mr. Kondratieff was sent to the Gulag Archipelago where he died a dreary death. Kondratieff's writings have been brought to light in the United States only recently.

Kondratieff viewed corrective capitalist wave cycles as the power behind marketplace behavior and economic change. His observation is, I believe, correct. His death and the reasons for it exemplify corrupted power and the danger of one group (Passive liberals run socialist and communist economies) functioning in a vacuum without the Active group.

Kondratieff believed a major war accompanied each fifty-year cyclical change. He believed wars every fifty years solved capitalism's economic downturns. No one bought his wave theory because the wars he said accompanied each fifty-year cycle did not historically fit... or, perhaps they did and that's why we have the industrial-military complex of which President Dwight Eisenhower once warned.

A careful study of American history proves that Kondratieff was correct when he identified the waves. The "wars every fifty years" part of his theory that caused it to be discounted is, instead, social battles for ongoing power or control fought between Actives and Passives. These battles are very similar to what we see in the anti-Trump protests seen all over America today.

I view the wave cycles as society's reaction to political corruption (Passive) or too much "pull yourself up by your own bootstraps" control (Active). In other words, Kondratieff believed conditions within the marketplace caused social change. I believe *social change causes conditions within the marketplace to change.* In my view, the mood of the marketplace defines and motivates political change.

The changes that occur in capitalism, referred to by Kondratieff as "capitalism's market corrections," are a fight by Actives who want to regain control, and Passives who want to maintain power at the end of each fifty year cycle. There is no definition other than war to describe the fights between Active conservatives and Passive liberals and neo-conservatives over the victory of President Donald J. Trump... political wars that destroy our nation.

Corrections are not market-motivated. Wave cycles represent society's rejection of political power abuse (Passive cycle) or too much responsibility (Active cycle). Society wields no power politically in socialist states. Thus, no such corrective cycles can occur in their economies. All socialism flows from Passive philosophies. Corrupted power gains momentum for lack of choice.

Perhaps Kondratieff was more right than "they" thought. The change from an Active to a Passive cycle represents a kind of "war."

If each group understood the purpose of the other and realized the positive result that comes from each of the fifty-year cycles, the world would be a more pleasant place for everyone.

On the other hand, Nature's Laws say balance results only when each group fights the other for dominance. The fight is supposed to adhere to rules of behavior.

It appears that society goes through cyclical mood swings.

The masses seek what is good for them at any given time in history. When the Passive group gains too much power over them, the masses reject traditional social values (a result of too much absolute power that has become corrupted). That is why in 2016 the American people elected a man named Donald J. Trump.

The people then begin to support the philosophical drive of Actives to regain control of their own lives or destinies and do away with the corruption. Or at least they try to eliminate corruption. Those who have become part of the corrupted system fight against those seeking to regain control of their lives... and the political winter and spring of 2017 certainly proves that statement to be true.

Perhaps it is to this on-going struggle to which Thomas Jefferson referred when he suggested a revolution in America every fifty years. Indeed, it appears we have one! A quiet revolution fought on battlegrounds with opposing philosophies at the core of each skirmish. It is a fight between Passives (for power) and Actives (for control).

During our last marketplace correction of the 20th century, corporate giants downsized as the old economy ran out of steam and a new one emerged. It occurred in the 1960s when we left industry and manufacturing behind as America's primary drive. That was when the number of new technology, information and service "industries" began to outnumber new industrial and manufacturing business start-ups. An economic base change occurred from industry to technology. It provided the engine needed for economic base change just as industry and manufacturing provided the engine to replace agriculture as the economic drive of the United States in the late 1800s and early 1900s.

Small technology businesses hired and trained workers who lost production line jobs. Workers learned to make computers and the chips for software that make them run. They learned to write software programs. In the process, they earned higher wages. This is part of the cycle. So, too, is increased productivity... the process of requiring fewer workers to complete jobs. The same thing happened when we moved from an economy driven by agriculture to industry. People had to learn new skills... it caused a massive economic depression.

Any society that thinks it can survive in the long-term by avoiding the realities of both sides of big/small business interaction is out of touch with history.

A MacGruder Axiom: Success means learning when to stop doing the important to take care of the necessary.

If you think things are better for American workers now than they were 25 years ago, think again.

In 1976, only 13 percent of American workers spent more than 49 hour per week on the job. In 1999, 19 percent work longer hours; the number keeps rising.

According to a Gallup poll done in 2013-2014, 39 percent of Americans work 50-60 hours per week; 11 percent work from 41 to 49 hours per week; 42 percent work 40 hours per week and 8 percent work less than 40 hours each week.

Since the implementation of Obamacare, the number of those working less than 40 hours weekly has increased substantially because companies prefer to use part-time labor when they can because no sick leave and hospitalization insurance benefits need to be provided.

According to Department of Labor statistics, the number of displaced workers totaled 7.4 million from 2013 to 2015. "Displaced workers" are those whose companies have been closed, whose jobs have been done away with, or whose shift working hours have been eliminated.

Since the economic base change of 1960, the number of mothers who must work for a family to survive has exploded. Women must spend time working at jobs outside the home. The impact of strangers raising children for whom they have no bond other than financial can be felt everywhere, from youth crime to drugs and sex and the accompanying diseases. It is easily seen in the "me, me, me" attitudes of Millennials.

Thirty years ago, people worked 160 hours less per year compared with today's work force (and based on the value of the dollar then versus now, they made more money). If you add the time people must spend today on over-crowded busses, subways, rapid rail, on freeways and streets going to and from work, those numbers increase exponentially.

Since the celebration of the New Millennium, some people work fewer hours... but their salaries are lower and their benefits are far less. That is the result of Passives not doing as nature tells them to do: Make those small businesses started from 1960 through 2010 bigger and more stable. That's what the greed for power of the abusive Passive cycle has caused.

And though the richest 10 percent of Americans controlled only 50 percent of all wealth in the 1970s, in the 1990s that number increased to 70 percent. As of 2015, America's richest one percent hold about 40 percent of private affluence. The lowest 90 percent of those holding liquid assets are responsible for 73 percent of all debt. Since 2009, another report states that 95 percent of economic gains went to the top one percent in net worth. In 2017, an Oxfam study reported that six Americans were among eight rich people who own as much combined wealth as "half of the human race" and that the average employee needed to work more than a month to earn what the company's chief financial officer earned in one hour.

In 2015, the top ten percent of two income households have incomes in excess of $100,000. The top one percent earn slightly more than $1.5 million annually.

It is tempting to blame hard-hearted Active conservatives for these numbers. Those who do need to remember that for 24 of the 29 years from which the statistics are taken, Congress was heavily dominated -- both the Senate and the House (with one short exception in the Senate) -- by Passive liberals. Of the last 24 years, America had Democrat presidents for 16 years and one Republican for 8 years.

Only a moderate number of Republicans holding office since 1994 are Active conservatives. The rest are "compassionate" moderates (the neoconservatives inserted into the Republican Party by the Bush family). Some are liberals. The public does not know how to tell when a candidate says he or she is conservative but really is not. They do not recognize the wolf in sheep's clothing who says he or she is conservative but is not and adds votes to the liberal side of the aisle in Congress. Hopefully, this book will change that.

Interestingly, Passive liberals honestly and truly consider Active conservatives as having no compassion for the poor. Equally, Actives believe Passives use people who suffer in poverty for political gain and ego gratification. They believe Passives seek ways to keep people in poverty as a means of maintaining political power. This example represents well the opposite nature of each group.

American taxpayers spent trillions of dollars on the poor during the years of Passive political domination. As of 2017, we are $20 trillion in debt. After all of those investment dollars, the attitudes inherent to wealth creation have yet to be instilled in America's ghettos. Rather, they are constantly presented with pictures of themselves as "victims," dependent upon "powerful others" for their sense of protected self. There is no better way to keep the poor dependent upon you.

Many of them were and are victims, but after the 1960s when the economic base change occurred, it was not necessary for people to remain victims. Unfortunately, those who think of themselves as victims find more comfort being shackled to that bed than they do buying an alarm clock, taking a shower every morning, and getting a job with a determination to start at the bottom of a company and work their way to the top.

A MacGruder Axiom: If you see yourself as a victim, you have a good excuse for a miserable life. You still have a miserable life. There are alternatives.

It is impossible to fight Mother Nature and win.

It is the nature of Actives to enjoy managing personal risks. That is required to create wealth and jobs.

It is the nature of Passives to avoid the risk management required of wealth creators. Rather, their natural duty is to utilize their talents to expand the work of Actives so more people can benefit from it. In the process, Passives solidify the existing economy, keeping the growth cycle spiraling upward. The cycle is broken, however, if over-regulation (whether implemented by legislators, bureaucrats, or Executive Orders) reduces the number of new business start-ups. The cycle is also broken when corporations use our military to create opportunities for them to expand while gaining access to cheap labor in poor nations.

Passives spread risk within a group to avoid personal loss. Risk cannot be spread around one-person offices where new economies are born. It takes disciplined dreamers willing to risk everything to keep working on their tomorrows in the face of today's numerous rejections and financial problems. Disciplined dreamers consider risk a personal responsibility for which they alone bear the burden.

You cannot demand that people be responsible for their own burdens -- business or personal -- as government does, then dictate on which shoulder they must carry it. That is for the person responsible for the burden of debt and production to determine.

CHAPTER 8

AMERICA'S FIFTY YEAR ECONOMIC CYCLES

A look at six Active/Passive energy cycles in American history offers good insight into how each of these groups weave threads into a beautiful blanket resulting in a capitalist country called America.

During the 1600s and through the mid 1700s, our nation was known as British North America. Diaries written by early American residents describe local economies dependent for survival on agriculture. Economies were local... they had not yet reached the point where they could be called regional.

There being little accommodation for visitors, tourism contributed a minuscule portion to local economies. There was minimal trade with European nations, but no efficient delivery system existed from one American community to another, especially inland communities.

Until the mid-1760s, America had local village economies driven by agriculture.

In 1760, the colonies entered a state of unrest. They also entered their first economic cycle driven by Active energies. Those energies motivated the Revolutionary War of the 1770s that ended in 1781. A rag-tag group of America's colonial soldiers defeated the most dominant military force in the world at that time. (A rag-tag group of terrorists called ISIS is trying to do the same thing to the most dominant military strength in the world in 2017.)

Patrick Henry's cry of "Give me liberty, or give me death" tells of a man motivated by the management of risk to achieve the moral objective of his right to self-destiny. His cry is the theme song for Active/self investors.

President Donald J. Trump's call to Make America Great Again – to reinforce our military power which has been so badly diminished by the prior administration – is another theme song for Active/self investors.

> *A MacGruder Axiom: To freedom-loving people, there is nothing more exciting than a positive possibility and the desire to make it a reality.*

Prior to the Revolutionary War (which gathered momentum from 1760 until the infamous tea party and resultant war over taxation without representation – the Stamp Act), the American economy and its political structure was controlled by the Crown... by outside forces.

What kinds of people leave a secure, well-ordered society in Europe for the insecurity of unsettled foreign shores? Part of the answer lies in the promise of land ownership and the right to self-destiny. Part of the answer lies in religious and other freedoms disallowed in Europe.

Which people are likely to be sentenced for crimes against the crown by various members of royalty... sentenced to leave Europe (especially England) to serve "jail" terms in the New World? What kinds of people would most likely survive the insecurity and discomforts of the New World? People motivated by security? Or, people with a tolerance for risk management who are motivated to gain control of self-destiny?

The answer is clear. The people who were sent to North America for violating a law or for being disliked by royalty were those capable of managing the risk of whatever might come. They were Actives.

Perhaps the risks people took that caused them to be forced to come to the New World were criminal... stealing from a London shop to feed their families. Maybe they hunted for food on the royal grounds. Or, perhaps they actively opposed the monarchy and their risk of political incorrectness brought them to American shores. Actives are notoriously incorrect when it comes to politics. Again, we can look to the public image and stance of a man named Donald J. Trump regarding his opinions about political correctness.

Regardless of the risks taken to get here, a large number of people who followed the Pilgrims were people motivated by the need to seek self-destiny, spiritual or otherwise. They willingly assumed the risks necessary to gain that status. They were not security-driven. No one looking for security willingly partakes of the hardships of an extremely uncomfortable trip and high risks of nation building in a hostile environment.

Our ancestors had no control over laws passed to govern them. They had no input into the political process, let alone any control over it. During the first fifty year cycle (until 1660), there were so few people on the continent, so little wealth, so much disease and discomfort that the American colonists were relatively free to pursue their own destinies. A difficult, high-risk destiny it was. There was no "economic drive." There was no "social agenda." There was no "political agenda" other than that of the English throne which viewed America as a means to expand both power and income from its new "colony." It was a high-risk environment -- but it offered land and wealth to those who could tolerate and manage risk.

Settling a wild, undeveloped land attracted those with Active energy whose risk management skills made them willing to wager their lives for freedom from religious persecution. They would no longer have to suck up to royalty. There were other benefits.

A MacGruder Axiom: No matter what errors people commit, they are not prisoners of their pasts. The future is a blank page.

They may have been taxed by the British Crown, their laws may have come from foreign soil, but until the 1700s, there was not a great deal of interference from the British King's military in the lives of American settlers.

The "nation" was so young during this time it could not really be defined as having an economy with a primary drive. The primary drive was survival.

From 1660 to 1710, that changed. America was a British colony with as many local economies as there were villages, all dependent on agriculture. Wealth began to increase. Free enterprisers established modes of transportation ... stage and shipping companies. Entrepreneurs built small inns and hotels for travelers and tourists. Farms were plentiful and roads were built.

As Madam Knight said in her diary about her trip from the Boston area to Connecticut, "It is a plentiful country for provisions of all sorts and it's generally healthy. No one that can and will be diligent in this place need fear poverty nor the want of food and raiment." Security and wealth were on the horizon and within the grasp of all newcomers.

Security and wealth attract ... what? The Passive energy group. By 1710, the risks of survival on American soil were reduced as the risk-managers completed the jobs nature gave them. Actives had established a functional social base. Opportunities for the wealth of future generations by land accumulation and the need for products and services in the new country needed to be broadened and stabilized.

Those with a lower tolerance for risk, motivated by the security of being able to own land, were attracted to American shores. The immediate objective changed from the risk management of establishing a workable social base (and the daily life challenges involved in doing so) to making things bigger and more secure. Remember, bigger is safer than smaller.

Members of the Passive energy group began the move from their homes in lands ruled by monarchies to the new land. The thrust of this 1710 to 1760 fifty-year cycle was to secure and stabilize what the founders of Jamestown and Plymouth had begun. It was dominated by those who sought power, and by those who curried the favor of the powerful. Politics and the power that go with governments that exercise control over the people began.

During the 1710 through 1760 fifty-year cycle, Passives dominated the cycle and brought stability and some comfort to the rough-hewn society of the New World.

New Englanders traded freely among themselves as did the colonists who had settled beyond the original Jamestown (or, James Cittie) colony. Thus, when the Active energy cycle of 1760 began, America's economy was driven by agriculture and was regional (no longer village, or local) in nature. It was still ruled by a foreign monarch. Economic base changes occur only under Active cycles... this change was from local to regional and agriculture was still the driving force. Shipping and tourism were expanding, too, and were part of the new economy.

By 1760, individualist Actives found themselves losing control of self-destiny. In 1773, the Boston Tea Party occurred; the Active cycle was a teenager of 13 years. Three years later, in 1776, Americans began the fight to gain control of their nation's destiny. They understood the risk-taking involved in forming a new nation. Citizens fought a war to change circumstances dictated by the Crown.

Some historians estimate the Revolutionary War was supported only by about forty percent of the people and was opposed by an equal number. Society today tends to be made up of similar percentages of Actives and Passives... about forty-forty. The remaining twenty percent are non-involved, non-political people who appear to have little drive, Active or Passive. They are takers, not givers, and are often a drain on society.

A MacGruder Axiom: People who think success comes to those who wait for it need to look around. There's a long line.

Passives dominated the 1710-1760 cycle and roads were made better, tourism expanded, farming was made more systematic. However, it is safe to say the period from 1760 through 1810 was dominated by the Active energy group. Most of the founding fathers believed in risk management, not elimination. Modern Americans appear to have forgotten what motivated (and won) their freedom-loving (often self-gratifying) lifestyles. Risk management, not risk elimination, is the rock upon which American freedom is founded. The Revolutionary War was fought by conservatives with Active energy. Their reason for fighting it was to gain and maintain the rights of self-destiny.

Our early patriots were willing to risk life and limb... provided they controlled the risks taken.

In 1810, the Passive cycle made us expansionary (expansion is related to power). The United States declared war on Great Britain in 1812. It began with a failed American invasion of Canada (we surrendered Detroit), and ended when we won the battle of New Orleans, fought after the Treaty of Ghent was signed.

Wealth was limited to a few and Passives set strict standards of conduct for those allowed into the exclusive club of the elite. Lifestyle -- especially in the southern states -- was typified by Tara in "Gone With the Wind." It was not so much the lifestyle of a romantic novel as in the holding of slaves and the plantation mentality. The lifestyle to which I refer is the secure sense that things would never change that dominated the South. Life would remain safe and secure. The cotton fields would always have Negro slaves in them and the comforts of the Tara-type lifestyle would continue.

As we neared the end of this fifty-year Active cycle of 1860, industry and manufacturing, in its infancy, began to replace agriculture as the primary economic force in America's northern states. Agriculture (particularly cotton) remained the strength of the south. The nation's economy was still regional (close to becoming national), but the regions expanded in size as industry solidified its toehold.

The threat of war sounded. The lifestyle of the South -- the sense of power enjoyed by those who exercised it -- was strong. It motivated a "fight to preserve our way of life and keep things as they are" response. This comment does not deal with the issue of whether or not the South had a right to secede from the Union (because I believe in state rights and I believe they did). This has to do with which 50-year cycles dominated our nation and when.

People motivated by power -- Passives -- will fight to preserve it. The Civil War, unlike the Revolutionary War nearly a hundred years before, was motivated in the South by the need to maintain power over others. Northerners fought to free a race of people from their bonds... or, so the history books say.

A MacGruder Axiom: We all have a place in time. How productively we use it is likely to follow us through eternity.

Passive wealth wants to keep things the way they are. To change things is to threaten existing power bases and familiar structures of security. Clearly, Passive energy philosophies ruled the nation from 1810 through 1860.

In 1860, the nation stood divided as questions about the abolishment of slavery abounded. It is reminiscent of 2016... a nation divided with violence in the streets perpetrated by those afraid of change – and loss of an existing power base.

In truth, Eli Whitney's cotton gin along with other industrial advancements made it possible for northern industry to process more cotton more quickly and less expensively than slave labor. Northern business wanted the slaves out of the fields in the South for a totally different reason: Commerce. Thus, America could become more competitive in world markets. This economic consideration was a major part of what motivated the Civil War. So, too, was the drive to keep the Union together, lawfully or otherwise. Moral questions about the inhumanity of slavery became an emotional issue to motivate the Union Army to fight the newly formed Confederacy.

The War Between the States – some call it the Civil War – began at Fort Sumter. It was very similar in purpose to the Revolutionary War if one views the freeing of humans to seek and control their own destinies the sole objective of the war. But it was not the sole objective. Nor was the war fought by a majority of slaves seeking their rights to self-determination. It was fought for them by those who value personal freedom.

There is little doubt that the majority of soldiers fought so others could enjoy the freedom of self-destiny. Active energies won this conflict. The decision to remove the right of self-determination from the states (as guaranteed them by the Constitution) was a political one and it was not driven by the marketplace.

Actives fight to preserve the right of self-determination -- theirs, or that of others. They see the two as intertwined. Passives always forget this fact. And, Actives always forget Passives fight to preserve their access to and ability to exercise power over others. The history of the War Between the States has been so rewritten from the reality of what actually occurred it is difficult to deal with it here. It requires its own book.

We need to remember our history. Prior to William Jefferson Clinton, only four Democrat presidents in the 1900's served two terms in office: Woodrow Wilson, Franklin Roosevelt, Harry Truman, and Lyndon Johnson (though President Johnson served only one elected term).

These Passive liberal presidents initiated American involvement in the four major wars of the 20th century: World Wars I and II, and the Korean and Vietnam conflicts. The total American dead from these four wars is 666,381.

Through 1992, there were five multi-term Republican presidents. The total number of years Republicans held the presidency during that 92-year period is 56 years. Or, the presidency was held by Republicans 61 percent of the time until the Clinton administration. No Active conservative president ever started a major war on foreign shores. George H.W. Bush (senior) initiated action against Iraq in 1991 when Iraq aggressed against Kuwait, but Americans killed in action deaths in the Gulf War totaled only 148. There were 458 wounded, 121 non-hostile deaths, and 11 female combatant deaths. Too, Bush is not exactly an example of conservatism. He is an evident believer in neo-conservatism and world government.

The evidence is clear that Democrat presidents are far more likely to start major wars than are Republicans. The evidence is equally clear that Passive liberals are motivated by power, Active conservatives by control.

Isn't power versus control the reason behind every war fought since David slew Goliath? Actives learned that little David could slay big Goliath with a very controlled weapon like a slingshot. During the Revolutionary War Active cycle, Patrick Henry's cry was a slingshot. At the time Abraham Lincoln first pointed to the moral wrong of slavery, his words were a slingshot. Donald Trump's positions on illegal immigration, illegal voter registrations, and his battle with what he calls "the lying media" and "junk news"... all of these are replicas of David's slingshot.

A MacGruder Axiom: We need to enjoy every ending in our lives. Each offers opportunities for new beginnings.

At the end of the Civil War, we began moving from a series of regional agricultural economies to a unified national economy. The new economy was based on industry and manufacturing. Traditional wealth lost its power base.

As has always been the case during changes of America's economic base, the drive from the previous economy maintained its strong presence. The majority of people were now employed by industry and manufacturing but that did not reduce the importance of our agricultural economy. Nor was agriculture viewed as inferior to industry and manufacturing. People understood the need to eat was primary to maintaining life. Agriculture was merely in the back seat, riding along in a new Model-T Ford that so exemplified the new economy.

The only era in American history we have not maintained the vigor and strength of the preceding economy is the 1990's. Rather, we have allowed our industrial base to be shipped to third world nations in return for cheap labor making inexpensive products... a practice that increased multi-national corporate coffers immensely. It is one of those historic eras that resulted in a huge lesson. The millions of unemployed or under-employed Americans are absolute proof of what the eight years of William Jefferson Clinton's and Barack Obama's Passive liberal Administrations did to this nation with Treaties like NAFTA and CAFTA.

In 1910, the new industrial and manufacturing economy that had been so resisted in the 1860s and created by Actives was in full swing. From 1860-1910, after the War Between the States, the economy became expansionary (typical of a security-driven Passive cycle). New fortunes were amassed and new wealth from the new industrial economy was now old enough to be considered respectable. The Passive Robber Baron era ruled the day.

Though energetically opposed by Actives, a central bank called the Federal Reserve (owned by banks and other private investors, not the government) was established. This fifty-year wave cycle clearly belongs to the Passive security-motivated, traditionalist group.

Two world wars were fought during the Passive cycle of 1910 to 1960. Both reflected increasing American world power and honoring treaties -- Passive purposes.

The Revolutionary and Civil Wars were fought on American soil under the political oversight of Active conservatives. Both were fought to put a halt to power abuses exercised by one group of people over another.

The new Active wave cycle began to emerge in 1960. The preceding fifty-year Passive cycle motivated the expansion of America's industrial and manufacturing complex. The Great Depression began under Passive dominance during this same time. World Wars were fought; Korea and Vietnam were, too.

Making small business big is a predictable occurrence under Passive energy rule. Then, economic stability began to be dependent upon and controlled by international, not national, markets. A new phenomenon emerged: the military and industrial complex. Change was in the wind and change is disliked by those with low-risk management skills.

In 1960, traditional social values were rejected by Hippies and Yippies ... a fitting end to that Passive cycle. A drug culture emerged. It was ultimate abuse of liberal power as students at Stanford University in California began chanting that "Western culture has to go!"

> **A MacGruder Axiom: Self-respect is based on one simple rule: Do the right thing because it is right.**

Traditional political values were questioned. Previously unheard of demonstrations against America's military and political involvement in the Vietnam war were almost daily occurrences. Those demonstrations cost President Lyndon B. Johnson his second term in office. He was so unpopular at the end of his first elected term, he could not be re-elected and he (and the Democrat National Committee) decided someone else should run for office.

There is little doubt that memories of that LBJ experience is on the minds of those who in 2017 demonstrated against President Donald J. Trump. They want to demonstrate Trump out of office as students did to LBJ. But they overlook the basic reason Passive liberals lost power: they abused power as students at Kent State University were shot down while demonstrating on campus against LBJ's Vietnam. Donald J. Trump does not carry that burden on his back and the demonstrations will not be as effective.

In 1960, we entered a cycle change, from Passive to Active.

For the first time since America's founding, those who fought wars for the ongoing right to seek self-determination were caught up in political issues in opposition to their very essence as human beings. Active citizens inherited in 1960 a government grown too big, too arrogant, and too motivated by power to control. John F. Kennedy became President and tried to remove the abuses. He was assassinated.

The economy began to contract and new start-up technology, service and information companies began to proliferate as an economic base change moved the nation from industry and manufacturing to information, technology and service. Economic base changes occur only when moving from Passive to Active cycles.

We moved from a traditional national economy to an international economy. Traditional wealth (including giant industrial corporations) began to lose their power base in this country as citizens found higher paying jobs programming computers than production lines. America's giant corporations were largely controlled by members of the Passive energy group. That group moved into the arena to fight for its ongoing right to power. Corporate leaders began shipping traditional American jobs overseas where they could get cheap labor.

If you go back to the first few pages of chapter three and re-examine the personality traits of the Active energy group, you will see why that group dominated the changes that occurred in 1760, 1860, and 1960.

If you re-examine the personality traits associated with the Passive energy group, you will see where that group's motives formed policies during the changes that occurred in the cycles of 1710, 1810, 1910, and which began again in 2010.

As I write this, we are only eight years into the 50-year Passive cycle and the unmanageable problems of corrupted power Passive liberals implemented during the 1910-1960 cycle were never brought under control because of the neo-conservative views of the Bush family. Senior was President from 1988-1992 and Junior was President from 2000-2008 thus effectively assigning the period from 1988-2016 to Passive power.

Under President Barack Obama, it took eight months for Passive liberals to cram Obamacare down the throats of the American people who, seven years later, elected to office a man who called Washington, DC what it is: a swamp; a man who called his opponent what she was: "crooked." Donald J. Trump rode into office on a horse named "Truth." Whether he will be able to maintain that seat is questioned daily by Passive liberals and their media. The point is, power abuse by Passive liberals is what got Donald Trump elected.

It appears one can take a cursory look at American history and project pretty clearly that Active cycles occur every fifty years, only to be replaced by Passive cycles that also last fifty years. The changes, as Russian economist Kondratieff said, do not come and go easily. He called the trauma of the economic base changes we see every fifty years "wars." Many people today say the American people are at war with one another: Passive versus Active. If one reads newspaper headlines, we can definitely be said to be in the midst of an uncivil war with one another. Which will be first to secede from the Union? California? New York?

Interestingly, back in the 1980s I was asked by Colorado-based Martin Marietta to project when the economy would be driven by technological advances supportive of space travel for the general public. The answer: Toward the end of the next Passive cycle beginning in 2010 and ending in 2060. It is interesting that the first testing of what is intended to become a public transport to outer space was completed in 2016. Thus, in addition to the success of my bank clients who created wealth creation private banks based on my research findings involving Actives and Passives, this prediction made in the 1980s is further evidence of its accuracy. Space travel will begin in earnest during that time.

What we lived through as we approached 2010, then, was a natural cyclical change, from Active to Passive. Actives began rejecting liberal values in the 1980s. In the new millennium, conservative voters did so even more aggressively when they reacted to Tea Party groups which let Republicans know that voters were fed up with politicians telling them they were conservative but voting as liberals once they were elected.

It has taken until 2016 for the momentum of the Active energy group to gain control. The movement is not yet over. Passives have continually lost power at both the national and state levels but will regain their lost power more quickly if Active political leadership abandons the conservative principles President Trump brought to the White House with him. President Trump needs to think seriously about that statement and recognize who the conservatives are among those that he trusts.

CHAPTER 9

ACTIVE INVESTORS: POLITICAL CONSERVATIVES

Power and control.

In the case of political conservatives, their most basic personal motivator is control. If you understand this single fact about them, you understand almost every conservative cause:

1. Make government smaller (small is easier to *control* than huge and ensures individual freedoms because small government has insufficient resources to constrain individual liberties);
2. Pro-Constitution and the original Amendments as approved by the framers of the Constitution (the Amendments which, along with the Declaration of Independence, clearly put American citizens in *control* of self-destiny and recognize that civil rights come to individuals – not groups -- from God, not government);
3. With each right comes responsibility. Personal responsibility and accountability are the price one pays for self-determination. One must *control* one's own destiny or turn it over to government. "Rights" is not synonymous

with "license." "Accountability" goes beyond 'apology' or saying "I'm responsible," to "a penalty suitable to repay the infringement." All are *control* issues.
4. To maintain American sovereignty is to keep political and military *control* in the hands of the United States Congress and the Executive branch of government. We should not give courts, the United Nations or any foreign country *power* over our military, laws, rivers, or national parks. Conservatives want control of America's international trade policies... of the inflow of goods into the United States to ensure -- or, control -- job growth and product quality for American citizens and they want to control immigration and limit it to legal aliens.
5. Immigration policies need to *control* population growth. Those unfamiliar with and disinterested by America's heritage, traditions, objectives, family values and the moral codes on which it is built must adapt. If they do not, we will lose our heritage.

The above represents only a handful of conservative issues but gives a graphic example of how control is at the heart of them all.

Conservatism is a philosophy. At the core of this philosophy is a belief in Natural Law. Many if not all conservatives believe Natural Law is a gift from their Creator. They believe it gives living examples each day of how to live life happily and without harming others. Some conservatives do not attach a connection between Natural Law and a Supreme Being who created the world and the nature that flows from its creation. They just understand the logic of living compatibly with nature and the laws that govern it.

> ***A MacGruder Axiom: Nature may dictate that the fittest survive, but our Creator dictates that survival is less important than spiritual evolvement and ethical existence.***

Conservative philosophy does not worship at the altar of Natural Law. It does, however, purport that to live compatibly with nature and people one must understand Natural Laws and function compatibly with them. Only then can human beings move beyond nature toward spiritual growth. Incidentally, only then can they be true environmentalists. Until people understand the Laws of Nature, it is impossible to be an environmentalist... without this knowledge those who claim to be environmentalists are merely ideologues trying to force their views down the throats of others who disagree with them.

Ayn Rand says in *The New Intellectual*, "Man's consciousness shares with animals the first two stages of its development: sensations and perceptions." All animals feel sensations from eating a good meal or pain from a knife cut or the sensation of good sex. All animals perceive fear or danger or physical attraction to another person. We humans share those ranges of consciousness – sensation and perception – with all other animal life.

Ayn Rand continues: "But it is the third state of consciousness, *conceptions*, that makes him man. Sensations are integrated into perceptions automatically by the brain of a man or of an animal. But to integrate perceptions or sensations into conceptions by a process of abstraction is a feat that man alone has the power to perform -- and he has to perform it *by choice*." No one can force you or me to be conceptual. No one can prevent it, either.

Human beings have imaginations. We know that death will follow life because of our ability to conceptualize reality. We instinctively know that truth will, in the end analysis, always win over lies. It may take time, but it will happen. We know love is stronger than hate and that to be able to forgive ourselves, we must forgive others.

Thus, Ms. Rand very succinctly explains why morality – or love, or hate – cannot be legislated. Choice cannot be legislated... only public assent. Thus, passing hate crime laws works in opposition to Natural Law. It will never work other than to support someone's sense of political correctness (which is designed to, among other things, prevent truth from being spoken).

That is conservative philosophy. And that is the base from which conservative legislators must write laws, policies, regulations, and, in general, run government.

The conservative philosophy, then, instinctively knows we must integrate animal sensations into perceptions that result in *positive concepts*. To do so, the human mind must first know the difference between positive and negative sensations. To gain this knowledge they have watched how certain modes of behavior have historically impacted society. They must be able to control the negative ones so the positives may flourish. That is perhaps why the word "discipline" is so big in conservative circles.

A MacGruder Axiom: Discipline is a trait shared by all animal life. Non-human animals employ discipline to survive physically. Humans develop it to survive spiritually.

It is Ayn Rand's third step that sets human beings apart from animal life and the laws of nature. They sometimes forget, however, that to try to take the third step – the step of conceptualization – without a basic understanding of the human inclination to worship at the altar of sensation and perception – ensures failure.

No being can ignore two-thirds of its nature (sensation and perception) and successfully live life in the remaining one-third (the ability to conceptualize and utilize imagination). To ignore that part of human nature we share with other animal life is to ignore reality. Ignoring reality is the ultimate ignorance. We are what we are. Two-thirds of what we are puts us on the same level with other animal life. Most humans prefer a somewhat higher standard of living. They seek to develop their conceptualization skills. Some do not ... and it is against them societies throughout history established functional social defenses.

It may be that the primary purpose of the concept of balance is to bring humans to a level of development where they grow beyond sensation and perception to conceptualization. The Ten Commandments help us to conceptualize positively rather than negatively... to do good, rather than evil. Love thy neighbor is a spiritual act, not an animal one.

No matter how good-hearted the lioness, she does not offer to share her kill for the day with neighbors.

To have healthy societies, humans need to understand how to use the power of conceptualization for good. For those who believe in the existence of a Supreme Being, the ability to move from sensation and perception to positive conceptualization defines the experience of faith and living in a state of God's grace. For Christians, it defines why "the Word was made flesh and dwelt amongst us."

Those who have no belief in a Supreme Being may find it easier to move from sensation and perception to *negative* conceptualization. Many, however, appear to work their way through life experiences to the positive side.

Religious or not, believer or not, conservative philosophy makes demands of its followers. For example, before recklessly pursuing the conceptualization of sensations and perceptions, human beings must first understand them. We must understand Natural Laws and the animal natures that are part of it. Only then can we control our own negatives and focus on the positives. Only then are we sufficiently aware of the dangers they present to protect ourselves.

> **A MacGruder Axiom: All it takes to succeed is one reason why. Forget the hundred reasons why not.**

Conservatism as a philosophy proffers that to control nature, humans must first (and honestly) understand Natural Law. If they do not, they must build dams (or arks) to protect themselves from negative physical (or spiritual) floods. If they do not, they will drown. To drown is to return to their animal instincts of sensation and perception and leave conceptualization and the human spirit behind.

Whether you believe God created the world and nature, Natural Laws come from a source outside of humankind. We can do nothing to cause or prevent hurricanes or tornadoes or earthquakes, or drought and blight. These natural occurrences are a warning to us that they not only occur in human nature, they occur in the world of spirit, too. We must prepare for them.

Whether people believe Nature's Laws are a gift offering guidelines from a Creator, conservatives believe they supersede the laws of human beings. To go one step further, conservatives believe if human laws are not built on a firm base supportive of Natural Law they fail. This is a critical difference between liberals (who place more credence in laws created by humans than those created by nature and/or a Supreme Being) and conservatives.

It was upon the precepts of Natural Law that the founding fathers wrote the Declaration of Independence and the framers wrote the Constitution. It is from the realization that Natural Law governs animal life and that humans must seek a higher social objective or live like animals that conservatism was born.

What is Natural Law? Some would term it Physics 101. Following are some examples:

1. All men are created equal and are endowed by their Creator (not their government) with certain unalienable rights of life, liberty and the pursuit of happiness (ownership of private property). People empower government. Government serves people.
2. For every action, there is an equal reaction. When there is a flood, there will be mud in direct proportion to the amount of water absorbed by dirt. When someone hates, another hates back. When a child is abused, the child often grows into an abuser. What goes around comes around. Nature is balance in motion.
3. For every cause, there is an effect. To have a positive society, we must have healthy children. To have healthy children, healthy adults must teach healthy values that must be lived-out in a positive, healthy environment. If

society devalues human life by accepting abortion and assisted suicide, all human life is devalued, whether in a Colorado high school, an Oklahoma City federal building, or in two giant towers in New York City. Nothing lives in a vacuum. In other words, it is logical to realize that life either has a purpose or it does not. If it does not, expect violence. Every action of every person impacts each of us, either positively or negatively. That is why we are to love and help one another.
4. The line of least resistance makes crooked rivers. Logically, then, the line of least resistance also makes crooked people.

The only way to reject the line of least resistance is through discipline. "Better" does not mean "easier." Giving in to the line of least resistance means doing what we want not what is best for us or for others. This explains the importance of controlling perception and sensation through positive conceptualization. It explains why conservatives instinctively know the damage done by the negative content of film and television. Both conceptualize *for* the viewer... viewer imaginations are not exercised. And, negativity (illicit sex and violence) sells movie tickets or gains television ratings. Too much time spent enjoying the conceptual talents of others results in negating our own creative talents which are motivated by conceptualization.

5. What goes up must come down. The stock market, the economy, our egos, our careers, schools, health, and a drug high ... what goes up must come down. Sir Isaac Newton was the first person who noted the laws of gravity. They are as applicable to our daily lives as to Isaac's apple. During good times, save -- money, memories, food, water, housing -- for bad times.
6. In times of trauma, the fittest who are best prepared survive. Because trauma of some kind will visit each person and each nation, to ensure survival we must be strong enough to protect ourselves. When we do not keep ourselves, our

defense industry, or our military fit, we send a message that we are not capable of surviving. Or, we send a message of over-confidence. Or we send a message of no commitment to the purpose of survival. Thus we have conservative support for a strong military, good personal health habits, gun ownership, and the best means of self-protection. Conservatives oppose crime and support the rights of victims of crime equally with the rights of criminal perpetrators. Passive liberals tend to support criminal rights.

Supporting a strong military does not mean forgetting that history proves the most frequent coups come from strong militaries that decide to overtake governments. In other words, military strength must be closely overseen. The same is true of intelligence gathering groups employed by government. Both are particularly dangerous when they join together in opposition to the people they serve.

7. All living things grow to maturity, level off and die. I will die, you will die. As Martin Luther King noted, how you die is relatively unimportant. What defines meaning in life is your cause -- your life's purpose. Meaning is defined by that for which you are willing to give your life. Though not all Christians are conservative, most conservatives believe in a Supreme Being. They find meaning in purpose, and purpose in ethical behavior. Conservatives believe committed relationships result in a healthy, more selfless society. History tends to prove this instinct accurate.

8. One weed in a garden multiplies quickly to kill the flowers. If the "flower" is family, this explains conservative opposition to same-sex marriage. If the "flower" is self-destiny, this explains conservative opposition to the weed of big government. If the "flower" is strong families with the financial resources to educate children, this explains conservative opposition to the weed of high taxes.

9. The cost of something for nothing is human dignity ... thus the conservative work ethic and opposition to career welfare.
10. Power corrupts; absolute power corrupts absolutely. The reason communism has failed worldwide is because it places too much power in the hands of too few people. Liberals appear to think if something sounds good, thinking or saying it equates somehow to doing it. Eliminating poverty sounds wonderful. But Marxist theories overlook this basic truth of nature ... ask the millions of Russians killed in the name of the communist collective. For freedom to exist, conservatives believe power must be vested in the people, not the government. History agrees with them and knows what Marx meant when he said socialism is the road to communism.
11. One must learn basics to progress beyond them. We must crawl before we walk. We must print before we write. We must add and multiply before we divide. If we teach birth control and safe sex rather than reading, writing, and arithmetic in our public schools, tools of logic and reason will always be lost from the learning arsenal of our young people. There are only so many hours for learning in each school day. None should be wasted. It is obvious in 2018 that young people lack critical thinking skills. Colleges and universities teach at the level of the last two years of high school. We need only look at the Snowflakes who cannot go to class after a lost 2016 election to validate that statement. Many feel the implementation of the new math program back in the 1970s was designed to strip youth of critical thinking skills.
12. Standards must be present for objectives to be set, achieved and rewarded. Right and wrong as standards are a matter of definable black and white, not ever-changing relativist gray. It is impossible to make positive achievements in a world of ever-changing standards.

There are hundreds of Natural Laws to serve as the basis of conservative beliefs and the dozen mentioned above represent only a few.

A MacGruder Axiom: Every time you think you've found the truth, question it until it is an old friend. Be willing to re-evaluate your truth when evidence to the contrary appears.

Welfare, in fact, is a perfect example of the 180-degree opposite views held by liberals and conservatives. Conservatives define compassionate welfare programs as those that reduce the number of people requiring aid. Liberals define compassion by an increase in the number of people receiving aid.

This reflects the conservative view that human dignity, comprised of ethics, character, and a positive sense of self, is the key to survival and purposeful lives. All contribute positively to the total social order by contributing positively as individuals. Productivity is essential to self-respect, which is essential to human dignity. Welfare kills the opportunity to be productive.

Based on my own experience with welfare, conservatives are right. I had to take advantage of societal safety nets, twice.

Because of a family tragedy, I was on welfare for three months in 1962. I had three-month and 18-month old babies and was unable to work. My husband was the source of the tragedy. I found my face on the front of the morning paper regarding something about which I knew absolutely nothing.

I was in an auto accident November 1, 1960. I was seven months pregnant with my daughter. She was born and multiple complications followed. I was re-hospitalized for a week in February 1961.

In June of 1962, I had to have surgery to correct problems caused by an automobile accident. My husband was in prison. I had not worked long enough to get sick leave at the law office where I got a secretarial job, but I had two babies to support by myself. The doctor said not having the surgery could cost me my life. So, I had the operation, stayed in the hospital for one day, snuck out and went back to work. Three weeks later, I collapsed. There was no family back-up system available to me.

I was most grateful for the welfare system, believe me! People think conservatives oppose safety nets like welfare. We do not. We oppose people using safety nets as careers.

> *A MacGruder Axiom: You can't have sunshine without shadows, good without bad, or success without failure. Nature says so.*

I am conservative. Like most conservatives, I believe in safety nets for people in their hour of need. I do not believe it enhances anyone's life to put men or women on a career dole. My own experience taught me that the cost of something for nothing is human dignity. Society cannot aid and abet in the removal of someone's human dignity by giving him or her something for nothing then act surprised or disgusted – or, compassionate – when that person behaves like a less than dignified person.

Aha! You may think my confession about being a conservative taints the validity of my research. Wrong. Until I became disabled in 1993, I was a totally non-political person. I did manage to vote. I changed my party affiliation many times over the years. It would be difficult to categorize me as either Republican or Democrat.

We viewed welfare quite differently in the 1960s. It was a horrible embarrassment – an admission of failure, not a career. I am glad that if I had to be on welfare during my lifetime, it happened when all of the pressure in the world was on me to get off the dole and back to work. I was like a wounded bird in those days. It would have been very tempting to just stay home and wait for my monthly welfare check. I was hurt and embarrassed and didn't want to face the world.

I started in the hole, but I didn't end there. In 1987, I was named one of the top 100 businesswomen in America (*What It Takes*, Gardenswartz and Rowe, Dolphin Doubleday). I was one of the founding members of The Committee of 200, the top 200 businesswomen in the country. It was during the process of re-applying research data to social and political issues that I realized I had unknowingly adopted a conservative philosophy without really knowing what a conservative philosophy was. That realization came after 1995, after my research was completed.

Had I been in need of welfare in the 2000s rather than the 1960s, I rather doubt I would have been able to achieve what I did. It is so easy – so socially acceptable – to be a loser today. I had a high school diploma and could type fast. I ended my career with a graduate degree, earning a low-mid six-figure income. In the 1970s and 1980s, that was almost impossible for a woman to achieve on her own. The public paid for no part of my university education.

All people make poor choices. I did. We all do. In the good old days when people paid an appropriate penalty for making poor choices, few people made the same mistake twice. All who overcame their errors were stronger after paying the price for erroneous behavior. It was a far better system than having a nation filled with victims who simply cannot display sufficient strength or discipline to behave responsibly.

I came by my conservative beliefs the hard way. I experienced the liberal solution to human misery and decided I wanted no part of it.

A MacGruder Axiom: Parents (or others) get thanks (or curses) for where I am when I enter adulthood at age 21. I can't blame another for where I go from there It's my choice.

Looking at the list of conservative personality traits on the first pages of Chapter 3 and at the basic philosophy to which these people subscribe, it is surprising *any* of them run for political office. In fact, few true conservatives run for political office. The way our political system is structured, it is designed to dissuade conservatives from running for office. It doesn't have to be structured that way, but it is.

Power is not the best motivator for the true conservative. Politics is a power game -- a blood sport. Those attracted to it seek power. Since conservatives are motivated by control and not power, few run for public office... until their way of life is threatened This has created a problem between conservative voters and their not-so-conservative political representatives.

A Republican who wants to be elected to office says, "I am a conservative ... I believe in smaller government and lower taxes" and conservatives give that candidate their vote.

Those two issues are on the conservative agenda, but represent only a very small part of a quite complex total philosophy. Because no one has ever provided a philosophy textbook for conservative voters, they often do not know what to ask to determine if such a candidate IS conservative. Instead, they say, "I'm for that, too," and vote for another moderate or liberal politician who is liberal but runs as a Republican. Consequently, America's conservative voters are quite under-represented in government. Because of this duplicity, conservative anger rejected traditionalist Republicans in 2016 and elected a non-Republican but very conservative Donald J. Trump as President of the United States.

Conservatism is a total philosophy from which social and political issues result. Philosophies do not evolve from issues. Issues evolve from philosophies. Liberals understand this. That is why it is so easy to get them to walk in lock step to achieve their objectives. They do a wonderful job of discussing their issues from a philosophical perspective. Conservatives have yet to learn this lesson. We think in terms of issues rather than the philosophy from which they come.

If conservatives adhered to a philosophy, it would unite them into a single, large group capable of effectively opposing liberal positions. Issues-based thinking keeps conservatives splintered into small groups. One group opposes abortion. Another supports the Second Amendment and gun ownership. One group wants tax reform, another small government, and others demand the right to pray in school. Some support immigration reform, others a balanced budget. Their interest in and support for all other conservative social and political issues stops at the end of their own noses. All conservatives suffer the lack of group unity caused by individualism.

Prior to the success of Donald Trump, the Republican Party did not necessarily represent a broad spectrum of conservative thought. The election of President Trump is testimony that the American people firmly reject the talk and do not accept the performance of traditionalist Republicans. It has become the party that most sincerely promises conservative voters the size of government and taxes will be reduced... and does nothing. Traditional Republicans had seven years to write a new health care plan to replace Obamacare and did nothing. Can there be better evidence that traditional Republicans do not understand conservative philosophy?

Republican candidates have identified a handful of issues supported by conservative voters and have committed to supporting them. Whether the GOP walks the walk rather than just talks the talk has consistently determined how long they remain a majority party. Their almost even split of the House and Senate after the 2000 elections indicates they did not walk the walk after the 1998 elections. Had they done so, they would have won or lost by a larger margin. The same is true of the 2016 elections... Democrats have not fulfilled their natural purpose of stabilizing and expanding business and commerce and began losing in the House of Representatives and U.S. Senate years ago. They were – and still are – more interested in power for the party than serving the needs of the people. That is why we have a President named Donald J. Trump.

Politicians are lured to that occupation by power. My research proved that people attracted by political power *have liberal rather than conservative beliefs. Liberals are power-motivated team players. Conservatives are risk-management individualists who need to control the risk management system in which they function.* That, in two sentences, explains why conservative voters are disgusted with and unsupportive of elected Republican representatives and senators who do nothing to provide what they need.

Those career politicians who say they are conservative because they support smaller government and oppose abortion and are fiscally conservative *do not necessarily hold conservative philosophies and it is apparent in their voting records.* Voters are beginning to realize this. The Republican Party is losing cohesiveness because of it. What is the Biblical story about seeing the mote in the other guy's eye? If Republican voters subscribed to a conservative philosophy instead of fragmented issues, they could identify and elect people whose political ideals match their own.

A MacGruder Axiom: Successful people see beyond the obvious to the subtle... beyond what people say to what people do.

If politicians support smaller government and oppose abortion and are fiscally responsible, they may be 49 percent conservative. They may also support increased controls on gun ownership or conceal-carry laws, or view the military as an extension of meals on wheels, or oppose prayer in school, or support the National Education Association or funding for the National Endowment for the Arts ... a 51 percent liberal. Such a person is a moderate. They just want to get along with everyone and really have no firm beliefs. They are the gray people known as "relativists" (see Chapter 5).

From 2000-08 we heard the mantra of how important it was for the Bush administration to "reach across the aisle and include liberals" and how George W. represented "all of the people, not just some of them." It almost sounds like an end run around the two-party system. What better way is there to eliminate the two-party system than to have both parties exercise equal power to achieve the same objectives? That is not the way it is intended to be. The two-party system is designed to make sure everyone – from labor to elitists – gain equal representation. It is intended to make sure the Constitution of the United States and the Rule of Law that flows from it are supported. Corruption in the Congress that involves lobbyist political contributions has perverted the system and both political parties. They serve themselves and their own survival, not the people who pay their salaries.

Mr. Bush did represent all the people. But it was not liberals who elected him. The same was true of Mr. Obama who strongly supported anything having to do with members of his own race and opposed anything having to do with non-members. I will never forget the new Black Panther group intimidating voters at a Philadelphia voting precinct, slapping clubs against the palms of their hands as voters entered the precinct to vote. I will never forget Attorney General Eric Holder ignoring them.

Natural Law says two opposing forces result in balance. That is why we are intended to have a two party system in America. Today, the two are not in opposition to one another. It is politically incorrect for either to act in a partisan manner... to argue with fervor for their beliefs. Rather, today both major political parties mirror one another. It results in political imbalance. The political teeter-totter has one end sitting on the ground, the other end firmly planted in the air.

CHAPTER 10

IT'S NOT NICE TO FOOL MOTHER NATURE

Conservatives need to understand that change in government takes time.

They do not.

Conservatives tend to believe government should function like a business and the reason it is so inefficient is because it is comprised of incompetent people who need strong leadership. If government just had good people and strong leaders, everything would move along smoothly and more quickly.

Wrong!

Government employees are civil servants and do not work under the same performance standards as non-government employees. It is almost impossible to terminate a civil service worker. You can eliminate civil service jobs sometimes, but you cannot terminate them. Too, even those who are committed and talented are bogged down within the system by departmental policies (written over many years by dozens of political appointees) and regulations (written by Congress or the courts or regulators). The cards are stacked so that government *cannot* function efficiently.

This is particularly important since the inauguration of President Donald J. Trump. He comes from the world of business, not government. He is used to managers that evaluate what needs to be done, who work out a plan to achieve his objectives, and then he makes changes if he wants or approves the plan and tells his managers to get the job done.

The problem with government productivity is that managers must research their plans in relationship to all of the policies and regulations that may impact them. What can and cannot be done needs to be determined... and that takes time. Often, the regulations and policies are written in such confusing language a legal opinion must be sought to provide answers to questions that arise. President Trump's hastily written Executive Order preventing travelers from certain nations was successfully challenged by a Passive liberal 9th Circuit Court of Appeals because of this particular learning curve. Steve Bannon is brilliant, but he is not politically experienced and was the one responsible for coordinating this project. The Supreme Court gave Trump a win in the end, but time was lost and so was credibility (the liberal objective from the start).

Conservatives have waited so long for meaningful change and President Trump is giving it to them more quickly than any President in history, but mistakes of varying sizes are made out of haste and highly skilled staff with no government experience. There are leaks... the government is filled with left-over Democrats and other people having real motives to cause the Trump administration to fail because it is good for them politically – even though it is bad for the nation and the people. Included in that group are traditional neo-conservative Republicans. Joined at the hip Senators McCain of Arizona and Graham of South Carolina are giant-sized examples.

The huge, unmanageable behemoth government was created by liberals, Republican and Democrat, who equate "big" with "safe." It is supported by the media which is willing to print any story, true or untrue, if it will gain public support for international government (previously known as the New World Order).

The biggest concern about Donald Trump has nothing to do with his temperament or his ability to act Presidential. It has nothing to do with his ego – he earned the right to a strong ego through his achievements. The only egos dangerous to others belong to those egocentric people who have done little or nothing in their own lives but come from a successful family or corporate environment (or is someone who talks a good game and even though they haven't done anything noteworthy, get elected to public office – e.g., Barack Obama).

What other people have accomplished in life through family, friends, corporate teammates, investment partners, etc. and who have never done much of anything on their own are the ones with offensive egos. My concern has to do with President Trump not being used to the slowness of getting his decisions implemented. He's used to Mach 4; government functions far below Mach. Also he's used to staff members who are loyal and who do not look for any word that can be twisted and leaked to Passive liberal progressive media members.

After fifty years of Passive liberal domination, it would be surprising if people were prepared to be responsible for their own behavior. Earlier chapters have described how Passive liberals avoid responsibility for their actions.

Wait a minute. Didn't I say numerous times in preceding chapters that the years 1960 through 2010 were dominated by the Active philosophy? If that's true, how can I say we've had fifty years of liberal domination?

First, what was accomplished by the Reagan administration was accomplished in spite of government, not because of it. Second, though since 1994 Republicans have at various times controlled either the House or the Senate or the Executive office, they have not controlled all three for many years (as did Bill Clinton, as did Barack Obama) and what they gave America was naïve military behavior in the Middle East and socialized medicine – both of which are huge failures.

The primary life-long message of anyone under 45 years of age has been "government will do it for you." Lest we forget, Franklin Delano Roosevelt began the "let government do it for you" era when he was elected in 1935 ... over eighty years ago.

That means everyone under retirement age has been conditioned to accept government as parent.

Having the opportunity for self-determination and getting government out of our lives sounds wonderful. Unfortunately, many people are ill prepared to accept personal responsibility, an issue so close to the heart of conservatives. Personal responsibility and accountability are at the top of every conservative Active's priority list. That does not mean saying "I'm sorry." It means paying a price for social or unlawful behavior that fits the action or crime. The problem is: What penalty can morally be imposed on a two-year old for irresponsible behavior? And yes, when it comes to understanding personal responsibility and moral issues, Passive liberals are two-year olds. The reason for their behavior? They believe the end justifies the means.

A MacGruder Axiom: From creative productivity flows self-esteem and self-respect. People who do not have these things are incapable of esteeming and respecting others.

Average Americans rejected liberal power motives and abuses when they elected Donald Trump to office. Please note I said "liberals," not Democrats because neo-conservative Republicans were also rejected. Neo-conservative Republicans also rejected (and still reject) President Trump. The people opted to gain more control over their lives and voted for Donald Trump. It represented a rejection of both political parties because Trump represents neither.

Since the Passive liberal cycle just began in 2010 and Passive liberals should have dominated the political scene for fifty years, the results of this election should not have happened. Passives, however, were not fulfilling the responsibilities given them by nature. When you abuse the power of nature, you lose that power – eventually. Politically, both Democrats and Republicans abused that power when they abrogated their natural responsibilities.

Passive liberals and many Republicans who say they are conservative but are not forgot that power truly vests in the people.

A free society doesn't work the other way around. History proves that. Logically, that brings to question the real motives behind the political objectives of both parties. Perhaps they fell in love with power and decided they could wield it better than the people. But it is not owned by the people... they merely pay rent on it. It is owned by Nature.

Let's go back a few years and look at why the Democrat party lost its majority in the Congress in 1994. We can then ask: Did they learn anything from their 1994 losses – or did they just continue with their lockstep divide and conquer mantra? If we look at what caused the 1994 losses and then look at what caused the 2016 losses, we can analyze whether or not Passive liberals learned anything between 1994 losses to Newt Gingrich and his Contract with America and conservative Donald Trump's victory... did they make any changes?

As authors Louis T. March and Brent Nelson point out in their 1990's book *The Great Betrayal: The Elite's War on Middle America*:

> "The majority (of Americans) were overwhelmingly opposed to forced busing for racial balance -- we have it.
>
> "The majority was opposed to the Panama Canal Treaties -- they passed.
>
> "The majority are opposed to current levels of taxation -- have been for years.
>
> "The majority are opposed to the massive federal deficits -- makes no difference.
>
> "The majority are opposed to the thirty-year crime wave -- whole sections of our major cities are not safe. Criminals walk.
>
> "The majority are opposed to massive illegal immigration -- so what? It continues year after year.

"The majority opposed the U.S. bailout of the Mexican peso -- too bad.

"The majority is opposed to so-called affirmative action -- it's still around

"The majority don't understand why their sons should be sent to fight and die for Somalia, Haiti, Bosnia and other parts unknown -- tough.

"The majority favor a Balanced Budget Amendment to the Constitution -- still waiting.

"The majority wants a better standard of living -- real wages have been falling for over two decades."

The actions, not the words, of U.S. Senators and Congressmen, the American President and Supreme Court Justices, engrave in stone the proof that government rules in opposition to the will of the people. For those who are unaware, that is called tyranny.

I wrote the above paragraph in 1995, right after Newt Gingrich and his Contract with America put a majority of Republicans in the Congress. Democrat Bill Clinton was President so they did not control the entire legislative arm of government but did control two-thirds of it. Here we are more than 20 years later and that list of "the public doesn't want it" is still the apparent priority of legislators. For example, had Donald Trump not been elected to office, we would have the Trans-Pacific Partnership (TPP), another international trade agreement Americans did not want.

Since 1995, thousands of American lives have been sacrificed in the Middle East, from Iraq, Kuwait, Afghanistan, Pakistan, Somalia, and other places. Americans are sick of it and now see our involvement in the Middle East as having more to do with maintaining control of the Afghani poppy fields and Iraqi, Syrian, and Libyan oil than with helping the people of those nations establish non-tyrannical governments. It opened the door to terrorism which, in turn, suggests that people living under Sharia Law may require tyrannical leaders to effectively manage government.

Since the time neo-conservative President George H.W. Bush set Kuwait up for an attack by Iraq's Saddam Hussein so America could justify entry into the oil-rich nations of the Middle East, our presence has brought the people of those nations nothing but pain and loss.

Donald Trump brought up topics like political correctness that withholds truth from the people better than any other strategy known to mankind.

The American public doesn't like political correctness, either. He brought up illegal immigration and economic problems that result from it – including loss of jobs caused by rotten trade deals other politicians had been too 'politically correct' (or financially rewarded for their vote) to mention publicly – and the majority of Americans agree with him.

Trump brought up the numerous violations of our Constitution by politicians... the people agree with him. He talked about foreign policy and wars being fought in the Middle East that do no good for anyone... the people agree with him. He talked about international trade deals that are more responsible for multi-national corporations moving their manufacturing overseas to gain access to cheap labor and which has stolen millions of American jobs... and the people agree with him.

If you are a Passive Democrat reading this – and I doubt Passives will get this far into the text because they have no tolerance for people who disagree with them (it's a threat to their need to feel powerful) – those are the reasons Donald J. Trump is now President of the United States, not Secretary Hillary Clinton or Senator Bernie Sanders.

Since World War II, we have fought to prevent Russia from establishing control of oil from Middle East nations. Russia wants to keep all of Europe dependent upon it for access to heat in the winter and fuel for their cars. There has been a lot of fancy footwork politically trying to make excuses to the American people why we're there, but it has little to do with anything called compassion and a lot to do with oil and money. It has a lot to do with why the immigration policies of European nations have brought so many Muslims into their culture that they can no longer safely walk the streets – day or night.

Elected officials "govern" when legislation reflects the will of the people; they "rule" when they legislate in opposition to the will of the people.

If you need more evidence of the lack of legislative concern supportive of the will of the people, add to the above list NAFTA, GATT, CAFTA, legalized late-term abortion, gun control, foreign policy in the Middle East, the NATO bombing of Kosovo, foreign aid to nations that are America's enemies, the general weakening and deployment of our military, and lost national sovereignty to the United Nations. We could add the emergence of ISIS.

If Americans do not support these things, why are they happening?

What better indicator is there that not only did Passive liberals not learn why they suffered losses in 1994, they repeated the same mistakes, the same power abuses, when they assumed power in 2008 and history repeated itself in their 2016 election losses?

What better indicator is there that traditional and neo-conservative Republicans learned nothing about why they gained those victories than their behavior in 2016 towards the people's candidate, Donald Trump? The lessons should have been: 1) The public believes Republicans represent a liberal philosophy and have morphed into middle-of-the road Democrats; 2) When Republicans support liberal policies, they lose conservative voters and cannot win elections without them; and 3) Donald Trump presents the public with an alternative to liberal policies and he won the election. Republicans did not learn those lessons and the "Never Trump" groups evidence it.

There are two basic and primary reasons American voters rejected liberals ideals and philosophies. The same two reasons will cause American voters to reject Republicans who call themselves conservatives but support liberal causes.

First, there is nothing more arrogant in the world than one person (or group of people) thinking he or she or it is better able than an individual to determine another human being's destiny. The people are tired of such arrogance. It is true that young people (the ones who protest and riot, particularly) want a free education, a free cell phone... and cannot tell you the name of the Vice President of the United States today or the names of the founding fathers. They don't care who determines their destiny because they do not think much about it. They will one day, but not now. At the moment, their thoughts mirror those of their liberal progressive professors.

Second, after the 2000 elections it appears the nation was evenly divided in its support of liberal and conservative campaign promises. A closer look makes it clear that big cities, where the greatest number of "let government do it for you give-away programs" exist, support liberal philosophies. The rest of the country supports conservative philosophy. The votes cast for Al Gore versus George Bush certainly prove those statements.

The number of counties won by Al Gore in the 2000 presidential election was 677.

Bush won 2,434 counties.

The total population of counties won by Al Gore was 127 million.

Bush counties totaled 143 million in population.

Al Gore won an area of American soil on which American voters live totaling 580,000 square miles.

George Bush won 2,427,000 square miles.

Al Gore won 20 states; George Bush, won 30.

Let's look at what Passive liberals learned after neo-conservative George W. Bush won the 2000 election and was re-elected in 2004. After his eight years in office, Passive Liberal Barack Obama was elected to office. Did Obama do things differently... did he avoid the power abuses that caused the loss of power in 2000? He was in office from 2008 through 2016.

This election should have shown Americans just how important the Electoral College is. Here is why we need it:

As of 2016, there are 3,141 counties in the United States.

Trump won 3,084 counties; Clinton won 57. Does that sound to you like Hillary won the popular vote? If you count only voters in big cities, it does. More important – and something about which you hear little in newspapers or on television – Passive liberals lost about 1,000 state legislature seats nationwide the past few years. That is called rejection; big time rejection.

There are 62 counties in New York State. Trump won 46 of them; Clinton won 16. Because she also won in counties surrounding large cities where give away programs dominate, she won in the Chicago, Los Angeles, San Francisco, and Boston areas.

As Colonel Allen West suggested in an article after the election amidst claims that Hillary Clinton won the popular vote and was thus the legitimate President of the United States: "When you have a country that encompasses almost 4 million square miles of territory, it would be ludicrous to even suggest that the vote of those who inhabit a mere 319 square miles should dictate the outcome of a national election."

If Ivy League professors and students understood that perhaps they might understand the importance of the Electoral College.

These statistics paint a clear picture. America is an almost evenly-divided nation. The liberal big cities which compose a tiny portion of land mass are in total opposition to rural America. How we are divided is of significant importance.

Of those who voted in the 2016 elections, about half live in America's largest cities. They have high rates of crime, large welfare programs, teen pregnancy, always increasing numbers of children supervised by foster parent programs. They have food stamps and free medical care -- they are well on their way to socialism. Those voters selected Hillary Clinton to be their president.

The other half of 2016 voters live in large and small cities across the nation. Their crime rates are low and their quality of life is pretty high. Their problems are solvable and their selection was Donald J. Trump.

A MacGruder Axiom: It is an act of arrogance to try to solve the problems of others until you have your own under control.

When you give too many people too much that costs them nothing for too long, you create many of the social problems running rampant on the streets of America's big cities today. Studies say the promise of something for nothing results in youth violence. Schools and parents teach children they should be held in esteem and respected by others whether or not they have done anything to earn esteem and respect. It is a major reason for youth violence.

Liberals simply do not realize you cannot "give" people self-respect and meaningful lives. These are things individuals must define for themselves and then earn. It is in earning things (rather than getting freebies) that adds value and gives meaning to the words "self respect."

In a recent speech, I said America's greatest problem is lack of character... people who have no self-respect and lack meaningful lives (which largely define character). Telling youth that they deserve respect and esteem when they have done nothing to earn it is telling them that lies and deception make up their character.

Education to the contrary is critically important.

A MacGruder Axiom: Nothing can be given to others that is not first given to self -- love, respect, hope -- nothing. To have something to give society, you must first possess it.

Liberals refuse to acknowledge that their surface-level solutions damage the human spirit. Nothing is surface-level in nature. To understand the human spirit, we must look inward, where it dwells, not outward, where it exhibits itself. Liberals are externalists. They instinctively look outward -- away from themselves -- for all answers. That's why they think guns kill people and cannot understand that people kill people and guns are merely a tool they use.

As looking inward is not a liberal strength, looking outward is difficult for conservatives.

Conservatives' problems result from the inability to look outside themselves and their own philosophies, a result of being issues- rather than philosophy-driven. It is a mistake and creates social problems. It causes conservatives to cast a too-narrow net and makes them unable to rid the world of social ills. It prevents them from legislating effectively.

Conservatives, looking inward rather than outward, are frequently blind to the weaknesses of some people within our society. We need to realize that some weaknesses simply do not make a philosophy of "pull yourself up by your own boot straps" possible. Asking people who live in large population centers to stand on their own two feet after they sat on government couches more and more for years frightens them. It may be an unsolvable problem. This makes evident how important changing what is being taught in our public schools really is. If these problems are to be solved, it will take generations.

Consequently, conservatives often appear to have very narrow views of the country and its problems. As a total group, they do not, but in their splintered groups they appear so. In its own way, that makes many people feel disenfranchised. It points to the need to deal with political issues from a philosophic rather than an issues or a political ideology base.

Remember that politics is a team sport where leaders emerge. Getting a large group of individualist, competitive conservatives to behave as a team is more than just a challenge. They do not like game-playing partisanship. Why? Game playing involves manipulation. That, in turn, involves the exercise of power over others rather than control of self and that rubs conservatives the wrong way.

> **A MacGruder Axiom: What you think is true at age 21 is often no longer true at age 45... and may change yet again before you are 60.**

Truth and honesty are wonderful attributes, but are seldom popular. People don't like the truth when it frightens or otherwise destabilizes them. If you are curious as to why so many people dislike Donald Trump, that's why. When one political party that has been a relatively meaningless minority for years suddenly becomes a majority and begins announcing sweeping changes that impact everything, people whose only view of government was represented by the old majority react with fear.

One does not create a path to the hearts of the public with a machete. A Swiss Army knife and a small saw to start cutting down the overgrowth on the path to change must first be used. Conservatives do not understand achieving in small increments. Liberals do and that is how they have made so much headway over a long period of time... as I said, they think similarly to the Chinese. They understand "back to basics." They are right. That's where we need to go. But we need to get there a little at a time ... incrementally.

These are wonderful personal qualities -- honesty, truth, and self-discipline -- but conservatives must learn to better communicate with a voter base made up of highly diverse beliefs and values. Liberals have convinced the electorate there is such a thing as a free lunch. They have explained away the terribly high price tag – freedom – with spin. Conservatives who want to present moderate and liberal voters with the stark truth without consideration given to the shell shock caused by going from la la land to reality are asking for defeat. They generate animosity based on fear. They must tell the truth, but it must be done gently and with assurance that everything is going to be fine.

The two motivational hot buttons of conservatives are control and risk tolerance. They exhibit themselves in many ways. Politics is just one. The traits are equally seen in finance, and social and career endeavors. They are seen in any endeavor involving an investment of personal assets. They appear each time an investment in a new car is made or a new computer is added to a home office.

Conservatives tend to be self-employed. Or, they work for small companies. If they work for large companies, they usually do not spend their entire career there. They work hard and learn a trade and leave corporate life to start their own companies.

They hate the politics inherent to large organizations. Some go to work every day for 25 or 30 years and hate every day of it. Actives dislike compromise, a required function of corporate team members. Conservatives can -- are not always, but can -- be loners. They are far less social than liberals are... and far less dependent on socializing to gain personal fulfillment.

Conservative (not necessarily Republican, but conservative) politicians want to create an environment in which people can control their own destinies. Will they give sufficient problem resolution energy to this real, live, fact? A large number of people had their self-determination skills destroyed or seriously wounded during the years of liberal domination. Will their impatient conservative constituents understand that a half-century of liberal "let government do it for you" programs cannot be torn down overnight?

The control factor is the strongest of possible personal motivators for conservatives... just as the seeking of power is for liberals. These two traits, by the way, explain why liberals make such good leaders and conservatives have to work so hard at it. Good leaders exercise power (which does not come naturally to conservatives). Poor leaders try to control through manipulation rather than personal strength (and conservatives dislike power-based manipulation). Donald Trump exhibits strong leadership skills. His style offends some, but there is no doubt that he is a leader. This, too, frightens Passive liberals.

> *A MacGruder Axiom: Moses was a good leader because he didn't ask anyone's opinion when it was time to part the waters. He just did what God told him.*

A conservative political environment serves well individuals within American society who want self-determination. Many individuals within our diverse society want to look to government as replacement parents in its responsibilities to them, as citizens. For them, a conservative majority rule is a misunderstood shock.

Those people who are not prepared to control their own destinies are not restricted to welfare recipients and people living in ghettos. Rather, many of them have been taught by liberal college and university professors that to take control of self-destiny is selfish and wrong. They must function for the good of the social collective (which is another word for socialism). The disagreement between conservatives and liberals on this issue focuses on whether one can do good work for society without first doing good for self, independent of government. Liberals come down on the side of government, conservatives on the side of individualism.

In short, conservative politicians have a major education job on their hands: They must teach recipients of social welfare programs that they will be happier as productive people. The only way to teach that lesson is to create jobs for people who can work. People in control of their own destiny are always happier than are slaves to government.

They must also teach college-educated middle-class and upper-middle class Americans that to be self-sufficient is not the epitome of selfishness. They must reach out to people and explain why, to love others meaningfully, they must first love themselves. Passives must learn the difference between self and selfish love. Self-love is the opposite of selfish love. The best way to teach that lesson is to exemplify it.

Conservatives will also have to educate the non-productive poor along with corporate executives (and those on the way up), and other educated members of the business and social communities that government is not their mommy or daddy. People at all socioeconomic levels have been exposed to this image of government for a very long time.

Since conservative politicians are not talented at people skills -- including communication -- this is a difficult road for them. Not understanding their own weaknesses in the people skills arena has been politically costly to conservatives.

A MacGruder Axiom: Whatever path you find your feet on, beware cursing it. You are the one in control of your feet.

People who are into philosophies of maintaining a social environment that encourages self-determination and individualism (as are conservatives), seldom see the broader need to be public relations experts. Why should anyone need to be convinced that self-determination is good? Or, that the development of self-discipline required to achieve it is hard -- but very rewarding -- work? Doesn't everyone feel that way? No. They do not.

CHAPTER 11

CONSERVATIVES: THE MEDIA AND SOCIAL INVOLVEMENT

From the Freedom Caucus to Log Cabin Republicans, the GOP majority has problems caused by individualistic philosophies of self-determination.

For example, committees only work when individuals serve as members of teams. Politics is made up of one committee after another -- and conservatives are not the best team players in the world. Motivated by self-determination and control philosophies inherent to individualists, they often have difficulty delegating authority and establishing common goals. They are, however, wonderful at digging up facts.

Legislators are responsible for investing public funds into worthwhile programs for the total population, not just those who believe in conservative philosophy. They must reach agreement with hundreds of other people almost half of whom disagree about the definition of "worthwhile programs." Things become complicated.

In a setting where personal control of risk is lost to group dynamics, conservatives have lower tolerances for risk than their liberal counterparts. Perhaps that explains why, when they arrive in Washington, D.C., conservatives lose the strength of character that got them elected and they put forth Obamacare Light rather than a truly rewritten, restructured program for national health. Financial risk taken by individuals must be managed by individuals. When control of individual risk is lost to group dynamics and government rules and regulations, it is impossible for individuals to manage risk in private industry or government. The government insists via regulations that it will tell independent business owners and entrepreneurs which risks they must manage and how they will manage them – and Actives have refused to honor such rules.

I repeat, Active risk management tolerance goes down in direct relationship to the amount of control lost in any transaction. That is why Active conservatives sound so sure of themselves when talking about an issue when campaigning and after being elected they meow like pussycats when it comes to fighting for their cause once it falls under the control of the rules and regulations of Congress.

Liberals are used to risking the assets of others. It is a way of life for them. It is how they "manage" risk, by spreading it around and sharing it with others. Thus, in the face of lost power and the need for courage to fight and implement their policies, conservatives have a tendency to pull back and do nothing. Liberals will fight – after all, it isn't their money they place at risk. It's taxpayer money. Liberals have no problem taking risks that involve others.

Conservatives are far more tolerant than liberals who tend to be tolerant only with those who agree with them. You never hear of a conservative campus barring a liberal speaker from speaking – one whom many students and professors may strongly oppose. That kind of behavior belongs to Passive liberals... no tolerance because any opinion that opposes their views is a threat.

A MacGruder Axiom: A good leader knows when to lead, when to follow, and when to get out of the way.

It is in these two basic areas of personal values and personality traits that conservatives get in trouble with their own constituents.

Conservative voters and special interest groups (e.g., the religious right), function in their environments of self-determination. They have little sympathy with the elected who must, to some degree, compromise to fairly represent *all* of the people they represent. Conservative voters maintain their high tolerance for risk. Their views of how conservative representatives should vote, behave, and allocate runs at a higher risk ratio than is possible for the politicians they elect to office to achieve. This very predictable circumstance results in conflict between the elected and the electorate.

Just as liberals are the nicest, most sociable people in the world, conservatives, too, are nice ... but in a very different way. They are often poor communicators. The reason? They are far more concerned with getting things done than in talking about getting things done.

Conservative business owners do not have the same amount of time available for community service as liberal corporate employees. No one pays them a salary for taking time off to go and help others in their communities. They must earn a living by working at their jobs. Thus, logically, they are not as involved with neighborhoods, associations and civil rights causes as liberals are.

Conservatives are not "tribal" creatures by nature. Liberals are. Thus, conservative politicians do not have the same strength of community behind them. Most corporate employees – the ones who have time made available by their employers to work for community causes – are Passive liberals from large companies (who use such contacts to develop new business for their companies).

Independent business owners are too busy making ends meet and creating company growth and jobs to spend hours in worthwhile community meetings and endeavors. Since community meetings and endeavors receive good publicity from local media, liberals benefit from this circumstance. Conservative politicians suffer the lack of constituent community involvement and accompanying publicity. A case can be made that when conservatives do very worthwhile community endeavors, the liberal media finds a way to bury the story on the last page -- if they publish it at all.

Does that mean conservatives are not interested in the welfare of the community? No.

It does mean Actives express their concerns for the good of the community in ways totally different than Passives. A liberal banker may receive a salary from an employer while spending numerous hours putting together a plan to help train residents of poverty areas. He or she may help improve chances for meaningful employment for residents of that community.

Conservative business owners are the ones who hire and train the poor without benefit of all those meetings. They both do good works. One gets publicity, the other does not.

From the perspective of liberal journalists, a community planner who has never employed anyone does more good than independent business owners who give people jobs and trains them. To them, there can be no argument on this point. The causes and regulations and political candidates liberals support make it obvious: Passive liberals would rather exercise power over the poor than create jobs that will enable them to work their way out of poverty.

A MacGruder Axiom: It is individual effort that makes America so abundantly successful. Big government, sadly, does little to encourage individual effort. Rather, it punishes it.

Conservative politicians believe people should learn to do things that enable them to become self-reliant. Doing things FOR people rather than helping people learn to do things for themselves is a basic difference between Passive liberals and Active conservatives. Those who do things for people get publicity while people who help people learn to do things are ignored.

Liberals love doing things for people. First, it makes them feel good about themselves. Second, there is no better way to gain and maintain power over someone than to have them indebted to and dependent upon you.

A MacGruder Axiom: Leaders make the impossible happen because they lack fear and overlook all that opposes them. They focus instead on achieving their objectives.

For this reason, the true accomplishments of conservatives will not gain public favor via the elite, big media machine which obviously understands little of the importance of conservative accomplishments. They are, after all, dominantly and admittedly liberal. The mainstream media has, in fact, become the public information office for the liberal Democrat party.

According to an article in the liberal Washington Post, "A majority of American journalists identify themselves as Independents although among those who choose a side Democrats outnumber Republicans four to one." The statistics come from a study done by Indiana University professors of journalism, Drs. Lars Wilnat and David Weaver. If you add to those statistics the fact that most journalists have little or no idea how to define the philosophy of conservatism and think that being a fiscal conservative makes them conservative, the number of liberal reporters and their managers compared to those who are conservative is far greater.

This is not a new game. In 1910, twelve men from senior management at major newspapers were hired to provide a list of the most influential newspapers in America. They provided a list of 179 newspapers which, because of size and reputation, could control public opinion. Controlling interest in these papers was purchased by the special interests that originally hired the 12 senior newspaper managers. Their holdings were reduced to 25 newspapers with the highest circulation in 1915. For confirmation read the March 1959 Congressional Record where Congressman Oscar Calloway, a Texas Democrat, reported on these two occurrences.

Unfortunately for the media, their ongoing and unfair coverage of President Donald Trump (and candidate Trump through the primaries, and the campaign and election) has pulled the curtain on the Wiz. The people can now see the swamp filled with snakes and alligators. People now see them for what they really are: Not dispensers of news, but liars that cannot be trusted to report the news – and they are paying a huge price for their blindness. The newspaper industry has jettisoned hundreds of thousands of jobs due to falling advertising revenues. According to the Bureau of Labor Statistics, in 1990 daily and weekly newspaper publishers employed about 455,000 reporters, press/print specialists, clerks, salespeople, etc. By January 2017, the number of people employed had fallen to 173,900. For most industries, that would be a huge hint that they are doing something wrong. Technology advances caused part of the loss of jobs, but not more than 50 percent!

News and editorial opinion are two different things – or, at any rate, they should be. In today's modern media, editorial opinion is often included as news. From deciding which topics and stories are important to determining whether they will get favorable or unfavorable coverage, the media is now one big dispenser of views, not news. The media too often sees itself as the news rather than reporters of it.

Whatever conservatives achieve they need to communicate directly to voters the positive aspects of it. Donald Trump understands this. It's why he Tweets. Do I think Tweeting is good? No, I don't. It reduces the seriousness with which the Office of the President is taken. The fact is, until liberal Passives stop rioting in the streets and until the media stops lying about him, it is necessary.

One good example of this is the President's Tweet about Trump Tower telephones being tapped. It totally changed the direction of the "Russia" investigation. All of the events involving Former President Barack Obama's National Security Advisor Susan Rice would have never been found or investigated without that Tweet.

The fake news about members of the Trump administration colluding with Russia to win the election put Trump in opposition to the best interests of the United States. It was the primary story in newspapers and on television for an extended time and Maxine Waters still rants about it. Democrat liberals were (and still are) withholding from President Trump approval of his Cabinet and thousands of support jobs which need to be filled. At the point in time the Russia/collusion story came out, the fake news about Russian collusion was eating up the time of President Trump's limited staff (limited because Democrat Senators were withholding cabinet approvals; what better way to make the administration look incompetent?). It was impossible for the limited staff to focus on the President's agenda.

Thanks to Trump's Tweet, information came to light that removed from front pages and evening newscasts a story about the President colluding with the Russians and focused on the Democrats having tapped candidate Trump's telephones. After Trump won the election, the Democrats were, thanks to the new President's Tweet, on the defense about tapping candidate Trump's telephones at Trump Towers at the campaign. As a result, President Trump's new, inexperienced and limited staff was able to re-focus on his objectives rather than playing defense to Passive liberal media attacks. A year later, the information gathered appears to have caused this worm to turn and Passives may be playing defense for a long time.

Tweeting may not be dignified, but in an environment where the media is supposed to inform the electorate but instead is indoctrinating voters, it is an effective way to get the truth to the people.

Everyone thinks Trump made a mistake with that Tweet. If it was a mistake, it was brilliant. To get the Congress to investigate what was really happening required him to provide a headline even the mainstream media could not ignore.

It is almost as if the mainstream media has a death wish. By forcing conservatives to bypass them to inform the people, they make themselves unnecessary to many millions of people which, in turn, eventually reduces the value of advertising on their networks, radio stations, and in their newspapers. Subscriptions are down for newspapers and viewership is down for television networks.

Conservatives must inform the public on their own and without the assistance of the Passive liberal media. ABC, NBC, and CBS will not be there to announce the completion of good conservative works. They do not even see the good works of conservatives as good works. *Time*, the *New York Times* or the *Washington Post* will not, either. They cover their turf well ... liberal turf. They leave no footprints on conservative ground, however.

"Good" is interpreted by different people to mean different things. Those who believe big government is good for society will not laud the progress of those who take steps to minimize it.

On the other hand, conservatives can all take comfort in the downward spiral of the audience market share of the three major networks. They are losing viewers to cable stations that present news from a less biased perspective. The primary provider of news for average conservatives is the Internet.

No one wins when the Natural Law of balance achieved through two unfettered and opposing forces is ignored.

The Constitution of the United States says in Article I, Amendment 1: "Congress shall make no law respecting an establishment of religion, or prohibiting the free exercise thereof; or abridging the freedom of speech, or of the press, or the rights of the people peaceably to assemble, and to petition the Government for a redress of grievances."

What we are seeing in our news each day is not a reporting of the news. It is the selling of our nation to sources other than the people to whom the nation belongs. The following makes that clear.

The media was put in place to inform all people about all major news, not just news that pushes projects supported by one political group over another. The Public Broadcasting Service (PBS) is a particular offender of this concept of equality of access to public issues because all taxpayers, not just liberals, pay their salaries. PBS ignores this minor fact (as does the FCC).

A MacGruder Axiom: Only a truly arrogant person thinks he or she is capable of defining success and life purpose for others.

There is nothing wrong with liberal attitudes being over-represented in the major media provided personal beliefs do not impact stories presented to the public. But reporters responsible for broadcasting and writing news of interest to all people do not recognize issues of significance to half of those viewers. Thus, they avoid reporting it. Public broadcasting stations must be held to a higher standard than are cable news outlets for which people pay a fee to have access.

For example, on March 3, 2017, President Donald Trump Tweeted a message that threw the news world into a spin. He accused President Barack Obama's administration of tapping phones at Trump Towers during Trump's political campaign for the White House. Trump was not yet elected when the supposed wire tapping occurred. He was in campaign mode.

Trump Towers is the home of then-candidate Trump.

Senator Chris Coons (D-Del) Judiciary Committee went on MSNBC and said the following:

"There are transcripts that provide very helpful, very critical insights into whether or not Russian intelligence and senior Russian political leaders, including Vladimir Putin, were cooperating – were colluding – with the Trump campaign at the highest levels to influence the outcome of our elections."

On Sunday, March 5, 2017, Chris Wallace on Fox News Sunday asked Senator Tom Cotton (R-AR) who sits on the Senate Intelligence Committee, if Senator Coons' statement was true. He specifically asked Senator Cotton if he had seen any evidence so far in this investigation – hard evidence or collusion between what I will call "Trump World" and Russia or Russian agents – to interfere with the election.

Senator Cotton quickly and concisely said: "No. I have seen no evidence..." and he told Wallace's viewers what he told fellow Arkansans at a Town Hall meeting two days before this interview. The following paragraphs will provide you with evidence as to why you should not trust media reports that are based on "anonymous sources" as Senator Coons did.

"For six weeks now, President Trump has appointed members to his Cabinet and they have made deliberate statements that have been tougher on Russia than anything President Obama ever did," Senator Cotton said. He continued, saying:

"If you want to know what a pro-Russia policy would look like, Chris, here are some elements of it:

"You would slash defense spending;

"You would slow down our nuclear modernization;

"You would roll back missile defense systems;

"You would enter a one-sided nuclear arms control agreement;

"And, you would try to do everything you could to stop oil and gas production" (in America).

"That was Barack Obama's policy for eight years. That is not Donald Trump's policy. None of those things are good for Russia that Donald Trump has proposed to do... to roll back Barack Obama's policies."

Wallace pushed Senator Cotton on the issue of transcripts being available as Senator Coons reported on MSNBC.

"I would prefer not to discuss what transcripts may or may not be available because that would reveal what we do and do not know and our capability of knowing those things and I would just leave it at that."

Chris Wallace: "But you stand by your statement that you have seen no evidence of collusion."

Senator Cotton responded by saying (very quickly): "Yes."

Wallace then introduced his audience to Senator Coons... (D-Del) the same liberal who, it was reported on MSNBC a day earlier, told the American public: "There are transcripts that provide very helpful, very critical insights into whether or not Russian intelligence and senior Russian political leaders..."

Chris Wallace to Senator Coons: "Why would you suggest in that tape I just played that there are FBI transcripts that show — and I want to use your words... 'that provide very critical insight into collusion' between the Trump campaign and the Russians?"

Senator Coons then spent the next few minutes explaining the unexplainable. It was clear that he had lied in the statement he made on MSNBC about 24-hours earlier. "I don't have and I don't know of any conclusive proof one way or the other about whether there was collusion between senior levels of the Trump campaign and Russian officials. But I believe our intelligence community which is the most sophisticated in the world has intercepts – has raw intelligence – and it's important that the Senate Intelligence Committee (Author's comment: which is conducting an investigation) be given access to those intercepts... transcripts of those intercepts."

The above is the best example that can be offered regarding several statements made herein about the accepted standards that motivate the behavior of Passive liberals: 1) It is okay to lie if the liar believes the end justifies the means (in this case, if it will get Donald Trump out of the office of the President and make Vice President Mike Pence, who doesn't Tweet, President); 2) It is acceptable to lie to the American public on a news channel that is watched almost exclusively by Passive liberals and assume you can explain your lies away on a news channel watched almost exclusively by Active conservatives; and 3) a rat trapped in a corner will bite any hand extended.

Delaware does have difficulty finding elected officials who avoid getting caught in public lies, doesn't it? Former Delaware Senator and former Vice President Joe Biden represented them for how many years? One of Biden's attempts to run for the presidency ended when he was charged with plagiarism... using someone else's work and declaring it as his own.

The Passive liberal media has no moral or journalistic standards when they will attack the young son of President Trump and print vicious lies about him having a serious disease... an effort to minimize the family's positive standing in society.

There is something wrong with major media when it intentionally overlooks major news stories so it can provide propaganda about Donald Trump and Russia. One good example is ignoring Chinese espionage of our nuclear secrets. Would Bill Clinton have been re-elected had this news been reported as the major news story it represented? We'll never know because it was not disclosed prior to the election, but it is doubtful. Would Barack Obama have been re-elected if the truth about Benghazi been reported rather than the lie that a video was the reason for the uprising? No. Again proof that no matter how big the lie, to liberals the means justifies the end.

During late 1999, a teenage boy was brutally raped and murdered in Arkansas by two gay men. You never heard about it? It wasn't publicized. The story of a gay man beaten and murdered in Wyoming by two heterosexual men was major news... remained major news, even a year later. Of course it does. It supports Passive liberal views!

The Arkansas story, even more brutal, didn't make many papers and was a one-day short story in others. Why? The perpetrators were homosexual, a valued liberal support group. It is on this tiny head of a liberal pin that the daily news we hear rests.

People paid to report news on airwaves belonging to all the people, not just liberals, cannot recognize the Arkansas death of a teenager at the hands of homosexuals. They ignore the damage done to our national security by the loss of high tech secrets to China and needed uranium to Russia at the hands of Hillary Clinton. They go on national television and lie about the potential involvement in collusion of a recently-elected President of the United States and they lie about the President's family.

The result of the liberal media philosophy is elitist and autocratic. Their job is to keep the electorate informed. The people own the airwaves, not the media or the politicians. When news is distributed it should be to all of the people. "News" is not the same thing as "indoctrination." Instead of focusing on truth, today's media focuses on the beliefs of news writers and talking heads... or they reflect the views of stockholders who tell the networks what to publish and what to write. What we read in our newspapers and hear on our radios and watch on our televisions too often does not come from the actual news of the day. Too often a source for a news story is not named ("an anonymous source") – and another lie is told.

To Active conservatives, journalists and other liberals are "left-wing extremists." Of course, you never hear the term "left-wing extremist" on radio or television and you never read the term "left-wing extremist" in newspapers.

Conservatives do not read or write most daily news. That, by the way, is the fault of conservatives who are not attracted to positions of power in journalism. Neither are they attracted to positions of power as politicians. That is not the fault of liberals. Equally, you seldom read the word "conservative" without "right-wing" preceding it. You often hear the words "right-wing extremist" in the news. How often have you heard the words "left-wing extremist" used?

Liberals define themselves as progressives and open to change. They favor reform, and say they support individual freedom. They perceive themselves as tolerant -- and, as long as you support their liberal philosophies, they are. When you do not, no group can be more hateful. If one supports individual freedom, one supports the right for everyone to express their views. You do not attack them for expressing themselves when their views disagree with yours. The violence surrounding the political campaign of then-candidate Donald Trump is conclusive evidence of the intolerance of liberalism. The violence after his inaugural supports this conclusion, too. The constant attacks against President Trump all but shout "Liberals are the most intolerant people in the world!"

Amendment I to Article I of the Constitution is provided above. It guarantees the right of the people to peacefully protest. Thus, those in Ferguson had no right to the violent protests that were anything but peaceful. The violence in Chicago that forced a Presidential candidate to cancel his appearance was not protected protest because it was not peaceful. The violence at California University Berkley was not protected protest because it was not peaceful – so why was it not stopped? Police fear repercussions from doing what is necessary to stop the violence because of how it will be portrayed by the media which could open the door to total rebellion. This is a very important issue.

How do they protect themselves from paying any penalty for their hateful behavior? They create hate crimes, making it illegal to hate them. That is Passive behavior at its finest! The individual freedom in which they believe is defined by groups. It is tyrannically defined by them and is only open to change when it supports liberal views.

On the one hand, Passive liberals say they support giving individuals more control over their own lives. On the other hand, they say that government should be given the power required to remove that power. They overlook basic laws of nature. For example, power corrupts and absolute power corrupts absolutely. In essence, they say they are willing to rely on those corrupted by absolute power to ensure individual freedom. There is no better way to destroy freedom. Any thinking person can look at history and know that is true.

The logical outcome of the media editorializing rather than providing news will likely lead to an update on how to define a "free press" under the First Amendment of the Constitution. The framers of our Constitution did not envision limiting news to opinions as protected free media. It did not include liars portraying themselves as news reporters. A standard needs to be set and those who violate the standard need to be as vulnerable to law suits involving libel laws and slander as is the rest of the non-media world.

If conservatives understood their own weaknesses, they would identify conservative newspapers in small towns. They would organize them as a means of getting out their stories. Small town newspapers would be the editors with whom conservative politicians talked on the telephone, daily. Instead, conservatives fall victim to believing the majority of American voters read big-city liberal newspapers. They want their names in *The Washington Post* and *The New York Times*... even *The Denver Post*. Why? Their conservative constituencies do not read them. In fact, they hold them in low regard. I live in a county with a population of about 100,000 which is conservative. Rather than call the paper *The Daily Sentinel* they call it "The Daily Senile."

Donald Trump's victory proves that the mainstream media has lost the respect and trust of the American public.

More than half of Americans live outside the city limits of giant population centers. Importantly (to conservatives if not Republicans), these are the people who elected Donald J. Trump. And no one prevents groups of affluent conservatives from getting together to purchase newspapers and television and radio stations. They choose not to do so. Why?

Republicans control the Congress and the Presidency and thus one would think they also control the Federal Communications Commission. A Committee needs to evaluate the regulations in place that threaten Actives from investing in media and doing new media start-ups.

Years ago, I sat next to a man on a flight from Florida to Washington, D.C. He owned two television stations. He told me that if he broadcast conservative truth backed by facts he would lose his broadcast license within a week. He was on his way to D.C. to get his renewals.

This is just one very good example of how the bureaucrats, not our elected officials, control things that are obviously wrong with our government. Or perhaps it is just a good indication of the difference between "Republican" and "conservative."

When I was a vice president at United Bank of Denver, I sat on the committee that invited members of the community to comment on the performance of local licensed media relative to the renewal of their broadcast licenses. Few Americans know such resources are available. I will also add that I never saw any media changes made by the State of Colorado based on reports made by the committee.

Conservative citizens' groups should raise funds to sponsor programs reflective of their values on the Public Broadcast Service. If a totally tax-funded liberal group of broadcasters like PBS refuses conservative programming, sue them. If conservatives were better organizers (team players and externalists) the conservative story would be getting out in spite of the dominant liberal media.

Conservatives cannot blame the liberal establishment because most college professors are liberal. Actives are not attracted to positions of power, like education. They are not attracted to large employers like universities and colleges. If we want our children educated in conservative beliefs, we have a responsibility to become educators. We do not. Instead, we do what any controlled person does. We turn to home schooling. A responsibility avoided is a battle lost, in this instance.

Conservatives complain extensively about university programs that promote Passive liberal ideals and newspapers that support liberal causes. Passives are supportive of causes they understand. Conservatives must accept their own lack of attraction to these positions and resultant non-conservative professorships and jobs as corporate executives and journalists. It is a big part of the reason these problems exist. There is no law against conservative ownership of media outlets. Nothing prevents them from becoming professors and teachers. Nothing prevents their involvement in all of the social areas about which conservatives complain of lack of representation. Nothing prevents it ... except conservative preferences and personalities. Individualism is a good thing – until it costs your freedom and your nation.

These are normal problems for people who tend to be "internals" -- just as liberals suffer from the weaknesses inherent to their natural tendencies to be "externals."

> **A MacGruder Axiom: There are two sides to every story and there is a flip side to every coin. Every strength has an opposite and equal weakness.**

As worthy as Active conservative attitudes are, they tend to defeat themselves. Actives often have no insights into their own basic motivators. To understand their own weaknesses so they can build dams (or arks) to prevent floods, conservatives need to understand that with every strength -- and conservatives have many of them -- comes an equal and opposite weakness.

Conservatives tend to be positive, by nature. They frequently do not take sufficient time to look at how the negatives of their strengths impact them. They do not examine how their weaknesses prevent them from achieving their objectives.

Conservatives define true power as the ability to achieve self-determination. They are right. Self-determination is the ultimate power so long as it is achieved without infringing on the rights of other human beings to avoid self-determination. It is difficult to do.

A MacGruder Axiom: People can't always control what happens to them, but they can control how they react.

The control and strong risk management drives of conservatives help society become and/or remain independent of government. If our economy is to be based on free enterprise, it needs the entrepreneurial spirit of conservatism.

If the people to be governed are to maintain their freedom by controlling those who govern, if capitalism is to survive, the American government needs the ideologies of conservatives at this particular point in time. Without them, Americans will languish in the dependency of socialism, giving up much of their freedom in the process, just as Europeans (whom Americans so love to imitate) have done. Hopefully, Americans will show the same strength as the Brits in their rejection of European Union membership (BREXIT). Change is difficult and requires patience and understanding of just how difficult it is to "clean the swamp."

Many Passive liberal policies and philosophies have held back the dynamic growth of the new economy. Liberals are more comfortable with the traditional industrial and manufacturing economy of the past 100-years. If conservative Actives were employed as bureaucrats at the Federal Bureau of Investigation, that agency's computer system would be cutting edge. It would not take the Immigration and Naturalization Service years to review proper documents supplied by landed aliens (and it would be secure).

On the foreign policy front, conservatives are logical, stoic, objective-oriented, and pro-active rather than reactive.

Externalist liberals tend to react to everything rather than risking a pro-active stance. It often confuses foreigners and causes mistrust of America's foreign policy efforts. Conservatives understand the vacuums that result when strong military and political leadership is removed too abruptly. They will not make the same mistakes the risk averse Passives of the Obama administration did.

A MacGruder Axiom: Conservatives may be known as "hawks," but liberal and not conservative presidents led Americans into two world wars and numerous military actions from Korea to Vietnam to Libya to Syria.

All good leaders come to realize leadership is based on strong personal principles. They exhibit a greater concern to adhere to those principles than to seek popularity. This perhaps explains why so many Republican presidents have been elected to office when liberals historically dominate the Congress.

Few Americans have forgotten what a nice guy Jimmy Carter was. Liberals are very nice people. They have the ability to communicate their "niceness" to others. Few people, however, remember Jimmy Carter as a good leader (and his former Secret Service agents have written about how his "niceness" was totally phony). Nice guys are frequently viewed as being very concerned with what others think of them. They avoid conflict... elude adhering to strong personal principles that sometimes result in unpopularity.

Conservatives understand profit and are supportive of it. They realize from profits a healthy tax base evolves. We pay income taxes, taxes on business profits, property taxes and income and we also pay sales taxes. We even pay death taxes and capital gains taxes. Liberals view taxes from the perspective of income not loss of profit and investment opportunity (and growth). It is a primary difference between the two groups.

The needs of the newly emerging, profit-oriented technology economy is more compatible with conservative than liberal philosophies.

Not all conservatives are Republicans, and not all Democrats are liberals. One thing is certain. Today we live in a world of Active conservative versus Passive liberal, not Republican versus Democrat. Like a pharmaceutical company dream flu, it is spreading around the world – Theresa May in Great Britain, Marine Le Pen in France... who is next? In America, it creates the ideal environment from which a powerful, third party may (like the Phoenix) rise from the ashes of the social engineering mess both political parties have made.

Conservatives want us to live within our means. They want us to spend what we earn both personally and as a government. They do not want us to spend more than we earn. They want us to save. Without a stable base, it is impossible for Americans to become self-reliant (and this philosophy is deeply rooted in Natural Law). Too, if Republicans set a better example of living within their means when approving budgets in Congress, their story about how important it is would be more believable; at least it would gain more attention.

The question is, after years of over-spending on their credit cards, can Americans change their instant gratification mind-sets? Can they put away credit cards and become savers who wait until they can afford to buy what they want? Can our credit-driven economy withstand the shock if they do? The biggest (and one of the most dangerous) bubbles in our economy today is consumer debt. There is too much debt and too little actual cash to service it and it is very dangerous.

A MacGruder Axiom: America is a nation of consumers. There's nothing wrong with that, but it's a good idea to stop consuming before you eat your own fingers and arms.

Conservatives want us to return welfare and education powers to the states. It is a good idea but one which, when people understand the difficulties involved, may generate more enemies than friends. It is critical that corrective measures be taken. The political leadership that oversees this change needs to be more concerned with implementing correct policies than with being personally popular. In the world of politics, good luck with that.

In truth, Active internal conservatives are far more open to diversity within their own political party than are Passive external liberals. Security-motivated people like the predictable. They like group compliance with the rules.

> *A MacGruder Axiom: Groups do not have dreams. Individuals do. That is why individuals are guaranteed the right to life, liberty and the pursuit of happiness by the Declaration of Independence, a document dedicated to individuals (not groups),*

There is no doubt that Active conservative politicians are their own worst enemies. The reason they are their worst enemies may be motivated by principled beliefs, but they are still their own worst enemies.

CHAPTER 12

OBSERVABLE PASSIVE LIBERAL BELIEFS

Security drives result in power needs. Power protects and stabilizes those with low risk-management skills. Passive liberals are fear motivated which comes from a base of insecurity and that, in turn, makes them seekers of power for protective purposes.

When you have a dream -- any dream about changing your life -- one of nature's laws says that to pursue your dream you must place at risk what you have today to achieve what you want tomorrow. You can minimize risk to the degree possible, but change requires risk.

If you dream of an occupation different from the one you currently hold, you must manage the risk of going from one job to another. Will you really like it as much as you think you will? Or, will you cry yourself to sleep at night wishing you could return to your old job? Will your new co-workers be as nice as the ones you are leaving? Will they be worse?

Change requires risk management. Some risks are small -- like trading in your old car for a new one. Some are large -- like resigning a vice-presidency with a major company to go start your own business. Almost everything we do in life requires us to manage risk one way or the other.

Liberals dislike risk management. It causes them to look to government as the protector of everything, from health to retirement to pain-free death. If the American government did not take care of these things, Passive liberals would look to the United Nations. Passives always look outside of themselves for solutions because they are external people. They look for protection from a big source like government because "big is safe" – and they are security-driven people.

Liberal efforts to thwart risk of loss -- whether it is personal, political, social or professional – are achieved through groups. The need for group involvement is exemplary of individually insecure personalities. Liberals realize there is power in numbers. Thus, they play group cards: Race, union, rich/poor, male/female, young/old, and others to achieve political and social objectives.

One thing the protests against the Presidency of Donald Trump have taught us is how easily fear motivates Passives to exhibit violent hatred. This is evidence of how violating Natural Law can bring down nations... which is precisely what Passive liberals are trying to do to the Trump administration. They do not see the threat to their nation that results from their games of political ideology as Trump makes the changes he promised voters he would make. Or perhaps they do see the danger and are so lacking in mental capacity they believe it is worth losing their nation to get their way.

The primary motivator of Passives is the need for security. They want to turn the daily risks of living their lives over to an external force ... in this case to big, powerful government. It logically follows that security-driven people believe they need power or access to it to prevent personal loss.

A MacGruder Axiom: Creativity has its price; disciplined creativity is priceless.

When people are held accountable for making stupid mistakes, they can lose everything. Making mistakes places everything at risk: community standing, political office, investment portfolios, corporate position... and power.

What better way to ensure no one will be held accountable for stupid mistakes in any area of life than to create environments ensuring no one can make mistakes? How do you do that? Remove firmly established corporate, social, political and spiritual values based on unchanging principles. If there are no principle-based values there is no risk of loss. Anything goes in a world with no principled values.

What are unchanging principles? The Ten Commandments is one good example and thus the Passive need to destroy Christianity... or reinterpret the Holy Bible so it allows the principles it contains to be destroyed.

In the investment world, create mutual funds to "spread the risk" (three words close to the heart of all Passive/market investor liberals).

In banking, write risk elimination loan policies. What does it matter that the primary purpose of banks under capitalism is risk management? But realize that removing risk management from loans eliminates the potential for new companies and new jobs because new start-ups and company expansion are risky. Since the 1990s the banking industry has been eliminating risk from loans. Under new regulations passed under the Obama Administration, banker inability to evaluate risk as part of the loan process brought job growth to a standstill. Remember that 70 percent of jobs are provided by independent businesses.

What does it matter that the basic premise of free enterprise is risk management? The Passive answer to that dilemma: "I dislike risk and prefer socialism." They don't even say "please." They gather in the streets as all fear-motivated mobs do to force those parts of society that disagree with them and willingly use force to make us comply with their wishes.

If there are no absolute truths, no one can err. If none errs, who can be held accountable? This is how risk is removed from society. Political correctness reigns – and guess who gets to define for all of us what is politically correct? Liberal thought police exercise their power and eliminate the need for anyone to be responsible for anything.

A MacGruder Axiom: Successful people learn how to resolve conflict positively. People need conflict to grow. No conflict, no personal growth.

In a social context, "passive risk" is defined as the removal of conflict from any situation: corporate, social, personal, political, or spiritual. If there are no absolutes, no one can ever be wrong. No fault can be found and no one can be held accountable for anything. If there are no rules, no one can be held accountable for not following them. No one risks loss of face, fame or fortune. This makes sense to risk-averse liberals.

To conservatives, this line of philosophical thought represents the removal of the moral values responsible for the success of a great nation. Actually, the moral values Passives want to do away with are responsible for the evolution of the human race the past few thousand years.

As my research proves, Passive market/investor liberals support the removal of financial risk from investments. It is apparent that they use the same yardstick used for investments to establish social standards (or perhaps better said, a lack of them). No matter how degrading human behavior and social decadence become, it is free of any risk of accountability. This is the Passive liberal definition of "freedom." It is the total opposite view of the conservative definition which defines Passive behavior as "license."

A MacGruder Axiom: People today confuse the words "freedom" and "license." Historically, freedom requires responsible behavior. License does not.

For example, Passive liberals:

1. Oppose the death penalty. They support civil rights for criminals convicted of horrendous crimes against innocent victims. Conservatives believe victims are also entitled to civil rights. This goes to the heart of the difference between Passive liberal security-motivated philosophy and that of

conservatives: "If I support less punishment for others, when I make a mistake, the penalty will be less for me." In light of Passive liberal attitudes toward abortion, opposition to the death penalty cannot logically be motivated by respect for human life.
2. Support abortion. Liberals are externalists. They always look outside themselves for solutions -- to abortionists or an abortion pill, for example. How many dead, unborn babies have felt this icy grip of liberal compassion?

The answer to abortions lies inside the hearts, souls and minds of sexually active men and women. It is called "responsibility," "abstinence," "protection," and "when you behave irresponsibly, there are consequences."

When you have not behaved irresponsibly and it would be dangerous to a mother's physical health, alternative choices should be available.

A MacGruder Axiom: Social justice is a reflection of the moral values of the total society. If you don't have justice, check society's moral values.

3. Support women's rights. In the mid-1970s, I was in the first line of fire to help achieve equal rights for women. It is on the shoulders of the women of the 70s that today's women stand. None is more disgusted than I that feminism has been prostituted into sexual license and complete disdain for the miracle of conception which is the greatest gift given to women. Feminism has been degraded into just another anti-male philosophy.

In the scheme of things, women have historically been the keepers of social morality. We are created by nature to be more security-motivated than men. We bear and have primary responsibility for raising children. That requires a secure environment. Thus, the female of the species is naturally attracted to the cradle-to-grave security promised by liberalism. The problem is, government does not offer real security, which comes only from within the human spirit. Believers in a Supreme Being find security in faith... within themselves.

Simply defined, this is the much-ballyhooed gender gap. Gender Gapper women look outward (externally). They look to government for the protection once provided to women by men (until the feminist movement removed that consideration).

Conservative women look within... first to themselves, then to the spiritual strength given them by their Creator. The last chapter of this book deals with the security motivation of women. It points out that feminists are ignoring their natural strengths as females and the competitive stance they have adopted is one that utilizes the natural strengths of males, not females, to compete in the work marketplace with men. You never win the ballgame playing to the strengths of the other team. The same is true of equality.

4. Support gay rights. Many conservatives do not believe anyone should be judged for sexual preferences in their bedroom. What people do in their bedrooms belongs in their bedrooms and that is where it should stay. Well-adjusted heterosexuals do not discuss their sex lives outside of their homes and immediate circles of friendship... or with their psychologist (sometimes with a bartender).

Passives, however, made sure the homosexual lifestyle became a matter of civil rights... they gave a disease called AIDS civil rights. They made sure homosexual lifestyles were discussed everywhere... at the office, at social gatherings – and in public schools where children so young they do not yet know what sex is all about are told how normal the sex lives of a tiny minority of the population are.

Passives spent more money finding a cure or treatment for AIDS than for non-lifestyle choice diseases that kill more people... heart disease, cancer, etc. Do they feel guilty that people die of pancreatic or lung cancer each year because research dollars have been diverted to study a lifestyle choice disease? No. Passives are never responsible for surface level solutions they generate to deep and complex problems. They see only as far as changing the outcome of their immediate wants and needs. Short-sighted is far too tame to describe this fault.

Obamacare is another surface solution to a complex problem. It is natural for Passives to look outward for solutions rather than inward... to decency and moral principles that have served successful societies throughout the history of the world. The Passive philosophy towards healthcare is: There should be socialized medicine – a single payer system where everyone gets the same care and government should pay for it. Has it worked elsewhere? Not really; not when you look at how long it takes to have access to medical tests to determine if someone has cancer or not. Look at how much longer a person who has cancer lives in America versus Great Britain if you need convincing.

5. Support gun control. Both the security motive and the "look outside of yourself for solutions" personality traits are at work here.

This is part of the "you take care of me because I don't want to be responsible for myself" syndrome. It can be seen clearly in affluent liberal Passives (especially politicians, media, and movie stars) who surround themselves with armed guards but who believe average people are not entitled to the security offered by personal ownership of guns. Some liberals believe all guns should be confiscated.

The leaders of Venezuela did that... took everyone's guns. As of spring 2017, the nation of Venezuela doesn't have enough money available to keep lights, water, and other things many people consider necessary to life in the modern world available to the people; they do not have enough to eat and disease is becoming a danger. People without weapons cannot defend themselves... especially against government overreach.

This is, perhaps, the best example of liberal avoidance of responsibility for the licentious social order they have created. It reflects the licentious, instant self-gratification objectives they call "freedom." Their "give me your guns" attitude clearly paints a picture of people driven by power. This is a power, not a control, issue.

Passive liberals reject the idea that people use guns against society because society lacks morals, ethics, character and faith. They pooh-pooh the fact that parental responsibilities have been stolen by "the village." The valueless society liberals created, not the guns in people's hands, is responsible for the violence.

We are a nation with millions and millions of illegal aliens who are supported by Passive liberals. The illegals may be involved with the drug trade or with a system of government (like Islamic Sharia law that states its intent to defeat the Constitution of the United States). Passives believe it is access to guns that cause violence, not people who are willing to break the law to enter our country (and may thus have little sensitivity to other American laws).

Liberals always look outward, not inward, to find their answers. It makes them great public speakers. It makes them very poor problem solvers. They are emotional, not logical, people.

A MacGruder Axiom: Successful parents understand that teaching discipline is the price we pay for the privilege of parenting. Our children are our responsibility, not our friends... not until they become adults.

6. Support pornography as art ("Freedom" as "license," again). Liberals overlook the logical fact that when "freedom" negatively impacts others – especially society's children – they abuse the rights of free people. The Constitution guarantees *individual* (not group) rights to life, liberty and the pursuit of happiness to all people. Passives want group rights.

The basic purpose of government is to make unlawful all behavior destructive to the general society. Passive liberals do not tolerate an unkind word against a racial minority or a female (except when a female supports conservative causes and then they may be placed in the sty with the other pigs). They applaud and support artistic freedom that exhibits the portrait of a black Virgin Mary covered with buffalo dung and pictures of various private female parts. You can say the most insulting thing you can think of about Christians and religion with a clear conscience. Such are liberal values. In the liberal world, diversity exists only in a politically correct dictionary – and they get to write the dictionary.

Passive liberals argue strongly for federal support for the National Endowment for the Arts. They make it sound as if art did not exist before government funding and would disappear without it. Conservatives believe the best place to solve this issue is a clear definition of the word "art." Worldwide it is generally accepted to be that which uplifts the spirit of those who view it. It is difficult to see how a cross showing the crucifixion of Jesus Christ in a bottle of urine uplifts anyone but Satanists. If that is who is running the U.S. government, it would sure explain a lot of things.

7. Oppose the military draft. Liberals view conscription into the military as a form of slavery. They oppose it. They also appear to believe the military, not politicians, start wars.

The job of the military is to do whatever is necessary to protect American citizens. We have lived privileged, safe, secure lives in America. We can thank our superior military strength for that. Passive liberals take our security for granted. This could yet end up being the greatest future danger to our nation's security. Like a husband that is taken for granted by a spoiled wife, the temptation offered by another woman may bring the marriage down. Venezuelans thought they were secure until very recently.

Liberals think the military offers an opportunity to give "meals on wheels" to the poverty stricken in third world nations. The idea of empowering others feeds Passive liberal egos and power needs.

Do liberals teach the poverty stricken to fish -- to become independent of them? Good heavens no! Rather, they give them as many fish as they can and send taxpayers the bill! Otherwise, the needy in America and in third world nations would have no need of Passives... a classic exhibition of power.

Externalists are emotional, not logical. To be logical requires us to look within ourselves (among other places) for black and white guidelines that result in logical conclusions. Passives always look outward, *always*, and they live in relativist grey, never black and white.

8. Support the legalization of drugs. "I should be entitled to do whatever I want in a free country." Again, they wrongly define freedom. They confuse it with a license to depravity.

"I used drugs when I was young; I have a guilty conscience about my free love and nickel beer mentality while in college. Surely you don't expect me to be a hypocrite and oppose drugs and sex for my children?"

Liberals have done everything possible to make the war on drugs fail. Then they complain -- as a group, of course -- that the war on drugs is a failure. Drugs should be legalized. They point to alcohol as a legal drug and use the abuse of it as justification for legalizing other drugs. There is nothing logical in such thoughts. Using the same logic, we should release all criminals from prison. If anyone is in prison, our laws are obviously failing us and we should do away with them, too.

As a Coloradan I can report that 2016 was the first full year of legalized marijuana for the state. I've observed from recent statistics that traffic accidents are up and that in 25 percent of accidents a lack of driver awareness was found to be the cause. Before you wonder how many people were texting and thus unaware, please remember that traffic accidents caused by texting have been around for several years and so that number is already part of prior year statistics. Thus the increase logically represents driver unawareness resulting from marijuana.

If you think the State of Colorado is going to admit that "lack of driver awareness" means "under the influence of drugs" and create a threat to its increased tax revenue from the sale of pot... you must be a Passive liberal. Colorado issued a report the first week of April 2017 that heroine use increased by 50 percent during 2016. Yet pro-legalize drug enthusiasts say that marijuana does not cause people to move from pot to hard drugs. Wrong.

9. Oppose personal property rights. Liberals believe property rights are subject to how the state defines the property's purpose and value. When people plow their fields and find an endangered species in the way, stop plowing. Your farming must be put aside! When the site of your home could be better used to make money for the city or county in which you live, Passive liberals see nothing wrong with taking it from you and using their corrupted court system to do so. (Ironically, should the result be a food shortage they will see no connection between closing down farms and too little food.)

Property rights are less important than whatever liberals decide is more important. To Passives, there is no such thing as personal property rights today. This is a perfect example of the ways in which Passive liberals (and neo-conservative Republicans) abuse political power.

10. Oppose a strong military. Liberals support spending defense budgets on increasing the standard of living in other nations. This is another good example of looking outward (externalists). They have no concept of just how horrible a war within the borders of the United States would be. They demoralize our military and prefer they be sent abroad.

> *A MacGruder Axiom: Parents are the first teachers. How well children do in school and in life depends on the teaching job done at home.*

11. Passives oppose taking public school education out of the hands of the very people who ruined it. Liberal teachers protest giving school vouchers to the poor. They say people must support the public school system (even if it does not educate their children).

This could not be made clearer than a 2017 violent protest of newly-appointed Secretary of Education Betsy DeVos, a woman who has strongly supported charter schools and scholarship programs to get children out of failing schools. It is very apparent that members of the National Education Association (NEA) who are teachers are more concerned with their jobs and salaries than they are in educating our children.

For years polls have shown that a large number of teachers belonging to the NEA admit they send their children to private schools. To Liberals, the end justifies the means. There is no positive end when the means are destructive to other humans. There is only hypocrisy and tyranny.

12. At the start of the new millennium, two articles appeared in a magazine sponsored by a group of professional psychologists. The group gets substantial support from the liberal community. The first article explained how sex between an adult and a child is not necessarily damaging to the child. The second article reported research results proving children with fathers in the home had no social or educational advantage over children without them.

There is no such thing as truth and honor when relativism rules the day.

To be a liberal appears to mean believing the AIDS virus is spread by a lack of federal funding. It means believing the same person who can't teach fourth graders how to read is qualified to teach them about sex. Liberals appear to believe that guns in the hands of law-abiding Americans are a bigger threat than U.S. nuclear weapons technology in the hands of Chinese and North Korean communists.

To be a Passive liberal, you have to believe global temperatures are less affected by cyclical, documented changes in the earth's climate and more affected by suburbanites driving SUVs. If you believe Passive headlines, it is human behavior or cattle passing gas that causes rising temperatures. There is no doubt there is global warming just as there is no evidence it is caused by human beings or their SUVs. There is strong evidence that the earth has gone through global warming periods throughout its history.

If you are a Passive, you agree that gender roles are phony societal definitions. Homosexuality, however, is natural. You support the concept that a baby born as a male has the right to use the same bathrooms as females if, on any particular day, that person's mood is female rather than male. You support withholding assistance to the elderly and the poor (there is only so much to go around) so money can be made available to prisoners for sex change operations and therapy.

If you are a Passive liberal, you support the notion that businesses create oppression but government creates prosperity and jobs.

Liberal comments in newspapers and on television make clear they believe hunters don't care about nature. Passive activists who have never been outside a big city do, however.

And, the idea of self-esteem is more important than actually doing something to earn it. You get extra points if you believe the National Rifle Association is bad because it supports certain parts of the Constitution with which liberals disagree. The ACLU is good, however, because it supports certain parts of the Constitution with which Passives agree – but which are not mentioned in the Constitution other than in the Tenth Amendment which says "The powers not delegated to the United States by the Constitution, not prohibited by it to the states, are reserved to the States respectively, or to the people." Some call this kind of selective anti-Constitution opinion "hypocrisy."

The Constitution of the United States is the document upon which this nation was founded. No person, liberal or otherwise, has a lawful right to change that which by its very existence defines our laws and makes us a nation.

If you are a Passive liberal, you can make a good case that standardized school tests are racist, but demanding racial quotas and set-asides in colleges and universities is not – an exercise that defies logic.

Passive liberals tell us that the only reason socialism hasn't worked anywhere in the world it has been tried is because the right people haven't been in charge. You think big government knows more about what people need than they do.

And, if support is an indication of what people believe, homosexual parades on publicly-owned streets displaying drags, transvestites, and bestiality are constitutionally protected while manger scenes on government property at Christmas and Easter are not.

Regarding the above comments, there is no judgment in my comments. I merely read the Democrat Platform and come to logical conclusions. The above is merely an explanation of easily observable Passive liberal beliefs. Judgment is left to the conscience and moral beliefs of each reader.

The above is an accurate reflection of the issues supported by Passive liberals. If any statement above is untrue, someone needs to explain the untruth to millions of others who observe liberal behavior. Liberals are certainly vocal and protective of these issues. Looked at in concert with Passive aversion to risk and a desire to be protected from it, Passive liberal issues can be understood -- even by logical people.

> *A MacGruder Axiom: Socrates said something to the effect that there is none so blind as he who does not know he does not know.*

CHAPTER 13

PASSIVE SECURITY AND POWER DRIVES

The Passive Security Drive

As Adam Smith, the Scottish philosopher on whose ideas capitalism was founded, once said, "It is the highest impertinence and presumption...in kings and ministers, to pretend to watch over the economy of private people, and to restrain their expense.... They" (kings and ministers) "are themselves always, and without any exception, the greatest spendthrifts in the society. Let them look well after their own expense, and they may safely trust private people with theirs. If their own extravagance does not ruin the state, that of their subjects never will."

Corporate power in the form of company politics impacts the daily lives of all employees of any corporation and all independent businesses providing parts, technology, services, and supplies for it.

Passives are part of all socio-economic classes in America. They are people whose primary personality traits are security/power-based.

Some Actives who are part of the labor workforce have little choice. They must work for large companies because their options are limited. They didn't have a family that could afford to provide them with college educations or didn't have access to sufficient money to start their own small business. Though they are grateful for their jobs, they are seldom (if ever) happy with their work environment. They often work for a large employer long enough to obtain training that makes it possible for them to start a small business.

Workers in support roles may never make big bucks. Often, however, they are homeowners. Most own two cars and many have kids in college. Most but not all are Passive liberals. Outside of their retirement plans, however, they may never own a share of stock.

At management levels, corporate presidents exercise power over vice presidents by giving or withholding raises based on behavior and performance. Do you dress the way your boss likes? Does he or she like your haircut? Shoes? Friends? Dates or mates you bring to company parties?

The point: Power can go a long way in controlling both personal and professional lives of America's employed. It can impact your political decisions, too.

In journalism, a liberal corporate executive exercises the power to promote a reporter because of news story content... is the story slanted in a way designed to please the boss? A reporter's career can be stifled. The public no longer trusts media giants (and what's in local newspapers which are dependent on the giants for stories about national events).

Liberal media moguls need to be reminded that the airwaves belong equally to liberals and conservatives – and everyone else. Consequently, the media has an obligation to serve the news needs of all citizens, not just those who reflect the political beliefs of their executive management staffs – or intelligence agencies who use them to publicize leaks about political figures the intelligence agencies dislike or fear. If they do not serve the needs of all readers, they are not defined as media. Rather, they are defined as editorialists.

Politics is a team, power-dominant game with great appeal to those who are security-motivated, risk management-averse individuals. Feeling personally non-empowered, Passives use politics to gain power with minimum personal risk.

Security-driven people see as much immorality in stacking the deck to maintain the security of their jobs as the rest of us see when firing a gun at an intruder that threatens our security. The deck stacking is sometimes unlawful. Passive liberals do what one must do to protect one's self. There is, of course, a difference between protecting yourself from an intruder, and protecting yourself as the intruder.

Rationale is a wonderful thing. It enables people to see what they want to see. And, what security-driven politicians want to see is the good they do or want to do for constituents. In fact, too often they see the good they do (or think they do or want to do) as being far greater in moral importance than the "small" moral compromises they must make to maintain their positions of political power.

> *A MacGruder Axiom: People who think themselves humble seldom are. People who tell how they serve others often serve a need within themselves.*

A majority of politicians, both Democrat and Republican, have strong security needs and power drives. The exercise of power is line number one in political job descriptions. Lacking the need for security and power, people are generally not attracted to political careers.

The same is true of the bureaucrats who work for those elected to office. Social workers are a good example. After a serious auto accident (and having two infants to feed), I learned while receiving welfare for three months that the objective of social workers in charge of the program was to keep "a full load of clients." If they help people get off the dole, they have no jobs. If income taxes are eliminated, how many jobs are lost at the Internal Revenue Service? If our schools improve, how many administrative bureaucrats lose their jobs?

In the investment world, Natural Law says Passives have the primary objective of maintaining and managing existing assets and profits. "Affluence" is defined at individual levels. A low-income person may define "affluence" as a primary residence for which a family has had to work and save for many years. "Affluence" can also be defined as corporate, social and political standing and public recognition... or, as power.

Money at any level requires power or access to it to ensure security once attained. If this were not true, we would not need police and fire protection. Both symbolize security and power and make clear that not all human beings are honest or compassionate.

There is nothing wrong with the exercise of corporate power or with liberal attitudes... until they begin to believe they know better what is good for people whose personal beliefs are different from theirs. Even worse, they withhold the truth from the public so they can avoid negative reactions which would harm their shadowy objectives and their profits. They withhold truth for power and money. Passives are people who base a major portion of their philosophy on being open-minded but are amazingly close-minded to the ideologies of those who disagree with them.

Anyone who believes social order will somehow find its way into the hearts of human beings that recognize no moral, religious or social constraints is naïve – or they have a socio-political agenda. To think amoral people will behave in a manner beneficial to society rather than self is totally lacking a realistic view of the world (and of human nature). To think self-interest and social interest are compatible is naive. Very naive.

Passive liberal support of the issues discussed in this book exemplifies their unwillingness to accept responsibility for irresponsible social decisions they have made.

It appears long-term power corrupted what began as idealism with a social and political purpose. The liberal political time in history is ending with irresponsible individuals demanding non-existent rights to societal self-destruction. Nature says the privilege of freedom will be removed from such scoundrels. Ask the Romans. Ask the Greeks or the Egyptians whether nature was wrong.

Because they are security-driven, power-motivated people tend to be liberal, not conservative. Political life is a more natural state for them than for conservatives. It is equally true, however, that hard right conservatives – what the media calls "right-wing extremists" – are not attracted to the security/power elements so much a part of political life. They often withdraw from the system and do not run for office. Some are so disgusted by the anti-Constitution political environment, they don't even vote. For the most part, this leaves conservative voters with politicians, regardless of party affiliation, who are more liberal than conservative voters want them to be.

This kind of compromise is not exclusive to politics and government. The same kind of rationale heavily permeates every major corporation, every university, every hospital, every courtroom and every newspaper. Security. Power. They are the name of the game for those with low-risk management skills.

If you want to find a Passive liberal, look for any job that bestows power -- corporate managers, politicians, nurses, firemen, policemen, media, entertainment, professors -- and you will find them. Most of the people attracted to jobs as firemen, nurses, policemen, and the military are there to serve their community because they have a real need to help others. There are exceptions, however – and I won't call them "rare." Those who are there because of the power of position are almost always Passive liberals.

It is easy to see when power becomes corrupt. When it does, governments, universities, hospitals, courtrooms and all community-based organizations with ties to government -- groups that are supposed to help people -- function for their own benefit and survival rather than for the benefit of society. They abuse the very people they are paid to serve.

Interestingly, the Constitution of the United States guarantees rights to individuals, not groups. Liberal Supreme Court Justices may choose to apply their own more emotional and less logical views on this point. That does not change the truth – or history.

> *A MacGruder Axiom: People with too much power and too little common sense usually don't understand their customers, constituents, parishioners, or pets.*

The Passive Power Drive

Active conservatives look at liberals as naïve and regressive, not progressive, as seeking self-gratifying license, not freedom. Naive? Yes. Regressive? Yes. All you need to confirm that statement as fact is to look at life in the 1950s and now. Children could play on the streets unsupervised until after dark. Today, they would be taken and sold into a sex trafficking ring.

Until the new millennium, medical care was superior in America to anywhere in the world and it was affordable for all but those who are extremely poor (who often had access to Medicaid) – and so was health care insurance. Just compare the quality of life enjoyed by Americans a mere two generations ago with today's "progressive" society. Today's "miracle" medications kill over 100,000 people annually. Physician errors kill even more. Opioids kill even more.

If you have an ounce of logic, you can only conclude Passive liberals are regressive, not progressive.

The moment one controls someone else, they exercise power, not control. They are controlling... manipulating. To control is quite different (almost opposite) from controlling.

This is why power-motivated liberals propose programs like the War on Poverty. They have been supported in social engineering efforts by Republicans attracted to the politics of power... fiscal conservatives but social liberals (generally referred to as moderate Republicans). The public calls them RINOs -- Republicans in Name Only – perhaps better said, Republicans who want to get their name in the *New York Times* or *Time Magazine* and other major liberal publications rather than their local newspapers.

Providing cities and citizens with billions of dollars is a powerful position from which to maneuver ... or, manipulate. City and state politics can be controlled; the RNC and the DNC generally fund much of state party costs and candidates. If the DNC doesn't like the candidate the Colorado Democrat Party puts forth, that candidate may not get financial support from the DNC for his or her campaign. The same is true of the Colorado Republican Party. All that is required is support for specific political issues to qualify for a share of the golden goose's eggs.

This circumstance should suggest to you that your political contributions should be made directly to specific candidates and not to national organizations that use your money to achieve their aims, not yours.

That is precisely what politicians from both parties have done. They manipulate the political process to secure their positions of power and their "government will do it for you" philosophies. It is why both political parties are dying.

The downfall of liberal philosophy has historically been caused by power abuse. Liberals need to gain a more in-depth understanding of the power corrupts concept. Just as it deposed Nero, it deposed liberals in U.S. politics in 1994. It did so again in 2016. Did they learn from the experience? Looking at the violent protests at the University of California Berkeley and elsewhere, it doesn't appear so. What we refuse to learn from history, we are bound to repeat... whether we are Republicans or Democrats.

A MacGruder Axiom: Positive purpose does not exist when the end justifies the means.

The power of implementing costly social programs has grown. So too has the power needs of those responsible for determining what new programs they can add to gain more power, more money.

To continue building a power base, an even more liberal (security-driven, power-based) view from year-to-year was required. Government got bigger and bigger. Regulations doubled, then tripled. There is no better way to stifle new wealth/job creation than using costly, time-consuming and costly regulations. Welfare programs, offshoots of Roosevelt's welfare programs, were clarified and expanded by Lyndon Johnson's War on Poverty.

Social welfare programs and regulations that prevent new business start-ups can be uniquely laid at the door of security-driven, power-motivated people. The guilt of inheriting rather than earning money can result in a guilty need to give money -- not their own money, taxpayer money -- to the poor. Fear of losing wealth they know they could never, on their own, replace causes security-motivated people to put roadblocks in the way of new profit and affluence. They fear innovation and change.

By 1994, the majority of Americans were ready to reject ever increasing and obvious power abuses against average citizens. A too-powerful government always becomes intrusive. Blind arrogance travels hand-in-hand with corrupted power.

Voters rejected liberal needs to make government bigger and bigger in their quest for more and more power. They began to see how the government's path of abuse could easily lead to an average innocent citizen's door.

Passive liberal political power abuses caused its own citizen power base to feel threatened. Liberals either voted for moderate Republicans or stayed home in November of 1994. That is why the Democrats lost their congressional majority status even though they supported a liar and a cheat as their President... one who was about to be impeached.

A MacGruder Axiom: Fear of failure can only be countered by a clear vision of goals and a strong belief in your ability to achieve them.

Unless conservatives show more sensitivity than is the norm for them, they will never understand this most basic reason for their 1994 and 2000 political victories. They did not and they lost needed momentum to maintain it. It took until 2016 for conservatives – not Republicans, conservatives – to regain the power base of the Executive Office, the Senate, the House, a large majority of governorships and state legislatures.

What conservatives effectively did in the November 1994 election was remove liberal security blankets. They were taken from hands that desperately need them to comfortably function. Conservatives, both Republican and Democrat, removed from the hands of liberals the power to sustain their security. At some point, desperation becomes apparent. It always does when Passive security-bases are attacked. Some say the personal attacks and lies being leaked about President Trump represent the beginning of that desperation.

We have grown tired of liberals presenting us with a new "crisis" every day... from drinking water to health care. Not possessing the plant life mentalities politicians appear to think we have, the public recalled that our liberal Democrat President, Bill Clinton, had ordered an extensive study of Medicare. It indicated the program would be bankrupt by 2002. Because they are not stupid, the people supported conservative cuts in Medicare. They knew if cuts were not made, there would be no health insurance programs for the elderly. The purpose of Bill Clinton's report was to prepare people for Hillarycare. It didn't make the grade and failed.

Think carefully. What basic mistake did liberals make by trying to implement this strategy? Why did it fail? Why could liberals not see it would fail?

The basic mistake was to assume that because they are security-driven, everyone is. In a nutshell, that is the sum and total of their political error. They thought all people would be afraid of threats of loss of Medicare... a man pushing a wheelchair over a cliff with a grandma in it. They thought all people were, like them: security-driven. The results of the 1994 election taught Passive liberals one lesson: "We need to make more people dependent on government so we can gain more power at the voting booths of America." They created more "something for nothing" programs which attracted a lot of people. And they offered access to something for nothing to illegal aliens crossing the Rio Grande River from Mexico into our nation.

They created an economy that was unstable via their spending and taxation. Though liberals like to position Republicans as belonging to Wall Street, quite the opposite is true, and legislation allowing an investment product called mortgage-backed derivatives was made possible. They began a very effective program of divide and conquer that replaced Hillarycare with Obamacare. Again, they assumed the public would be too dumb to understand the source of damage to their nation and again they lost control: this time to a Republican House, a Republican Senate, and a Republican President.

It didn't dawn on liberals that people might respond by saying, "You say in one breath our water supply is not safe. In the next, you say Republicans are eliminating effective water conservation and purification methods you put in place. Liberals ran Congress for forty years. If your water purification methods were so damned good, why are you telling me water is contaminated with 'human feces' within six-months of the Republican takeover of Congress?"

When people begin to believe their own lying rationale, trouble usually follows.

They thought if they told us our water was dirty, we would be as frightened as they would be if someone told them the same thing. When they told us school children were going to starve, they expected us to react defensively. They thought if they threatened the existence of medical care for the elderly, the elderly would be frightened. Some were.

Polls done in 1999 indicated the strongest support for Republicans comes from seniors.

They thought the slaughter in Waco would scare people rather than push them so far they would stand up against the evil it represented. Many people remember the decision to use tanks to attack the Davidian compound and burn so many women and children to death. It was power run amok under the Passive liberal administration of President William Jefferson Clinton whose Attorney General, Janet Reno, approved the attack.

They thought the same about Ruby Ridge. And, the threats did scare some people. The less powerful people are, the more likely they are to be frightened by government threats of violence against the citizenry.

A MacGruder Axiom: We live in a society that does not know it is as wrong to kill someone's spirit or sense of individualism as it is to kill their physical being.

Security-motivated/defensive people who are driven by power think because they would be frightened into silence if DEA agents broke into their homes and shot innocent people, others would be frightened into silence, too. One good way to gain more power is to frighten people. At least, it's a good way to gain power if your adversaries are security-motivated liberals. Conservatives bought guns to defend their homes.

The problem is, most average Americans who live outside of big cities are not part of the elitist liberal movement and are more conservative than they are liberal when it comes to matters of freedom. Joe Six Pack does not worship at the door of big and intrusive government. He is more incensed than frightened by such actions. Thank God for Joe Six Pack and for rural America.

The liberal power base continued to erode because they never came to grips with the responsibility that is inherent to positive power. Only the desperate worship at the altar of negative power where divide and conquer defines their holy communion.

Polls taken in 1999 indicate the greatest source of displeasure Americans had with their government: The total lack of accountability. The people were and are incensed by those who violate their oaths of office, constitutional law, and the trust of the people. The people in 2016 were even more incensed by precisely the same things.

The thing liberals like to talk about most: how they can empower people. A nation that is based on constitutional rights does not recognize government's right to empower people. Rather, it recognizes the rights of the people to empower government. Liberals must reckon with this issue... but they do not and likely will not.

Power irresponsibly used and corrupted is to no one's advantage. Those who think it is try to utilize it. They become corrupted by it instead. It has caused the downfall of a political party that once represented social compassion in opposition to conservative support for business. The two opposing views, as nature intended, resulted in balance. They no longer do.

Passive Liberals and Externalist Talents

Externalists function best when using public expression. They use facial expressions and body language (Senator Daniel Moynihan, Patricia Schroeder). They cry (Chuck Schumer). They are socially involved (Senator Ted Kennedy). They are eloquent public speakers (Walter Cronkite, Franklin D. Roosevelt, William Clinton, Barack Obama... to name just a few).

By contrast, conservatives have produced only a handful of leaders capable of establishing rapport with the people. Even fewer can be defined as "eloquent." Abraham Lincoln was, of course, the first. Ronald Reagan was the next... but he was a trained actor with learned communications skills. No one would call Richard Nixon or Dwight Eisenhower wonderful communicators. Gerald Ford and George H.W. and George W. Bush also put their share of people to sleep – and they are neo-conservatives, not conservatives.

Donald Trump woke everyone up!

The point is, because liberals are externalists by nature, they always out-perform conservatives when competing for votes. They are showmen and women. It is a talent which the 2016 Passive liberal candidate did not and does not possess and that, along with not putting forth ideas for positive growth, is why Hillary Clinton lost to Donald Trump who, like Ronald Reagan, is a performer.

Conservatives must come to grips with this weakness. They need to become more effective communicators. They need to utilize alternative modes of communication other than radio and television (e.g., the Internet, conservative print publications, email, Tweet, etc.). Only then will they stop losing this battle. Conservatives, quite the opposite of liberals, are internalists. They may come up with brilliant solutions to social problems, but have a very difficult time communicating why they are brilliant.

A MacGruder Axiom: Because creative individualists each hear different drummers, it can be difficult to get a good parade going in the same direction.

All externalist Passives need to understand they have this strength of self-expression. They also need to understand their weakness as externalists is seeking the most obvious, not the most meaningful or accurate or best, problems and solutions.

Internalist conservatives have a tendency to the precise opposite strength and weakness. They see the more meaningful expression and the more logical solutions. They are, however, frequently unable to express them well. When they do they ignore the need to reach out to the publics' hearts to motivate an enthusiastic response resulting in votes. Their logical explanations cause yawns, not applause. One does not have to be boring just because one is logical. Conservatives need to learn this lesson.

A MacGruder Axiom: Real solutions go to the heart of a matter. They are internal. Spin finds solutions from the heart that offer external, exciting and emotional rhetoric.

Passive liberals give children a wonderful education about how to be more sensitive. They don't appear to teach much about how to read, write, add, subtract and divide. They even lack proper training in the history of their own nation, but they are learning to be more sensitive (mostly towards themselves, if Millennials are any example).

Rationale based on the natural liberal inclination to externalize their sensitivities causes them to distort truth to exemplify the need for sensitivity. One need only look at Passive liberal and former Vice President Joe Biden to accept that statement as true. Nobody does it better than Joe... though many liberal politicians try – and so do Republicans... I didn't say conservatives.

Liberals are not lacking in intelligence. They do not commit these errors of logic because they lack mental capacity. These personality preferences and drives run very deep and motivate sincerely felt moral compromises. When you fear risk, you usually rationalize your moral compromises into plausible sound bites that make you look and feel good. The compromises are always presented as if they are made for the benefit of others who prosper in some way from them. In reality, they are made for the benefit of the person making them.

Passive Liberals and Compassion

An externalist considers outside factors of greater importance than internal ones when determining who is entitled to compassion. Note: An "internal factor" is defined as personal character and a strong sense of ethics.

> *A MacGruder Axiom: Compassion may be a kind word or deed. Or, it may be an expectation of those we love that they live up to standards worthy of people blessed by God.*

All externals are high on compassion. Liberals, however, define compassion quite differently than conservatives because liberals emphasize external factors.

To Passive liberals, compassion must express itself in a way that makes someone else responsible for events (and dependent on liberals), or it is not really compassion.

Look at the opposite, internal conservative nature when it responds to the question of whether someone or something is worthy of compassion: "You are the one in control of your choices."

Regarding compassion, no difference of attitude could more clearly delineate attitudinal differences between conservatives and liberals than this example.

The conservative answer of "you are in control of your choices" has as many short-comings in its own way as the liberal answer of "everyone but you is in control of your choices – but don't worry, I'll take care of you." People are only in control of their own choices in an ideal world, and we don't have one. On the other hand, in a civilized society people must be held responsible for their choices.

This is the eternal conflict of the civilized world.

Liberals consider conservative statements of self-responsibility and "you are in control of your choices" as totally inhumane and lacking in compassion. Conservatives view truth, logic and self-responsibility as inherent factors of compassion. How compassionate is it to let people function in a world of untruth just because it makes them feel better?

A MacGruder Axiom: Freedom of speech doesn't mean much if the only people with the ability to reach the masses are tyrants.

Logic doesn't sound beautiful and doesn't make people melt on the inside. Seeking justice isn't a feel-good business.

Ronald Reagan exemplified how to speak about conservative issues: Be such a nice, likeable person with a good sense of humor that people listen to what you say because they like you and want to hear you speak. Externalist priority structures place visible criminal perpetrators higher on their compassion list than invisible victims of crime.

One fact cannot be disputed: The system of justice established by liberals during their long-term control of America's Legislatures gives nothing called compassion to victims of crime. That is totally apparent in the Passive liberal attitude towards people who enter our nation illegally. Passives want no borders and totally ignore the fact that the only thing that makes a nation a nation is its borders. Passive liberals want the uneducated poor from Mexico because they are easily manipulated into the corrupted system created by Passive liberal politicians: They will become Democrats. If the rich and well-educated were pouring over our borders, Passive liberals would oppose them with great vigor.

Socialism places responsibility for the people in the hands of big government. It removes responsibility for risk management from the hands of the people.

Government provides your education, your job, your life's purpose, your housing, and your medical care. No wonder the risk-elimination of socialism holds so much appeal to security/power-motivated people. And, best of all, it sounds so compassionate to people more concerned with the obvious than with the meaningful.

A MacGruder Axiom: Security in life exists only when you, not an employer or a government, control your destiny.

If human nature were not corrupted by power, perhaps socialism would be a more compassionate form of government than it has proven to be. People corrupted by power, however, are seldom morally fit to run their own families, let alone the whole of society as socialism requires.

Liberals enjoy being part of the human race. They enjoy people… enjoy interacting with them at all levels. They love to party, join clubs, partake in team sports, and work at large organizations with a lot of other people on the team.

Liberal compassion also plays an important role in our failing educational system.

We had school busing which, though it may not have been a planned outcome, introduced the violence of ghetto poverty to middle class American teenagers. Liberal compassion expects positive outcomes but often suffers the precise opposite. This philosophy assiduously avoids dealing with pragmatic realities and logical outcomes. Liberals tend to start with faulty precepts and leap to erroneous, illogical conclusions. Passive liberals seldom, if ever, pay attention to the ruined lives strewn around because of their surface-level solutions to complex problems.

We have multiculturalism which de-emphasizes the nationalistic (pro-American) culture held dear by a majority of citizens. We have outcome-based education wherein two plus two may not equal four if, indeed, a slow-learner cannot perceive that it does.

Liberals will not isolate slow learners or others with learning or non-English language disabilities so their difficulties can be effectively handled. Better not to hurt kids' feelings by identifying their shortcomings. Better to pass them on to the next grade than to hurt their feelings whether or not they qualify scholastically. Better that good students who could learn far more if they were properly taught have their education process de-railed than remove from classrooms those who suffer from learning disabilities. Liberals, big on feelings, call it compassion. It sounds like placing more importance on emotion than on intellect.

Rather, though it is an unintended but logical consequence, better to hurt the learning (intellectual) process for the rest of the class. It is compassionate liberals who insist no child's feelings be hurt by being held back a grade because they haven't learned the required material to move forward to the next grade level. An unintended but logical consequence of that "compassionate" act is high school graduates who cannot read their own diplomas. Students capable of and wanting to learn are prevented from doing so. Their teachers are too busy trying to make non-learners feel better about themselves.

Liberal compassion in education hurts achievers to avoid hurting non-achievers. Their compassion in our criminal courts hurts victims to avoid penalizing offenders.

A MacGruder Axiom: Compassion isn't always tenderness. Sometimes, tough love is compassionate. The teaching of discipline to children is compassionate... to them, to others.

We have abortion on demand -- probably the best example of liberal views which give priority to the rights and sensitivities of irresponsible behavior while demeaning the rights of less obvious victims, aborted and thus quieted (non-voter) unborn babies.

This is a distinct contrast with conservative views. Conservatives consider the unborn victim the primary priority.

Passive liberals allow their natural compassion to distort an honest view of responsibility, too. Without responsibility, there are no rights. The liberal cry of rights without actionable responsibility is falling on deaf ears. Too many victims strew the path called compassion as defined by liberals. It has little credibility to many American citizens.

This particular peculiarity of the liberal mentality created a welfare system that rewards single women and girls for having babies who will be raised without fathers and who often compensate for that loss by joining a family called a gang.

The compassion of liberals has created a foreign aid policy that uses bribery as a way to manipulate foreign governments. It has resulted in a hatred of Americans worldwide. People know the difference between true compassion and self-indulgent exercises that allow powerful people to feel good about their exercise of power over others.

The compassion of liberals has created a system of criminal justice in which there is no consideration of the real victims of crime. Police are hampered in their investigations. Black Lives Matter decided in 2016 that "cops should be burned like bacon" because they are "pigs" and it became open season on police officers as those perverted by Passive liberal philosophy shot them in the back from shadowy places where no one would see them… cowards. Jurors are hampered in reaching fair verdicts by directions given them by judges who are corrupted by the distorted Passive liberal views of the law. Information and evidence is withheld from them by Courts presided over by liberal judges.

An idealism that violates Laws of Nature cannot survive. People's attitudes cannot be legislated. Rights without responsibility cannot exist. Only when people assume personal responsibility for the rights claimed do rights gain respect from society in general. To declare otherwise in the name of compassion denigrates the very meaning of the word.

Passive liberals do not understand that – and that is why we are $20 trillion in debt.

As we look at the strengths and weaknesses of liberal and conservative politicians, it is very apparent that for society to be civilized, both groups are a very necessary part of a total attitude. We get into trouble, it appears, when one attitude prevails for too long or one party dominates... becomes too strong for too long. Power abuse results in tyranny which tends to bring an end to power.

There is a greater need for true compassion than conservatives appear to understand. Liberals have the right personalities to offer it, but mistake the obvious for the meaningful. They turn compassion into abuse by one group over another. Liberals seldom deal with individual issues and, thus, their misdirected compassion tends to impact groups of people, not individuals.

To find true compassion, a balance must be struck between conservative and liberal definitions of the word. As the two dominant political parties have allowed polls rather than philosophy to dominate their agendas, the balance resulting from two opposing ideologies clashing and compromising has been lost. Today, we must be bipartisan.

The two party system is intended to be very partisan. It is the only road to balance.

The streets of America are littered with those grievously injured by the good intentions of unrealistic liberalism.

Passive liberals need to understand power attracts them like a moth to a flame. They need to understand why, when they abuse the privilege of power, their wings get burned.

CHAPTER 14

SOCIAL VALUES

Feelings are the most unreliable faculty of the human condition. They change from day-to-day, and from one moment of body chemistry to the next.

The United States was not built on feelings, it was built on moral virtue and personal integrity, and that included integrity to speak one's mind, regardless of the *feelings* of the listeners. Equally important, it was built on a strong work ethic.

Democratic institutions that exist in a Republic are not sensitivity seminars. We are a Republic that uses the democratic concept of one person, one vote; that does not make us a Democracy. Debates over real life issues are rife with discord. If discord hurts your feelings, you should remember that if you can't play with the big dogs, you should put down the dog leash and go back into the safety of your house.

Everyone talks about values today. Yet few appear able to give a specific definition of the word "value."

Whenever I ask, "What do you mean when you say 'values'?" a rather long, vague, philosophical answer is given -- like "Values begin with the family. They are taught to children by parents. When the family fails, our society fails. When society fails, it is because our values have failed."

It sounds very nice. Moreover, it's true. It still does not define "values". What are they?

Values derive from principles. Principles do not derive from values.

What does the word "principles" mean? It is defined as doctrine, ethics, morality, ideology, and primary beliefs. Principles are unchanging. Thus, finding a philosophy in a book that has not been tested for a long period of time does not qualify it as a principle.

Dr. Spock is a good example of the truth of the last sentence.

Dr. Spock wrote a book that became the textbook for childrearing in the 1960s onward. Until Spock directed new mothers otherwise, babies were put on a feeding schedule by the time they were a month old. Spock commended demand feeding. "Feed them when they get hungry and cry." This same philosophy removed from the lives of infants and young children the need for scheduled bedtimes (let them sleep when they want to sleep), and, in general, removed all "old fashioned" child-rearing beliefs that had withstood the tests of time.

Spock watched and saw the impact of his philosophies on two generations raised under his theory of human behavior. It made these infants and young children unable to muster self discipline when raised under Spock's demand theories (which gave birth to the "me" generation). They were given everything when they wanted it, not when it was time for them to have it. They became drug addicts and people who believed if they wanted something it should be given to them: NOW!

If you believe in a Christian God, then that is the base of your stated principles. If you believe in Jesus Christ, then that is also the base of your stated principles.

The principles of Christianity are found in the Old and New Testaments of the Holy Bible. The principles include the Ten Commandments, the virgin birth, the crucifixion, the resurrection, the forgiveness of our sins because of the sacrifice Jesus Christ made in assuming all sin in the world as He suffered one of the most horrible deaths imaginable. It includes thousands of other values (many of which Christians ignore).

If you believe in Allah, the Koran explains your stated principles. Sharia law decides the penalties Muslims pay for disobeying those principles.

If you are a Jew, the principles of your faith come from the Torah. Some Jews adopt values from other sources but if they are not clearly tied to the Torah, they are preferences, not values because they are not firmly attached to the unchanging principles of the Torah.

Understanding that values come from principles is key to understanding the meaning of "values." If a social "value" is not strongly tied to an unchanging principle, it may be a form of social behavior you or someone else accepts, but it cannot be defined as a value. Indeed, it may do great harm to society ... be of no value. To be defined as a value, the value must be tied firmly to an unchanging principle.

Principles are unchanging. Values change as society progresses -- or, regresses. By bonding values that change to unchanging principles, societies throughout history have maintained stability in the long-term and flexibility in the short-term. It is a difficult -- but necessary -- balance. No stability (e.g., a lack of unchanging principles) results in social chaos. No flexibility (e.g., no changing values) retards social progress.

History books prove this traditional method of determining positive social values to be largely responsible for the survival and progress of the human race.

For example, America's founding fathers proved they understood the concept that changing social values must be tied to an unchanging principle when they stated in America's Declaration of Independence that our rights are unalienable and come from God. That is why the Constitution was written in a way that restricts government in its exercise of power over citizens. The principle: all human beings are children of God and it is God not government that grants humans unalienable rights. The value: the purpose of government is to write laws that do not infringe upon the any individual's right to life, liberty and the pursuit of happiness (including ownership of private property).

In other words, writing laws that violate God's granting of the primary freedoms stated in the Declaration of Independence changes the entire meaning of that first and most important document. It demands independence from England and grants American citizens freedom from being ruled and imposes limitations on government preventing it from acting as a ruler and forcing it to govern.

An equal and opposite example can be given involving Russia's early 1900s movement from a monarchy to communism. This historic event is 180 degrees the opposite of what happened in 1776 in America. The new communist government told the people the government in essence replaced God. The government took over the rights of the people to life, liberty and the pursuit of happiness (ownership of property). In other words, they put in place a form of government that did not tie changing social values to historic, scientific and unchanging principles.

The new communist government took away all rights to own property, to own profits from their labor (profits go to government which also gets to define how much money you need to live) and the property and equipment used to make society function were owned by the government. In all of the Soviet states, government said there was no God other than government and the right to worship any God other than government was gone.

Russia did not immediately begin its expansionary quest to overcome the governments of other nations but created the United Soviet Socialist Republics (USSR) in December 1922 making clear its intentions to do so. The USSR killed millions of people – it is estimated that Stalin alone was responsible for the deaths of 40 to 60 million people – and it failed long before the Berlin Wall fell in 1989 or Gorbachev declared it a failed system in 1991.

The failed Russian system did not last very long. It removed the one known way to have a successful society: tie changing social values to unchanging principles. The greatest problem we face in

America today is the drive by largely uninformed people to do the same thing.

We humans are imperfect beings. The majority of us want to build positive societies by choosing the best long-term solutions to social problems. Positive social environments reflect what the majority of people define as "positive" and others -- a smaller number -- define as "negative." At least, that is the way it is supposed to be. That is the way societies throughout history have evolved and bettered themselves.

No society has ever been able to remove the malcontents or criminals. It may try, but passing laws does not change personal beliefs or behaviors. Passing laws to deal with amorality is like putting a bandage over an infected wound. It may hold in the stench of the infection, but it does not eliminate the problem. The wound is the problem and in this social context can be defined as a lack of absolute standards.

A positive social environment *primarily* supports those things that give it, the total society, strength.

A MacGruder Axiom: Social justice reflects the moral values of the total society. No justice? No moral values.

Marriage and family are two good examples of social behavior proven through thousands of years of testing to offer the most positive environment for the total society. When romantic commitments become legal ones, fewer children do without fathers. Regardless of what the fringe left says about how unimportant fathers are in the home, dads are important in raising physically, mentally and emotionally healthy children.

A positive social environment *secondarily* seeks ways to enhance the lives of all citizens, not just those who are physically, mentally and emotionally capable of giving society that which it needs. It exhibits compassion to those unable or unwilling to fit the mold that best supports the social order. Take care, however, when defining "compassion."

A good case can be made that the social order in much of Europe and America has reversed these two priorities. Modern society rewards behavior destructive to it and penalizes behavior supportive of it. Does society have a death wish?

During the 1990s, the dropouts of the 1960s climbed to positions of power. They brought others with them who, like themselves, were society's historically traditional misfits. They displaced the rule of natural order that tells all successful societies to hold tight to unchanging principles when establishing changeable social values.

Traditionally, social conservatives seek principles that promise to improve the human condition. They do so by utilizing nature's unchanging principles. Her values, because they change with the seasons, are easily observable. The sun rises in the east every day, but in winter climates it rises on trees with no leaves. The sun rising in the east equates to an unchanging principle. A lack of leaves on the trees equates to changing values that reflect nature's progress from season to season.

For example, an observation of nature tells us the line of least resistance creates crooked rivers. This principle tells nature what path a crooked river has taken: it took the easy way... the line of least resistance.

> ***A MacGruder Axiom: There is no sunshine without shadows, good without bad, or success without failure. Nature achieves balance by pitting opposing forces against one another.***

Conservatives apply that same concept to human behavior and conclude the line of least resistance creates socially crooked people. Humans who take the easy way through life (the line of least resistance) will have difficulty walking a socially straight line. Nature's principles become a conservative societal principle: The easy way is often not the best way.

Current experiences (rather than historic) and human behavior (rather than Natural Law) establish the basis of how liberals determine social values. The way liberals and conservatives define and establish social value is the most basic difference between these two groups. Unfortunately, this key difference is often ignored by both groups.

Passive liberals believe values should reflect human experience. They combine the current social environment with their views of what human behavior in that environment is most comfortable for them. From that analysis, a liberal social structure of values is created.

In a liberal world, human behavior determines social values. In a conservative world, it is reversed: values determine human behavior.

Liberals are very in touch with their feelings. They want social values to reflect it. If they want drugs, they should be legalized. If a liberal wants promiscuous sex, not only should it be available, but also the public schools should teach all children that promiscuity is the new norm.

Resultant pregnancies require easily accessible abortions. Abortions must be legalized (and people must be conditioned to accept this alternative to promiscuity as moral behavior).

Medical care for sexually transmitted diseases must be available. Research for cures to new diseases caused by promiscuity get a high priority. They become more significant than cures for plain old diseases that kill... like cancer and muscular dystrophy.

The problems that result when we ignore Natural Law are like the ripples in a pond when a small stone is dropped onto its peaceful, calm waters. They spread, and spread and continue to get bigger and bigger... until society again becomes attuned to nature's laws.

A MacGruder Axiom: Positive purpose does not exist when the end justifies the means.

Since values are tied to unchanging truths, and liberals prefer values that change as often as their wants, needs and feelings do, the resultant value structure is unprincipled. This is not a moral value judgment. It is simple, extended logic. If your changing values are not tied to unchanging principles, your values are unprincipled.

With no unchanging truths to guide people, all things become relative: Truth, honor, integrity, ethics and all human behaviors that contribute to rather than detract from society change on a whim. Without non-changing truths, society becomes amoral. Amoral does not mean immoral. It means totally lacking in moral principles. This is a logical result. If social values are not tied to social principles, principled values do not exist.

Principles based on Natural Laws accurately reflect daily occurrences, like what goes up must come down. For every action, there is an equal reaction. For every cause, there is an effect. All living things grow to maturity, level off and die. A garden untended is quickly overtaken by weeds. There is no such thing as a free lunch. Power corrupts; absolute power corrupts absolutely. These are just a few of the unchanging principles of nature.

How does "There is no such thing as a free lunch" translate from an unchanging principle into a social value? It supports the work ethic so valued by conservatives.

Power corrupts and absolute power corrupts absolutely explains conservative opposition to government grown too big to be held accountable... government unable to serve citizens because it serves itself.

Other principles of life represent modes of behavior that are honored because they have a long history of positive societal results.

For example, respect your elders. Smiles get you further in life than frowns. We are all in life what we have prepared ourselves to be. If you are bored, you are probably boring. If you lay down with dogs, you may get up with fleas.

It is in this category of social principles that liberals and conservatives find some common ground ... until liberal relativism enters the discussion.

"Not all people," they say, "have the opportunity to prepare themselves to be anyplace but where they are. All things are relative."

It's a true statement, but has little or nothing to do with the equally true statement that we are all where we have prepared ourselves in life to be. For some, the preparation process was easier than for others. And lack of opportunity has not prevented many wonderful people from leaving ghetto mentalities behind and becoming successful. I know from my own experiences how difficult it is to start adult life in a losing position ... and all I had to contend with was the shape, not the color, of my skin.

> *A MacGruder Axiom: If you see yourself as a victim, you have a good excuse for a miserable life -- if that is what you want. There are alternatives.*

Social observations have been made by people millions of times. The process started when humans found they were different from other animal life. Historic observations are part of conservative philosophy.

Respecting your elders is an historic principle. The means by which you respect them -- active love, concern, and care for their physical well being – are social values derived from the "Respect your elders" principle. You may show your respect by mowing their lawns and shoveling snow from their sidewalks. You may take them to doctors' appointments when they are unable to take themselves. You may listen to their ideas, helping them find ongoing life purposes after they are too old to work. You may visit them in nursing homes where so many of our elderly must spend their final days.

Spiritual principles come from a Supreme Being, from our Creator. You shall not kill. You shall honor your father and mother. Love your neighbor *as* yourself. The Ten Commandments are spiritual principles to be applied in the physical world. Other religions offer principled guidelines from which values flow to people who worship in their houses of spiritual learning.

Spiritual values derive from spiritual principles. The value of family and its positive impact on society derives from "Honor your father and mother." The value of honesty, morality and trust derives from "You shall not steal," "You shall not covet," and "You shall not commit adultery."

> ***A MacGruder Axiom: Successful people develop moral principles they do not compromise -- not even "just this once" or "when no one is looking."***

I know people who teach their children things... the wrong things. They aren't teaching them principles from which values derive. They teach them valueless behavior based on no principles. Unfortunately, by the time parents figure out they've been teaching their children negative rather than positive values, the kids are drug addicts, gang members, or pregnant teenage girls.

Values used to hold a place of honor in America. That has changed. Today, people talk about values as if they are relative... gray, rather than black and white. Indeed, today it is politically incorrect to have black and white, absolute values. Those who cling to them are called "radicals" and "extremists" by Passive liberals.

To be politically correct is to be gray. To be politically incorrect is to live in a world governed by clearly definable principles from which positive values flow.

There are many different kinds of "values."

There are marketplace values... the value -- or, cost -- of business and consumer goods.

There are family values... philosophic principles of loving behavior designed to strengthen relationships between people related by blood and, generally, living or being (or having been) raised in the same household.

Different people define "love" in different ways, however. Incestuous parents insist the sexual invasion of their children's innocence is an expression of love. How can a free society control such parental abuses?

> *A MacGruder Axiom: When you abuse power, you lose power. All tyrants must learn this lesson... even if the tyrant is a parent.*

We control abuse by asking one question: Does parental behavior increase or decrease the value of a child to itself or to society? Since mental illness results from this kind of parental abuse, incest can be defined as aberrant behavior. It is of no value to society and is valued only by the perpetrator for self-gratification reasons. Incest gets relegated to the trash barrel and those who practice it cannot be accurately defined as parents. Those who sexually abuse an innocent child are not "parents." They are predators. If the word parent is properly defined, a predator cannot, by definition, be a parent.

We speak here of values, not a lack of them. We speak of parenting, not abuse. Parenting is a privilege, not a right. If we treat it as a privilege, far fewer children will live in long-term abusive situations. Since all truth is relative, there is no absolute definition of "parent." It is impossible to hold accountable that which is not definable. (Our government is learning that in the Middle East.)

There are business values... principles to guide commerce, industry and technology in a way that benefits workers, consumers and stockholders. When laws written to protect people against unprincipled business practices are ignored, the giants of industry are eventually toppled. Investors withdraw their funds from the public markets (as United Airlines recently learned). Business slow-downs cause millions of lost jobs. Everyone in the total society suffers financial consequences.

We had a work ethic until the past few years. After all, we conservatives have been soundly chastised for expressing opinions about people's behavior on the job. We have been told that how people behave personally while engaged in their professional lives is none of our business.

Perfect evidence of research conclusions on this point is Quarterback Colin Kaepernick of the San Francisco 49ers. He thinks it is appropriate to show his lack of respect for the American Flag by sitting on the bench or kneeling – as he adjusts his black lives matter practice socks which are decorated with pigs dressed as policemen – while the National Anthem is played pre-game. He thinks it is okay to display his personal beliefs at his office... the playing field.

Kaepernick's quarterback job description is much different than mine was as a banker, but off of the football field he is free to support any cause he wants – and there are plenty of causes to support in San Francisco that aren't terribly popular with the general public. For one thing, it is a sanctuary city for illegal immigrants. For another, if you can get in and out of San Francisco without being aggressively approached by panhandlers on the streets, you have had a unique experience. Why go there?

The moment Kaepernick takes the field in a stadium paid for by the public and working for a corporation which pays his overly-large salary (considering his playing skills or lack thereof), the rules change. Neither the majority of the public – nor the team for which he plays – support his personal issues with the American flag. At least, the 49ers say they do not. The San Francisco NFL franchise pays Kaepernick millions of dollars a year for his ability to throw a football – not protesting. He is not free to use the media which is owned by the public to force his personal beliefs on the rest of us! If he wants the public to be aware of his hatred of the American flag, let him do what John Q. Public must do: Pay for a newspaper ad.

There are educational values. They are supposed to support principles of effective learning. They are supposed to determine the most critical curriculum required so people can function in a manner most supportive of themselves and the total society. It should be noted that to function effectively in society requires the ability to read and do basic math. We need look no further than this most basic standard to declare the public school system a failure. Our children are taught about their feelings, not how to read or multiply, divide, and subtract.

There are social values... principles by which a culture's people live. Social values determine the moral climate in which we all must live.

A MacGruder Axiom: People motivated by self-gratification see the world in relationship to themselves. Those motivated by self-fulfillment see themselves in relationship to the world.

Everyone lives by a values-based system. Some people hold negative values; some hold positive values. Values are based on relative truths or they are based on absolute truths. There is no in-between. Relative and absolute truths are both open to change as new facts emerge. The word "absolute" does not mean unchanging. It means, "based on the facts I have today, this is my truth." Until facts, not public opinion, justify changing that truth, it will remain so. We must all grow... or, we die. For how many years did people believe the world to be flat before determining it was a globe? It was an absolute truth until science and social growth changed it.

How can people tell if they subscribe to positive or negative values? Positive values in any endeavor produce win-win results. Negative values produce win-lose or lose-lose results.

History has held out as examples of positive corporate values executive managers at companies like Enron which were investigated for fraud. They lied to investors and auditors. It appears they were abetted in their fraud by a highly respected accounting firm, Arthur Andersen, which has now gone by the wayside. Enron was not an example of positive corporate values. It is anything but – but you would not know that from headlines preceding that company's demise.

Investors lost huge sums of money. Worse, employees lost retirement benefits for which many had worked long, hard years. Those individuals within a few years of retirement will be badly hurt for the remainder of their lives. Those who lost their jobs may lose forever many things they considered theirs a short time ago -- homes, cars, private schools, college for children, etc. Enron is not the only example – Qwest is another example from years ago – it is simply the easiest to see as an evil entity which utilized deception to earn a fortune for a few and cost thousands of people the security of jobs and savings for a secure retirement.

Isn't the real reason everyone is so upset about corporate misbehavior is that they thought we had a work ethic in America to prevent the Enrons and Qwests of the world? Unfortunately, all truth is relative today. "Hard work," "deserves," and "labor rewarded" have lost their firmly defined meanings. Those who are upset only because they lost a bundle in the stock market need to learn the lesson that investing is safe only when rules are written in black and white, not relativist gray.

We do have a work ethic and it usually stands us in good stead... as long as positive values remain firmly anchored to positive principles.

What causes corporate executives at giant corporations to commit fraud? Greed; power abuse; a total lack of business ethics and values and/or a total lack of personal character are the guilty parties. Moreover, let's not forget: Social values that hold no one accountable for aberrant acts. If there is no accountability to the law of the land then total lawlessness will encompass the entire society. In a relativist world everything is grey. There are no black and white truths on which trust and hope can be based. People who are driven by profit are not nearly as dangerous as those driven by power of which they can never get enough.

Personal character is an interesting thing to ponder. It is like having the flu. Either you have it, or you do not. You do not have it while you are on the job and suddenly lose it when fulfilling personal needs. A man or woman who violates the vows of marriage – a lack of values in one's personal life -- is far more likely to have a lack of business values than one who does not. It's like zebras and stripes. More often than not, they do not change unless a massive change in personal beliefs occurs and causes a person to totally redirect their entire life, both personal and business.

One of the most interesting world happenings to which the above information about values and principles can be applied is the Middle East.

Because of Sharia Law, Muslim values are unchanging. Unchanging values cause society to remain locked in place... because no unchanging values, no social progress. Islam ties unchanging values to unchanging principles. Perhaps that is why there is so much reference to Islamic nations as being 750 years behind the rest of the world in social development. When one looks for Islamic hospitals with major breakthroughs in cancer research, they do not exist. When one looks for peace-loving social order with close-knit, loving families, they are not there. Rather, we see mothers strapping bombs on the chests of their ten-year olds to go kill others.

The concept of changing values being tied to unchanging principles so positive social growth occurs may sound insignificant.

If we want to solve our social dilemma caused by years of changing values that are not tied to unchanging principles, it is one of the most important chapters in this book.

CHAPTER 15

RELATIVISM AND OUR CORPORATIONS, OUR COURTS, OUR CHURCHES, OUR FAMILIES

Conservatives are right when they become outraged over political leaders who behave without character in their personal lives. They are right because such people also behave without character in their professional lives.

In short, that is why Enron, Qwest, Global Crossings, Bernie Madoff, Lehman Brothers and their abuse of mortgage-backed derivatives, Goldman Sachs and the fines they have paid for various violations of the law, and all of the banks that have been fined for manipulating the financial markets are causing economic turmoil in America today. The list of offenders is long.

It is hypocritical to suggest private sector leaders should be punished for their behavior when the liberal media ensures political leaders are in no way condemned for it. It is a double standard... or, better said, no standard at all. Elites of politics and business are not held to the same standard of law as the average person is... and no sane person supports such a system for very long.

The result of abused corporate power is lose-lose. The abuse of power at any level results in a lose-lose deal whether it occurs in corporations, politics, courtrooms, churches, or the family unit.

Employers that utilize business "values" offering high salaries to executive managers but no rewards to workers use a win-lose philosophy. As this is written, one of the nation's largest airlines is facing bankruptcy. A case can be made that part of the airline's bad management involves compromises made with unions demanding more in wages than the public will pay in ticket costs. Labor can be as greedy as management. That, too, is win-lose.

In April 2017, the evening news presented us with pictures of a 60-year old physician being dragged down the aisle of an airplane to throw him off of the flight.

The initial reaction of the CEO of United Airlines was to congratulate his crew members for enforcing United's rules that insist paid passengers be removed to make room for United employee crew members when necessary. The physician who was the passenger who was violently removed from his seat refused United's demands that he depart the airplane. He had patients awaiting him in a Louisville hospital and refused to leave the flight. He was forcibly removed and was injured in the process.

After United's stock began falling, the CEO came to the realization that it was, indeed, the public that holds power in their hands, not his "Let's Pretend" airline. His story changed more than once over the next few days. Finally the CEO apologized and the policy was changed.

Is there a better example of lose-lose? It's doubtful.

The truth is, the CEO's first reaction accurately reflects the attitude of UAL towards the public. All of this because United flight attendants who fly out of Chicago want to live in Denver or Des Moines or Atlanta and catch a plane from their home to Chicago when it comes time for them to go to work. Did the CEO change that policy? No. Those flight attendants still live in Denver or Des Moines or Atlanta and still commute to Chicago. This is a perfect example of surface-level Passive liberal solutions to complex problems.

A MacGruder Axiom: If you bargain with life for a penny, that's what life pays. If you demand more than you are worth,

you may get it... but will pay a big price. Ask unemployed flight attendants and pilots at Eastern and Braniff.

Passive liberal changing values with no tie to unchanging principles are based on relative truths and represent the philosophic perspective that nothing is ever totally wrong, nothing is ever totally right -- all situations have gray areas. Truth is in the eye of the beholder. The values that result from relative truth are always gray, never black and white.

When there are no absolute truths, when all truth must be determined by relative justifications, there is no truth. There is merely a rationalization of an opinion and whoever can rationalize best is deemed to hold the truth in his or her hands. It is good to be rational, but rationale does not replace truth. Not ever. When there is no truth, there are no values.

Modern American values... marketplace, family, business, educational, corporate, political, and social ... are based today on relative truth. Thus, they are based on no truth at all. And, that is why we are so conflicted in modern America.

Relative truth is the perfect closet in which the insecure can hide.

This philosophy is designed to sustain security-motivated Passives. Risk-averse people do not want to be found wrong. It increases risk -- social, professional, political, and physical risk. Relative truth requires no commitment -- to family, friends, husband, wife, children, or church. Whatever was said yesterday has no meaning because someone's mind changed this morning and along with it the truth by which they live has also changed.

Relativism lets those who wish to escape into anonymity from commitments made do so with immunity. All risk is removed from society when there are no standards to be violated. When everything is relative, it is impossible to err. When it is impossible to err, it is impossible to be found wrong or lacking. It is impossible to take a loss... especially of face.

Values based on absolute truths represent the philosophic perspective that all things can be judged right or wrong and that nothing is ever relative -- especially truth. All people must define and judge truth for themselves. Each must live his or her life based on those truths. We cannot judge others and the (lawful) truths by which they live without trying to be God. We can, however, judge whether the behavior of others is destructive to us. We can look at the lack of standards by which others live their lives. We can fight to keep that behavior from society's mainstream.

Each individual views truth from his or her personal perspective. If I see black and you see white or I see purple and you see yellow, which of us is right? Should you be forced to see purple because more people see purple than see yellow? Must you live your life based on purple principles because those who see purple outnumber you and can force their views on you?

A MacGruder Axiom: People value truth, but dislike those who tell it. Good leaders are truthful (and that's why it's lonely at the top).

Each person is entitled to his or her own truth ... until that truth becomes harmful to other members of society. If your truth says murder or robbery or rape or child molestation has value and that is the value by which you choose to live, then I have the self-defense right to impose the judgment of my truth on you. My most basic value -- the most basic value of the world -- is that no individual's truth has value if that truth allows one human being to harm another. This concept becomes difficult because liberals and conservatives strongly disagree in their definitions of what is good and what is bad for people.

In America, people are free to believe in whatever absolute truths they wish so long as those truths do not impose burdens on others. When you force others to bear your burdens because of your absolute truths, then you are not exercising your rights. You are exercising license and when you involve government rules or regulations to abet you, you are depending on tyranny to assist you in your effort. It is a license to harm others. No one has the right to live life in a manner that is harmful to others.

If people wish to believe a bearded Billy goat is God, they are free to do so... as long as the bearded Billy goat doesn't start eating its neighbors' grass. If people wish to believe in no God, that is their right, too... unless their lack of spiritual guidance makes them think murder and theft are okay.

In general, values based on absolutes are those with the greatest potential to positively impact society. They are also the ones with the greatest potential to harm society when they are abused by those we elect to public office to protect us. They harm us when they are used to justify unjustifiable behavior.

Relative truth offers no anchor to define right and wrong for the total society. Relative truth changes from day-to-day and so values based on relative truth change from day-to-day. Values of right and wrong that change hour-to-hour, business-to-business, family-to-family, or courtroom-to-courtroom are of no value to society. They lack the very stability society needs to thrive.

Society is only in control of that which it can define. A conspiracy theorist might suggest that is why the definitional meaning of important words is blurred today. Absolutes have standards that don't change from day-to-day. They may change from generation to generation as new truths are discovered, but black and white is always black and white. It provides stability.

"But," you may say, "all things change as society changes. If values are to keep pace with economic, family, social, and political progress, don't they, too, have to change?"

Absolutely. Values need to change to meet the needs of the societies they serve.

When society changes – when we move from an agricultural economy to industry and manufacturing, and then from industry and manufacturing to technology, values must change. The specific values required by a forward-moving society will not be the same as they were 1,000 years ago. They won't be the same as they were 100 years ago -- or, even 10 years ago. *The societal principles on which values are based, however, do not change. Principles do not change! Only values change and they must be tied to unchanging principles to maintain their value to society.*

That is where American social order failed. Passive liberals began untying social values from unchanging principles. By doing so, they placed our values under relativism. No more black and white values that were clearly understood by society. Our values today are relativist grey and change at the drop of a Passive liberal hat.

It is as wrong to murder today as it was 2,000 years ago. It is as wrong to steal today as it was 2,000 years ago. It is as wrong today to avoid your social responsibilities and commitments -- to lie -- as it has always been. It is as wrong to commit adultery today as it was 2,000 years ago.

Two thousand years ago, society thought when a man died it was a good idea for his brother to marry the dead brother's widow (even if the living brother already had a wife).

Older women with children might not find new husbands. Societal values at that time made men the breadwinners. Women often found it impossible to care for themselves and their children after the death of a spouse. To ensure their well being, it was okay 2,000 years ago for a brother to marry the dead man's widow... to assume legal responsibilities for the fatherless family.

Based on today's social values, such an action is called bigamy. It is against the law. Today, we have life insurance and women can work to support their families. They don't need to marry their brothers-in-law to ensure they and their children survive.

Does that mean the PRINCIPLE that says adultery is wrong has been changed because a social VALUE 2,000 years ago allowed a man to marry his brother's widow (though the remaining brother already had a wife)?

No. What it means is values 2,000 years ago said when a married person had sex with someone not his or her mate it was called adultery. Adultery is defined the same way today. The PRINCIPLE that a healthy society rejects adultery as acceptable behavior remains the same. The VALUE that allowed multiple marriages then versus now has changed to keep pace with societal change.

VALUES, then, are directly related to PRINCIPLES. Gray people -- liberals -- are very good at redefining values. They are not good at keeping redefined values directly bonded to unchanging principles. And that is why, in the end analysis, liberal values will not stand the test of time.

Societies that structure their value systems on principles offer long-term stability. Everyone knows what is socially right, and what is socially wrong. Parents know what to teach their children. No human being can always attain the high standards resulting from positive, principled values. We are only human. Nevertheless, it is far better to have high standards in place and attain them only half the time than it is to have no standards at all.

Only when right and wrong are clearly defined can all people within a society, through disciplined choice, control their own destinies. Only when you control your own life are you truly free. That is the biggest reason I became a conservative. I am motivated by control, not power. My twenty-year research project taught me one thing is certain: human beings born of this world are motivated by power or control.

There is only one entity in this universe with true power and that is God. However, humans are, according to the Bible, born in sin and their lives are lived in the sinful physical, not the sinless spiritual, world. And, in the physical world, all people are motivated by either power or control. Both are part of the physical, not the spiritual, world. Christian objectives must be to increase spiritual faith and understanding. We must strive as hard as we can to let the spiritual dominate the physical world as we are directed by the Lord's Prayer... "On earth as it is in heaven." We live in the physical world but learn to let our spirit dominate.

I want to have the confidence in myself to take a chance on my own abilities to solve my own problems. I want me, not government, to control the risks I take. Otherwise, I take unacceptable risks... I am dealing from an unpredictable deck of cards dealt to me by legislators, most of whom have never run their own (or any other kind) of business and many of whom are egregiously unhappy people who have little (if any) understanding of personal and social responsibility. We are to grow in spirit and emulate God's Son, but we live in the physical world and need to understand the difference.

We are in life where we have prepared ourselves to be. Who and what we are is determined by a series of choices we made. We made those choices as we progressed through life. If you do not like where you are, do some more preparation and make better choices.

A MacGruder Axiom: Successful people tend to understand how to make the better choice of two bad options.

Children who are not taught positive values often make poor choices. They don't finish high school or go to college to prepare themselves for challenging work that pays a sufficient amount to have and enjoy a family. Or, they seek ways to escape reality... drugs, crime, pregnancy/welfare, violence, etc.

That has a devastating impact on the social order. People with positive values need to help those less fortunate than they are progress to a better life but we need to be very careful of how we define "help." We do that by holding tightly to societal values that change but keep them tied to unchanging principles and by teaching, through example and the helping hands we extend, just what those standards and values are. We need to teach those unskilled in values what their parents didn't teach them: Life without values is life without meaning and purpose.

Passive liberals think it is compassionate to "understand" the negative behavior of people who hold no values. Judges set criminals free for committing heinous crimes, implying by word and/or action that people shouldn't be punished for crimes because their emotions controlled them and they were filled with rage caused by racist or gender attitudes.

That is like saying, "I understand you have cancer ... and because I'm too compassionate to hurt your feelings, I'm going to withhold the cure from you so no one thinks less of you... so you won't be afraid because you're going to die. If I gave you the cure, everyone would know you are sick... we can't have that now, can we?" Rather than wasting so much creative energy trying to understand them, we need to help them understand how the world works and how their world can be improved.

How would you like to have a physician discover you to be very ill but withhold the information so you won't get depressed or feel socially ostracized or because you might go bankrupt in an effort to save your own life?

> *A MacGruder Axiom: What some people call "compassion," others call "cruelty." How we define words is reflected by our behavior.*

Liberals are right. Children who are not taught positive values have been abused. You do not, however, correct the abuse by sympathizing with the lack of values these youthful victims carry with them into adulthood. Rather, you correct the abuse by teaching positive values.

Some are capable of learning. Some are not. Each person has the free will to decide his or her path.

Thanks to the relative truths of the gray people, business standards change on the whim of a manufacturer's interpretation of "what the market will bear." Major corporations, led by one of the nation's largest accounting firms, commit fraud. Their employees lose all retirement benefits and investors get scalded. Lives are ruined.

Cars with faulty gas tanks are produced after the fault is identified. People are killed because there is no black and white right or wrong. Tires that blow up continue to be produced after the fault is found. According to reports published in 2015, about 300,000 people are killed each year while being treated with questionable medications in hospitals around the country.

Corporate executives prevent employees from selling their company stock. It is held for them in retirement accounts. They, the executives, dump their stock before the company fails and the stock price tanks. They lie to investors, lie to employees, lie to their accountants. They make fortunes at the expense of investors and employee stock holders. It isn't against the law, so it must be okay to do it.

Welcome to the world of relativist thought! The fraudulent practices with which we became so familiar in 2002 when this all began are perfect examples of it... there is no black and white right and wrong in the business world any longer. Enron taught us that.

Liberals and libertarians push to have drugs legalized because "liquor is legal, after all, and it's just another drug." Yes. It is. We should learn from prohibition that once a door to escapism is opened – whether alcohol or drugs – it can never be effectively shut again, regardless of the obvious damage done. No one can look at the number of drug deaths in this country every day and deny that obvious damage is being done because of tolerance of the unlawful.

"Drugs are a victimless crime," liberals and libertarians say. My daughter foster parented for children of those who committed this "victimless crime." The drugs helped parents forget they had responsibilities more important than their addictions.

"Drug laws do not work. We have lost the drug war. We need to legalize drugs," liberals and libertarians say. Based on that logic, we should open the doors to all of our prisons and set every criminal convicted of every crime free. They are proof that our laws do not work and so we should eliminate the laws.

Passive liberals complain about the immorality of big business... but Passives created the relativist social standards by which big business functions.

In our courtrooms, relative values change on the whim of gray areas one judge sees in a criminal case versus the relative gray another judge sees in the same case.

One judge in Washington State sees an error in an Executive Order signed by President Donald Trump and makes a decision that the Order cannot be imposed. A panel of judges who sit on a

Court that oversees only the 9th District supports the Washington judge's decision and everyone in the 1st through the 10th Appeals Court Districts are forced to live with a decision made by the 9th District Court of Appeals which has more decisions overturned by the Supreme Court than any other -- as this decision was.

Welcome to the world of relativist law!

The biggest problem we have with our system of justice in the new millennium is that policemen function from the perspective of absolute truths -- violence comes to us in black and white offering no shelter under the aegis of relativism. Judges, safe in their courtrooms, function from the perspective of relative truth. The lawyers most talented at painting the best gray areas -- those most compatible with judges' gray areas -- win. The concept of justice has fallen victim to the gray people and the gray principles they use to determine "truth."

In politics, standards based on relative truth change on the whim of a politician who sees things one way (usually the people's way) at election time, but another way while serving in the legislative or executive branch of government.

Society cannot control that which changes on the whim of those who produce it. The good old days of my childhood are based on this premise: What is right today will be right tomorrow. What is wrong today will be wrong, tomorrow. The values with which my generation chose to identify were firmly rooted in black and white ... absolute values. They are the reason Tom Brokaw called us "The Greatest Generation." All of society functioned from the same playbook. We all knew what was good, what was bad. There were no relativist interpretations of either. Whims change daily... hourly.

Should truth be relative? Or should it be absolute? Should values be relative? Or should they be absolute?

A MacGruder Axiom: The things that hurt us most in life occur because of the differences between our dreams and our realities.

When we assert that there are no absolutes, we assert there is no absolute giver of law or life... there is no God. Arguably, that is the greatest evil in America, today. This is the primary reason I am a conservative. I believe in absolutes. I believe in God who is the only unchanging Truth in the universe.

Gray people reject absolutes. Many gray people say they are Christians or Jews or are of some other religious faith. It appears to me that rather than worshiping a Supreme Being, they are trying to replace Him: their law in place of His law.

Deciding what things I will stand for requires me to walk out of the gray areas of life and take a stand that certain things are right, certain things are wrong. Period. By selecting the things for which we stand, we define the "who" (as opposed to the "what") part of ourselves. We define our character. Everyone does. We must be careful about which black and white things we choose to support.

Gray people may intellectually toy with the idea of a God, but by rejecting the absolutes our Creator gives us, they reject the idea that an absolute authority exists... an absolute authority called God. Or, Buddha. Or, Mohammed, but they replace the laws of a Supreme Being with man's laws. The dismal results speak more eloquently than any writer ever could.

No society has ever willingly subjected itself to physical, emotional and spiritual slavery. That is what results when people give over power to an elite group that tells society there are no absolutes. There is no God. No society forced or manipulated to accept elitist dogma has survived the test of time.

America desperately needs God, but God does not necessarily need America. Truth and people willing to pay the price required to honor and make it a way of life will survive someplace; America's survival depends on what she finally decides is (absolutely) true.

There is only one logical answer to the question "Who controls social behavior in the new millennium?" It is this: People who rebelled against traditional values in the 1960s. They are now parents of adults raised with no absolute values. Parent and child (and, often, grandchild) stand firmly in gray areas, lacking absolute definitions of right and wrong. Otherwise, society wouldn't be so confused. It wouldn't feel so out of control. It wouldn't be so frustrated. We wouldn't have the current trends and epidemics of children killing children; children having babies; children and adults seeking escape in the foggy world of drugs and other addictions.

If average Americans controlled their lives, children wouldn't be taught relative values that contradict historically honored moral teachings observed by every successful, happy society.

A MacGruder Axiom: Compassion may be a kind word or deed. Or, it may be an expectation of those we love to live up to standards worthy of people blessed by God.

American sovereignty is not a matter of relative truth. It is an absolute priority if average citizens have their way. Crime is running rampant ... there are no absolute guidelines preventing it.

It is implied that if children once suffered abusive behavior, they are exempt from moral, principled behavior as adults. Somehow everyone else is responsible for the rage these people allow into their lives.

Isn't that really the greatest frustration people feel today? We have no control over society and thus we have no control over the standards by which we choose to live our lives. When justice is in the hands of gray people, it is non-existent. Justice cannot exist without absolute truth.

When today's values change tomorrow -- and, again the next day -- we are prevented from making decisions about the right or wrong of anything. Nothing stays the same. What is right today is wrong tomorrow.

Gray people suggest those of us that stand in black and white areas are intolerant. We are lacking compassion. We are hate-filled mongers who would hold others to our standards of behavior and beliefs.

A MacGruder Axiom: When a little voice says, "Don't do that!" it is morality and comes from its home in your heart. You can kill the voice if you ignore it too long.

Rather, quite the opposite is true. Passive liberals force us to live with their lack of principles and beliefs. They force us to live by their theories of relative truth, relative morals, and relative values. Since everything is relative, there is no truth, morality or values.

How do liberals exercise such power over all of society? The air waves (radio being the exception), the courts, the newspapers, and our universities are dominated by liberal philosophy. If the airwaves, courts, and public universities were privately owned, that might be acceptable. Since all belong to every American citizen, it is not.

If people do not stand for something absolute, people stand for nothing. They dwell in gray, relative shadows. That which is relative is rudderless… as those protesters who call themselves students at the University of California, Berkley, are. There is no sense of direction in modern society, whether on Wall Street or University Avenue. Society cannot create items of permanent value because it has no sense of permanence. Pseudo-values have no anchor in philosophic principle. Further, those defined as "students" must be made to understand that they are at university to learn, not make demands about who has the right to speak on their campus and who does not.

Liberal educators teach our children that "Truth is relative" and "There is always gray." They live their lives by those same standards. They forget that children taught there is no right or wrong rarely develop discipline required to create and achieve. Why should they? Today's society penalizes the disciplined and rewards the undisciplined.

Relativist gray people say everything has some truth, but that nothing has all of the truth. It is an accurate statement. Everything holds some truth. We must logically ride each truth to the end of the race before selecting the best (rather than the most comfortable -- or easiest) mount, however.

This single belief -- that nothing is totally true -- has rendered Americans moral schizophrenics and spiritual cowards who refuse to take stands on moral issues. Moral chaos results. And, that is where we are. In a village filled with moral chaos.

A MacGruder Axiom: When the powers that be reward the non-productive and penalize the productive, people are motivated to be non-productive.

There is nothing vague or general about values. Based upon the objectives a society wishes to achieve, the values required to achieve them are very logical. It does not take a terribly bright person to figure it out. It only takes an intellectually honest one.

It does not take a village to raise a child. It takes parents with absolute convictions about their own values who live life in a way that exemplifies to their children what those values are and how to live by them. In such families the values of the village are of little consequence.

The village without changing values tied to unchanging principles is morally schizophrenic and chaotic... much as America appears to be today.

CHAPTER 16

WOMEN AND THEIR PLACE IN THE WORLD
ARE WOMEN PASSIVE OR ACTIVE?

A MacGruder Axiom: Women are equal to men because they are their opposites. Men are equal to women for the same reason.

About 150,000 years ago Neanderthal appeared and 40,000 years ago was replaced by Cro-Magnon. About 10,000 years ago, history documents the beginning of farming. The human race, both male and female, is very old.

Throughout almost all of that time, the male of the species has been accepted as the laborer outside of the home and the female the laborer inside of the home – whether the home was in a cave, a tent or in suburbia. The male was the historian, family provider, the lender, the borrower, the business and property owner, the worker, the head of government, the physician and the lawyer. He has been the philosopher of the human race. He has written the Bible and the Koran. He is the inventor who sailed (and mapped) the world.

How did things get out of balance? At which point did the sexes take different paths leading to our modern identities? What is it about male/female identities that in the new millennium create such imbalance? Would the imbalances exist if nature's laws were being observed? And what does "Women and Their Place in the World" have to do with Active/conservative and Passive/liberal philosophies?

A lot! Just as men and women have been around since the beginning, Actives and Passives have always existed. We have always had opposing forces and the intent of creating opposites has always been to establish balance. It's nature's way.

It all started in the cave.

A long time ago, people lived in a mobile society. It was necessary to hunt, fight a hostile environment and be fast enough to either attack or retreat successfully. Then, people returned to the cave to cook the day's catch (once we figured out how to use fire).

It was obvious to both male and female that pregnancy was not particularly conducive to running a successful footrace with Mother Nature. Originally, it was common sense for the superior physical strength of the male to make him the dominant partner. It was a survival of the fittest life. Man became a manager of risks – an Active. Woman became his opposite – the risk-averse Passive who sought the safest cave for a family home.

Women have one additional Passive link. We have had this link from the beginning and will have it until the end of time. It is an Alpha and Omega deal. We are the bearers and nurturers of progeny. We carry babies, we birth them, and we nurture and raise them.

Women who bear, nurture and raise children need one thing above all else: security. Without safety, children cannot develop properly. In and of its self that tends to make most women more compatible with a Passive than an Active philosophy. This simple, basic fact explains why women tend to support political candidates that promise them security. Most conservative political candidates do not understand this basic hormonal female need and, thus, are unable to properly counter it in political campaigns. In truth, conservative philosophies provide much more security than liberals ones do but too many conservative politicians do not understand why that is true. It is true for one basic reason: you are much more able to take care of yourself than government is. Liberal promises are just that: promises. Is our border secure? Is the crime rate down? Are salaries up or stagnant? Are jobs being created so your children can find meaningful careers?

No. The reason: society stagnates when it becomes dependent upon government to provide necessities (like security).

Donald Trump understood both the up and down sides of this concept and used it to defeat not just an opponent, but female candidate Hillary Clinton and the philosophy that supports liberals. Establishment Republicans haven't got a clue that is what is behind the Trump movement! Until they learn it, they will lose elections.

That need is basic and will remain a strong drive within – until women learn being protected by society or husbands or government often provides less security than they can provide for themselves. It often means abuse. And men did abuse the power they held over women for centuries, personally and politically.

A MacGruder Axiom: You are what you ingest mentally... what you believe. If you do not like yourself, change your beliefs.

Men and women experience life. Men cannot have babies. Women can – but cannot change history.

Only when people realize that security lies within are they capable of making honest choices based on their own personal philosophy. It is at this point of personal growth – the realization of a sense of internal personal security – that beliefs are based on choice rather than external factors including fear. Prior to the time a person (male or female) reaches that level of maturity, political and social decisions are based more on societal security needs than on philosophical beliefs.

All males and females come into the world very dependent upon others. We are quite insecure. We are unable to control our environments for fifteen years after birth. Thus, one prime objective of pre-adolescence is to learn to control fear so we can control our lives. Almost all of us achieve this objective, to one degree or another. How well we overcome fear is largely dependent upon how well our parents or some other adult caregiver coach us on facing it. When adults teach children to avoid childhood crises they never learn to face fear and overcome it. They will grow up to be Passives.

Nature provided an environment to help children grow through their fears. When that is accomplished, we become independent people. Until the modern feminist movement, women were primarily the protectors of children. Because women are generally the physically weaker of the two sexes, men protected them. Under normal circumstances, that provided a secure environment enabling women to protect children. There were abnormal circumstances.

Feminists decided it was demeaning to women for men to protect them. In truth, men gave feminists a lot of ammunition. They lied, cheated and stole from their wives and children. They deserted them. They skipped out on child support payments. They became sperm donors rather than fathers. Women found themselves serving as both mother and father. As lawmakers, unless a woman was on welfare, men did little to help find fathers who deserted their families and did nothing to support their offspring.

Consequently, women fooled around with Mother Nature's plans. I was one of those women who supported the early feminist movement. My children's father deserted his family. I had to work three times as hard as I otherwise would have had to because of it. I went to the District Attorney. They found him. He lived in a southern state with a post office box for an address. In that particular state, government did not think it important to respond to inquiries from a northern state about fathers whose prior families suffered as a result of male neglect. They did not care how hard I had to work or how little time I had to spend with my children.

I was one of those women of the 1960s who were paid half of what men earned, just because I was a woman. Did I support equal pay for equal work? Does bacon come from pigs? I did not support what the feminist movement became, however. At one point, in fact, the National Organization of Women asked me to become active in their organization... to speak at gatherings and counsel other women. I refused. Graciously. By the time the request was made, feminism was headed in a direction I did not care to go. They did not want equality. They wanted superiority.

When feminists convinced American society that it was socially and politically incorrect for men to protect women, children lost their protectors.

Today, no one protects women who busily emulate male behavior to compete more effectively in the business world. Not all women do, but too many do. The fact that business standards are based on male views of the world is not the fault of females. It is simply a fact. It is a fact because, since business began, men and their personalities dominated it. It is only natural that the business world reflects the standards of its creators: male personalities.

Compartmentalization is one good example of male business behavior.

Compartmentalization reflects how men segment their lives. It reflects how they keep separate the various elements of career, wife, and children from their jobs. Women have long complained of the male capacity to leave home in the morning, forget about a sick child and go be a breadwinner. Women are now adopting the same behavior patterns.

It is to no avail for any element of society to try to ignore the laws Mother Nature sets down. Look at the dinosaurs. Well ... you cannot look at them because they ignored Nature's Laws and are now extinct. Dinosaurs are a thing of the past.

Women, as the world has always known them, may be headed in the same direction. They need to get a strong grip on who they are and what their substantial value to the world is. Passives have a specific purpose and value in the world. Actives do, too. And, so do males and females. As you would expect of opposing forces, their purposes and values are quite different.

The political gender gap that results because women have natural security motives is serious. Women appear to be giving political support to those who promise they will take care of them: government. We naively respond to those who pander to the natural inbred security needs today's feminists deny they still have. Even worse, women vote for them!

> *"Every time that we try to lift a problem from our own shoulders, and shift that problem to the hands of the government, to the same extent we are sacrificing the liberties of our people." --John F. Kennedy*

Unfulfilled promises do not change biology. Nor has biology changed females. We still bear babies and raise children. To raise healthy children, we still need a secure environment. I didn't say we still need security because we have always been capable of providing our own security but have only recently become aware of it. It is internal. A secure environment is a different issue and reflects the involvement of government and the society it supports. Many women confuse the two.

Women who look to government to fulfill their safety and security needs give politicians too much power. We vote for their promises, not their performance. Though it seems insignificant that those who tell the lies take the world further from safety, it is not. Those who create problems will seldom solve them.

When we compare the lives of children two generations ago with the lives of children today it is easy to see that government has failed to provide the security it promises. Today's children cannot go to the school playground alone without the threat of potential violence. The perpetrator may have anything in mind, from rape to selling a young girl (or boy) into a sex trafficking ring. It is unnecessary for me to prove the statement that government has failed in its efforts to protect children. Daily newspaper headlines do that for me.

Women who support big government are the same ones who reject male protection. Could it be they seek safety in the arms of government? Has Big Brother become Big Daddy?

The biological necessities of our early ancestors that defined male-female roles are not applicable to today's technological society. Still, they impact many modern women's views.

It does not take a lot of physical strength to program a computer or design a spaceship or perform surgery or argue a legal case in court. Sales and marketing skills require little physical strength. Unless you want to become a model or a movie star, a good mind gets you further in the modern world than a good body or a beautiful face, male or female. But many generations of social conditioning are not reversed overnight.

Though the percentages are becoming more equalized, men still dominate.

A MacGruder Axiom: Little advantages become big opportunities to those who seek them.

Women are no longer totally incapacitated by pregnancy. Medical advances have shortened the recovery period from childbirth. We have progressed from the cave into suburbia. Physical strength as an integral part of leadership has largely been replaced by technical skills and the potential to develop them. The color or shape of one's skin is meaningless. Perhaps better said, it is meaningless to everyone except those who use them to gain advantage over others. Such people also do not seek equality. They seek superiority.

History teaches that because of the childbearing role and weaker physical constitutions, women were -- and would always be -- placed in a more sedentary role than men. That is simply no longer true. Since the social condition through most of man's existence cast him in the role of leader, policymaker and problem solver, it has been assumed -- erroneously -- he is better suited to it than woman.

Until the 1970s, man has been the one to leave the safety of the cave. He left the cave to learn to read animal tracks and to hunt food. He left the cave to sit in the United States Senate to determine policies that affect women as well as men. Men had little understanding of what women needed. Women did a poor job of telling them (but societal values placed great pressure on women to avoid telling them).

Man has been the explorer of the human race. His instincts for survival have been honed to a fine tolerance level. He has learned to compete with everything from nature to corporate counterparts and large offensive lines on the football field. He has passed, both genetically and by example, those same traits on to his sons, generation after generation.

Now, it appears, young males who exemplify those traits are supposed to take Ritalin. School administrators and teachers -- many of them women who do not understand male traits or value them-- want little boys to behave sweetly. Little girls are sweet. Little boys are ... little boys.

Women have the natural ingenuity for reading animal tracks. They also have the ingenuity for political leadership -- and for everything else women through my generation were conditioned to believe was man's exclusive domain.

The fact is that women have not had their instincts for survival and all that encompasses it finely honed for centuries. Competition, exploration, physical fitness to defend against attack, decision-making skills, leadership and dominance, and a sense of team must be exemplified by women for their daughters if these traits are to be made a natural part of the female personality. These things have not been finely honed and passed on from mother to daughter, generation after generation.

Most women have never had to face the natural fear that comes with trailblazing. They have not had to deal with it because with rare exception they have not been trailblazers. Instead, throughout most of history, women chose to stay in the cave and behind the throne. There were exceptions, but they were precisely that: exceptions. Though many women have challenged their fears of self dependence and won the battle, the vast majority of women have not.

A MacGruder Axiom: You can climb any wall if you know what you want and it's on the other side.

News of females being protected by males shouldn't shock anyone. It is repeated billions of times daily by all living things in our environment. Bugs, birds and bees all do it. Bugs, birds and bees do not have the power of the vote, however.

Some women are Actives, most are Passive -- and, there is a reason for it. Some men are Active, some are Passive. Gender does not determine if people are Active or Passive. Personalities that evolve from very basic behavior motivators – parental example – make that determination. Dependent men and women tend to be Passives. Independent men and women tend to be Actives. Insecure people who are risk averse and for whom safety is a primary life force drive are likely to be Passive. Secure people with risk management skills are likely to be Actives.

There is no pejorative in these titles or explanations of them. There are very positive things about dependent human beings. Marriage is usually much easier for the dependent than the independent. The more socialized we become, the more dependent humans, as a species, become. Equally, there are positives and negatives associated with being independent. It is no more wrong to be risk averse than it is to be too willing to manage risks. These two opposing forces just are. Each is... a fact. Each group has its own strengths, its own weaknesses.

I've stated this same thing numerous times on previous pages. I re-state it here to emphasize that whether a person is Active or Passive has little to do with gender. Though at this particular point in time it is true that women are more likely to be Passive liberals than Active conservatives that picture is changing. It is an evolutionary process. The gender gap will melt away as female insecurities do.

In 1997, for example, there were 5.4 million women-owned businesses in America. That is over one-third of all businesses in the nation. These companies provided jobs to almost 7.1 million people and generated about $818.7 billion in receipts. By 1999, the number of women-owned businesses almost doubled. In Colorado, women in 1997 who held ownership positions totaling at least 51 percent of that state's 114,800 privately-held firms indicates over 20 years ago, women owned 28 percent of Colorado's independent businesses.

As has been mentioned several times in this book, over 90 percent of the self-employed are Actives. Thus, women are planting their feet firmly on solid Active ground, becoming independent, learning to not just tolerate but be challenged by managing risk -- and we like it.

Nationally, the trend includes minority women. In 1996, one of every eight women-owned businesses was owned by women of color. Slightly over one million minority women employ nearly two million people and generate annual sales of close to $200 billion. Like their sisters, most of these women are well on their way to the independent Active lifestyle.

> *A MacGruder Axiom: Greatness can be found in small things. For big things to occur, someone needs to do the groundwork.*

In 1999 in Colorado, the Women's Foundation and the Institute for Women's Policy Research said full-time female workers earned 75 percent of what full-time male workers earned. But another study done by the Department of Labor indicates women who work between 35 and 39 hours a week earn 98 percent of what men who work the same hours earn. It appears we are back to the liberal explanation that it all depends on what "is" is. This is a good example of how carefully studies done by groups with a vested interest in the outcome must be evaluated.

Men and women, like Actives and Passives, are total opposites. The strengths of one are generally the weaknesses of the other, and vice versa. Nature's laws say that should create balance. It has not. Why? When humans fool around with Mother Nature's laws, the balance opposing forces is intended to create is lost.

It is well to remember that Natural Law that creates balance is based on opposing forces of *equal* strength. For thousands of years, men had almost total power over women. For the past fifty years, feminists have tried to gain power over men. So far, no balance has been achieved because there has been no equality of force in the opposition. There will be none until the two sexes each accept the other in their normal state. To do that, both genders appear to need coaching.

Why is there a political gender gap?

Active conservative messages say "You have the freedom to be who and what you want, but you are accountable and responsible for your actions and decisions (you are independent of government). To be free is to be accountable. The best kind of security you can provide your children is freedom (independence)."

The Passive liberal message says "Government will take care of you, from the cradle to the grave. We will educate you and your children, provide your health care, take care of your career and eventual retirement (you are dependent upon government, educators and other bureaucrats for happiness, health... everything)."

A MacGruder Axiom: What others think of you depends on how well you communicate your beliefs. Who you really are is determined by the truthful statement of your behavior.

What appears difficult for conservative political candidates is to state issues so they clearly define security versus personal safety. Conservatives have no understanding (and appear to have very little sympathy) with the security drives of Passives. One good place to start is to provide a list of current government programs. Over the years, many promises of enhanced security have been made. To date, what kind of security has the government provided?

Is Social Security strong and healthy? How about Medicare? How about Obamacare (which won the election for Donald Trump)? How about education? Do you love what government bureaucrats have done to your local public schools? Can anyone argue with the stability of Amtrack?

How about the arts which, if they do not demean women or religion are considered outdated? How strong are the values of Americans? Does the post office run as efficiently as FedEx? The nation's airports? How safe are all of the things government has taken over and promised to make better – and safer? Is America's infrastructure better and stronger now than it was twenty years ago? Fifty years ago? If government cannot do basic things well, why do women naively believe it can handle their complex security needs? How about citizen safety on our own land... on the soil of America? We have terrorism of 9/11, San Bernardino, Orlando and other terrorist attacks.

Is the protection dilemma the result of feminist attitudes? Alternatively, is feminism the result of males who, in the 1960s, stopped protecting women? Are American women living their lives with no husbands because men seek wives in Russia and China and other nations where women still think it is honorable to be feminine and to seek male protection? If that is true, who, in the end analysis, is winning this ridiculous game?

A MacGruder Axiom: *When you abuse power, you lose power.*

It was not long after men began abandoning their wives and children that the feminist movement began. There are dots to be connected here. Are men and their mistreatment of women what motivated women's liberation? In many ways: yes. Whether the abuse was physical, mental or emotional, women historically stayed in the home until male behavior made the home unstable.

Divorce laws -- written by men, of course -- made it easier and easier for older males to divorce wives who devoted their entire lives to establishing and maintaining a family. Why did they want to leave? Younger women gave them a new life line to aging genitalia and the fear of aging. As nature motivated libidos to lower levels, it ran into ego-based male stubbornness. Men refused to accept their diminished sexual appetites and looked for new appetizers to put on their plates. There wasn't anything wrong with them, just with aging mates who no longer excited them. Many people believe this to be a natural state -- a law of nature. Shame on you! Until Hollywood influenced moral standards, men and women loved one another more not less as they aged. Sex and love are not the same thing.

Younger women got... what? Why, the security older men have to offer, of course! The first wife often worked to put her husband through college. Her objective was to provide security later in life for the total family. Her only job training for the next twenty years was as mother, wife and homemaker. She had no career to which she could "return." Many such women ended their lives in abject poverty. And so began the feminist movement. Men abused power and they have lost power as a result.

> **A MacGruder Axiom: For every action, there is an equal reaction. What goes around comes around.**

The younger woman got the first wife's dessert. The point is when male legislators made it easy for men to desert lifelong companions, the absolute need for women's liberation arrived.

Liberal feminists rejected male protection after male protection began to desert wives and families. No wonder women largely support big government. How else, they wondered, can we replace male protections lost to feminist rejection? Most women seem to look to government as their new protectors. Many of us look to ourselves and rely upon God to be our protector. That is one reason to motivate women to start and run their own businesses.

Unless women face their security needs honestly and find a sense of individuality reflective of their natural needs, they will continue to become pseudo Passive liberals.

There is nothing wrong with being a Passive liberal or an Active conservative, male or female. There is everything wrong with being a pseudo anything. It means supporting something because you fear what you perceive as weakness too much to face it. Having a security need because of nature's gift of motherhood is not a weakness. Personal philosophies about social and political issues result from self-knowledge, not the lack of it.

Until women figure out that security comes from developing internal strengths rather than looking outside of themselves for someone or something else to provide it, they will listen to Passive liberal security-based promises. They will continue to kid themselves that intentions are good even if results are poor. Women will continue to vote for political candidates because of natural, normal female security-drives and liberal promises. And they will continue to be disappointed by those who make the promises.

There is nothing wrong with the need for a secure environment in which to raise our children. There is a great deal wrong with looking to politicians to fill the need with promises that, after more than fifty years of experimentation, have yet to be fulfilled. Nature gave women a strong security-drive. She gave us mates to provide it. She did not create senators, representatives or even presidents of nations for that important purpose. A social order that is failing did.

I really do not care whether men or women are Passive or Active. I readily admit I am an Active. I realize that because I am an Active it is difficult for me to see the Passive side of things. I also see that it appears impossible for Passives to recognize the Active side. With them, it's "My way or the highway."

I respect people who believe a philosophy – even one that totally disagrees with my own – because it reflects who they are. I disrespect people who accept a philosophy because it panders to natural personal weaknesses.

> *A MacGruder Axiom: Nature controls our need for oxygen, food and water... and the female security-drive. Women control how they react to these needs.*

Women as voters are frightening. They watch as the public school system is torn apart by the giant bureaucracy of government.

Yet they convince themselves politicians really intend to provide secure schools with high learning standards. In light of all evidence to the contrary, why would any intelligent person believe such promises?

"We just need more money ... class size is too large." Regardless of the massive failure of the system, women who really are not liberals -- just Passives -- attach themselves to liberal promises of security. Why do they ignore the negative outcome? Because promises of security are basic to their natures. Because as Passives they are externals who think the solution is "out there," somewhere. They look outside of themselves for answers.

Why do Passive liberals make promises they cannot keep? They defeat their own intentions. How? Passive liberals work hard to preserve and protect existing power structures that are the precise cause of the failure. New things over which they exercise no power imply risk and Passives avoid risk whenever possible.

Women watch the health care system disintegrate. Still, their security drive makes them support liberal promises that government can provide better care than the private sector. Women ignore the reality that American health care was the best in the world until government got involved with it. Passive politicians gain support through fear. They know it appeals to the security drives of constituents.

Women watch their own children suffer the results of cradle to high school non-parental care. They give over to government the responsibility for raising their children. They are confused by the divorces and delinquent children that result from failed marriages.

One thing about "me first" attitudes: When one parent is inflicted with it, the only way the rest of the family can survive is to adopt a "me first" attitude, too. Family conflict is the logical result. A self-absorbed society is the logical result of that kind of family conflict.

Real feminism is accepting one's self as one is and as what one can realistically achieve in life. Long-term objectives should always be aimed star high, but they should be based on the possibility of achievement, not on hopeless dreams. If you aim for a star and land on the moon, you're doing well. Positive thinking is based on truth. Negative thinking is based on lies... to others and, even worse to you.

To truthfully evaluate what you are capable of doing in life, you must first honestly know what you can do and you need to understand why you can do certain things better than others. And that includes your many strengths as a woman.

Author's Note: *The chapters which preceded this one were written to point out the differences between Actives and Passives and the unique philosophical perspectives from which each group functions. The purpose of this chapter is to provide a map that shows how the two groups can work effectively together and compatibly. Since men tend to be Actives and women will always have the motherhood security drive (even when they are or become Actives), it seemed a good idea to combine two groups of opposites in finding ways to establish a productive, compatible political, social, marital, intellectual and corporate environment.*

CHAPTER 17

WOMEN: A NATURAL INCLINATION TO... WHAT?

As long as we were an agricultural or industrial society, the law of male dominance that prevailed in the cave continued. Survival was based on physical strength. Only the most foolish woman will argue that women, as a total gender, are men's equals in that realm.

As long as character and ethics dominated society, women could count on men as providers and protectors, and children could count on women to protect them. Relativism meant character and ethics no longer mattered. When that happened, women rightly sought alternatives. Equality became the objective.

> *"Reason obeys itself; and ignorance does whatever is dictated to it."--Thomas Paine*

American women went through numerous crises -- from the Revolutionary War through World War I -- with our identities and life purposes totally tied to being the "keeper of home and family" and never heard the word "feminist."

As with outstanding women achievers in other areas, women's contributions to the military have been exceptional. It is always difficult to make meaningful contributions when social barriers prevent you from doing so. Thus, the contribution of America's military women is even more worthy.

For example, in 1866, Dr. Mary Walker was the first woman to receive the nation's highest military honor, the Congressional Medal of Honor, for her service during the Civil War. In the Spanish American War, more than a thousand women served as Army contract nurses -- 20 of them died.

> *A MacGruder Axiom: To truly live requires a personal, committed sense of purpose. We were all put here for a reason. To have a happy life, we must find it.*

During World War II, more than 400,000 women served in non-combat military jobs and 87 female nurses were prisoners of war in both theaters of operation.

During Vietnam, 7,500 American military women served. Eight died.

The vast majority of women between the ages of 18 and 30 did not involve themselves in America's wars. The vast majority of men of the same ages did. Their nation required them to do so. That is the point.

Until World War II, women's place was in the home -- as, with rare exception, it has been throughout history. The war effort recruited an untrained female work force into factories and "Rosie the Riveter" was born. Women took over jobs normally performed by men.

There weren't enough men to do these jobs because they were sent to fight on the battlefields of Europe and the islands of the Pacific. We needed our instruments of war -- our ships, our planes, our rifles and parachutes. Someone had to make them. My mother and her peers went to work. They left their homes and their children to become an industrial force.

A lot of women found they liked the independence, sense of self-worth and individual purpose having a job outside the family gave them. Women of my era (and every era which preceded it) worked their buns off (so to speak) and no one ever handed them a paycheck. It is a time-honored way of showing appreciation for time, skill, and dedication.

World War II and Rosie the Riveter's appearance on the scene was the true birthplace of the women's movement for equality in America. What has happened to that movement in recent years may be a disgrace to the reasons behind it, but the actual birth was honest and beautiful.

Before the war, life was simple. There was a peacefully naive beauty in the 1940s and 50s. Things were... predictable. You may say "How dull!" You would probably be right. But we sure didn't have people keeling over with stress-related illnesses as Americans do in the new millennium. We had no drug problems like those of today. Today's drug problems are reflective of a society afraid to look at itself in the mirror so instead it chooses drug- or alcohol-induced escapism. In the good old days, half of the people who got married didn't end up in divorce court and children had traditional families. It was a beautiful predictability.

Pre-1950, black families stayed together while today more than 75 percent of black babies are born out of wedlock. A very large percentage of black families today are made up of a female who has numerous children by different fathers. The mother and children are supported by the welfare system and the father is more often than not uninvolved in the lives of their children. It has resulted in a destructive black youth violent crime rate (double that of white and Hispanic youth combined). When more children are killing one another in Chicago than men being killed in the Afghanistan war, no sane person can say society has more character today than the standards pre-1950 provided. Stable families produce a safe, secure society. There is no doubt which is better for a good social order.

It would be inaccurate to suggest white families do not have family problems because they do. Rather than deaths of violence, white kids suffer death by drugs. The problems are generally caused by a strong lack of identity. White kids have been given too much without having to earn it – especially respect for doing nothing worthy of respect, a Passive liberal theory that purports "if we give them respect they will act respectful." Passives have a problem with the concept that respect is something that cannot be given, it must be earned. White youth do not have the gang problems of blacks and Hispanics but they are getting hit over the head with so many messages about why they should feel guilty about being white it results in confusion. They are told they are either supremists because they are white or they are responsible for slavery.

The "guilty about being white" theme comes from the Passive liberal power drive of elected black office holders who, more than 150 years after the end of the Civil War, blame today's white kids for slavery. In other words, they blame white kids for the lack of leadership in black communities... leadership they have failed to provide.

White kids don't know who they are and have parents who are too busy earning money to buy things they don't really need to help them figure out their identity. They see football heroes kneeling in disparagement of their nation's flag and, thinking they can make a statement that they are not racist, join in an anti-America protest. Because they have little sense of self inside of them, they try to establish some kind of stable identity by decorating their bodies with tattoos and they attach "jewelry" to their eyes, mouths and cheeks... and they take drugs (and wonder why they cannot get a job).

Bear in mind that drugs like heroine and other opiates could be purchased over-the-counter in the 1940s... evidence that it is possible for drugs to be legalized *in a moral society*. In the amoral society of today, legalizing drugs would be like handing a lit match to a pyromaniac.

> ***A MacGruder Axiom: A lot of people who want to leave their footprints in the sand sometimes have a hard time finding the beach.***

During WWII, Rosie the Riveter made her entrance on the scene and traditional family values blurred. After the war, a drive began to put women back in their proper place: the home.

Our brave soldiers left Europe's shores to return home to America. Every magazine was filled with stories explaining to young females why successful, happy women did not work outside the home. Every movie glorified housewifery. Rosie was being pushed from the factory back to the kitchen.

In short, we females under age 15 when World War II ended were brainwashed to believe we would be inferior females if we worked outside the home. We would lose our femininity. After all, nature's natural leaders, men, were coming home. They were here to resume their natural leadership roles. Government did not need us in the world of business anymore.

I was eight when the war ended. The next eight years of my life were spent looking at movies with strong but subtle plots and subliminal messages: "Women are much happier when they become wives." Another theme was "Motherhood places women at the zenith of fulfillment and happiness." Watch any Doris Day movie; watch any episode of Father Knows Best.

I was firmly taught a female's place is in the home. Beautiful movie stars told me so; in living color... on big screens. I was confident I would spend my life at home, raising children. I loved to write, so would do that as a hobby... hopefully a profitable one.

By the time I was 16, I had a clear view of who society dictated I was supposed to be and what everyone – except me – expected of me. I fell victim to the old adage: "Send your sons, not your daughters, to college. Girls don't need a costly education to have babies." I had been taught to play classical and pop piano, entertain, cook, clean, etc. I was a singer. I was still going to university in my 40s to make up for that error.

Unfortunately, social engineers of the 40s and 50s didn't know I would have to support two children alone throughout the 60s and 70s. The number crunching male social engineers did not project the millions of women who would be forced into the role of total family provider. They did not calculate the number of men who would drop out of sight and refuse to support their children.

In other words, they did not calculate the harsh results of forcing relativism on society.

Neither did I.

> ***A MacGruder Axiom: If your dreams say one thing and your realities another, you'll need to change one of them.***

As I began my career in the white male-dominated world of banking in the early 1970s, I knew my limits. Society had taught me well.

Don't compete too effectively or you will threaten male egos. Don't be too bright, too intense, or you invite competition -- and, it's not ladylike to compete with men. It's even less ladylike to win.

It was men in my world of banking that expanded their views of my capabilities. They were the ones that took me out of the socially acceptable woman in marketing role. Fiscally conservative males put me in the non-traditional female position of managing a major credit and deposit portfolio at Denver's largest bank.

Men who had to fight social views taught to them by preceding generations supported and promoted me.

I'm not sure who had the toughest time with attitude, the bankers who helped me learn and succeed; or me. I have often thought that many of the men who supported my becoming a credit manager expected me to fail. Some consciously, some subconsciously, hoped I would fail. Those that wanted me to fail wanted things to stay the way they were. Passives are threatened by change which, to them, embodies risk. They wanted to be able to say, "See, women cannot assume a role that forces them to make major credit decisions. They are simply not emotionally equipped to do so." Most, however, did what they could to be helpful and non-judgmental.

When I did not fail, many of them changed their attitudes. It opened the doors for more women to progress into the male-dominated world of bank credit.

I constantly fought the sense of displaced housewife and mother and all the inherent feelings of guilt that accompany both. When there are no parents in the home, children suffer the consequences. No one can effectively argue to the contrary. At one point I worked 60 hours a week, sat on five boards, and attended school working on my graduate degree so I could continue my upward mobility. I had to pay for braces on teeth, a home in a good neighborhood, and nice clothing for all of us. Some Sunday mornings when after a Saturday spent cleaning the house, washing and ironing, and doing the shopping for the week, I made time to take my kids to the mountains. We'd get a campsite by a mountain stream and cook breakfast out of doors. I look back now and wonder how in the hell I did it.

The psychologists who tell the world that kids raised in fatherless homes really do not suffer any sense of loss need to go back to school – and study something else.

One of the most difficult things all women of my generation achieved – those who went beyond the social career norm of the day – was going beyond the limits set for us. I've always been grateful that men more Active than Passive were the ones that invited me into their ballpark to play their game. I'm glad it was they who taught me the rules.

I thank God they did not change the size of the ballpark or reduce their demands on me as a player to accommodate my status as a female. That's what Passive liberals would have done. It is what they have done in the battle for racial equality. It puzzles my logical mind how people can demand set asides and social and educational advantages and call it "equal rights." If you require an advantage to be equal, are you really equal? That goes for both race and gender equality. You may need an initial favor or advantage, but not for more than one generation.

Logic tells me that you cannot say you are my equal and, at the same time, demand special favors and protections. Women must demand equal opportunity but avoid demanding privilege or advantage. Requiring advantage to be equal proves we are not equal. Equals require opportunity, not advantage.

The conservative men of 45-years ago who gave me my pre-affirmative action opportunity are scurrilously attacked by Passive liberals. The picture painted of them is that they are uncaring about females and minorities. They have not in my experience deserved these attacks.

In fact, had the Passive liberals of the new millennium been the ones teaching me to be a banker, their own rhetoric about empowering people dictates they would have condescended to me. They would have set lower standards of performance for me. They would have viewed me as a victim, not an equal. They would count on my gratitude to them and be confident I would overlook the fact that it is not the government's job to empower anyone. In a Republic, it is the job of the people to empower government.

How dare Passive liberals think me less capable than them and lower standards of excellence to "accommodate" my inferior female capabilities! All minorities should react to this kind of condescension with outrage. It is insulting, to say the least!

A MacGruder Axiom: If you mistreat people, watch your back for someone who casts a larger shadow than yours. Shadow sizes change with the movement of the sun.

There is an old saying that dictates water seeks its own level.

What does that mean -- water seeks its own level?

Aside from meaning like attracts like, it means that wherever you as an adult find yourself in life, you are there because that is where you have prepared yourself to be.

Water seeks its own level -- or, like attracts like. It means nature has rules. Some people think they are better at balancing the many delicate life forces that, when left alone, function compatibly. When people mess with Mother Nature – which Passives make a habit of doing – things become unbalanced.

Women are precisely where they have prepared themselves to be in life. They allowed men to keep them in positions of dependency. Most of us enjoyed the advantages of being the keeper of home and family. It gave us the opportunity to love and raise our children.

Yes. It is right that women be equal with men. It is equally right that women understand that to be truly equal, they must earn that status. We must prepare ourselves. There is much about business we largely chose to ignore through the years.

Feminists argue that women were forced to stay out of business. Men preferred to keep them tied to the refrigerator, the stove, the bedpost, and the maternity ward. They don't appear to get it. When women admit that men have forced them to do something, they admit the superiority of men -- even if the superiority is vested only in physical, emotional or economic strength.

Strong, intelligent people do not spend thousands of years complying – against their will – with the desires of others. Intelligent but weak people do. Dumb but strong people do. Intelligent people who are strong do not. Intelligent and strong people may be caught in a social trap for one or two generations before they find an escape. They soon find an escape.

Too often women, typical of Passives, compare their plight to how much worse it can get if they do not play the male dominance game.

If you listen to most Passive liberal arguments, you will hear comparisons with lower, rather than higher, standards. It is a "things could be worse" mentality.

"Sure, we could be doing a better job with our schools. But we are still very good... we rank much higher than (name third world nation ranked 50th) in education (or health care)."

If you listen to most Active conservative arguments, you will hear comparisons with higher standards. It is a "things can be better" mentality.

"Not long ago, our schools were the best in the world. Today, we rank thirty-second in the world in education (or health care)."

Feminists argue that women were inundated with psychological brainwashing throughout history. They were told that the kitchen, bedroom and nursery were their strengths, their havens, and their need. Women needed those things to be happy. The brainwashers may have been largely right. A very large percentage of women do require those strengths to be happy.

I lived that life, understand it, and agree with the statement. Again I say: strong and intelligent people do not let others define for them their life's purpose. Brave women throughout history have understood this concept. They achieved in spite of social restrictions placed upon them. They did not wait for someone to give them a hand-up into the saddle. They put their foot in the stirrup, lifted themselves up, and rode to their destinations. They were the exception, not the rule. Until women understand that is what they must do, they resist the very responsibilities that make them male equals.

Within certain parameters, female destinies are in female hands. Important parameters of responsible commitment must be honored, however.

After childbirth, women have one primary responsibility: Motherhood. Women who want a career should have the opportunity to compete on an equal basis for that career. Once women have children, however, a choice has been made. A woman may be very devoted to her career, but children come first. A purpose has been created. This is your saddle and this is your stirrup. This horse you will ride to the parenting destination. Ride well and proudly... and prepare yourself for your career which can be more dedicated after the kids leave home.

Children need the loving hands of a mother to put small feet on a path to self-love and self-respect. If their own mothers do not love them enough to stay home and see to their well-being, why should they have any sense of self-worth? They need the interested ear and the loving hands of a mother when they come home from school in the afternoon. Social circumstances may make it impossible for women to be there immediately after school, but by understanding that their children need their love, affection and attention it can help women create the highest quality time with their children it is possible for them to create.

Does any thinking person believe a day care stranger knows enough about each of the many children they tend to fulfill the child's need to be loved? Children need the involved heart of a mother when a bad day shatters youthful dreams. How significant are school bullies in the lives of children when there is an attentive parent at home to share their sense of degradation and despair? Does anyone think young adults share such feelings of inadequacy with a stranger?

There are cases where there is no choice. I had to save my children from a father who had caused and would continue to cause egregious harm to them had I stayed. We had breakfast thirty years later. He told me I did the right thing when I left. I had to leave. It happens.

Once you have children, your life responsibilities and priorities focus on them for the next eighteen years. If you do not want to meet those responsibilities, avoid parenting until you do. There is no way to give to children what they need when you are not in the home to greet them each day. If I have one regret in life, it is that my husband's errant choices caused me to miss much of my children's growth to adulthood.

Today's world demands mothers, both married and divorced, work. If you want to both work and be a mother, it requires a deep understanding of what quality family life is all about and planning skills to help you achieve the quality time required. It means family dinners where there are no cell phones allowed; just family conversation. It means children learning to adhere to schedules and house rules because children need them to learn self-discipline. It can be done, but it isn't being done in today's millennial families.

A MacGruder Axiom: How do we, as women, define equality? By walking out on our responsibilities as mothers?

I remember very well taking my first step into a man's world. Actually, in the 1970s there was only one step. Once taken, it could not be reversed. Like Eve, once a bite from the Tree of Knowledge was been taken, you could not pretend you did not see your nakedness -- or that of Adam. Those who make and implement business decisions are more assertive than are those who do not make them. Assertiveness becomes a natural part of the personality... a trait I was taught was unfeminine.

I worked at United Bank of Denver. I was a single mother with no child support from a father who deserted his children. I was the one responsible for being both mother and father. Physical, financial, mental and, to the degree possible, emotional support for three people is a huge (and very tiring) job. It becomes bigger – and lonelier and more tiring – every year that follows the first one. Even mothers, at some point, want to enjoy a sense of human individuality.

There were no role models when I took that first step over the line... from a support role in marketing to a credit management role. "Support role" in banking means a non-lending job. Specifically, it means having no credit authority.

In the 1970s, it was totally acceptable for women to hold bank management and vice-president titles in marketing and personnel ... credit support roles. It was not yet okay for us to take higher-paying lending jobs away from men or to wield the power of large credit authorities. It was not okay with other women in the bank for me to move from a support role to a credit management role. It totally surprised me. I thought I had opened new career doors for them. Rather, they viewed me as having removed their excuses not to work hard enough to make it into credit management jobs.

> **A MacGruder Axiom: Women view men who walk away from their family responsibilities as scurrilous dogs. Why is it okay for women to desert their children for the workplace?**

I think it must be lonely to be the first woman to do anything. In those days, you were suddenly playing by "their" rules. I remember very well making logical management decisions and feeling a loss of my sense of femininity. It was a different era, remember. As I said, other women were less than helpful. They had their standards of feminine behavior and I was expected to live up to them... or, be considered less than feminine. In the 1970s, decision-making in an area exclusively reserved for men was an unfeminine trait.

The men on the management team on which I found myself also had their standards. Unlike the women, their standards had to do only with my management role, my performance as a credit manager and officer of the bank. The fact that their expectations of me conflicted with feminine behavioral standards of the time was noticed only by me. I sometimes felt like I was being cut in half.

A MacGruder Axiom: You are what you think ... and you are the one who controls your thoughts.

Did decision-making cast doubt on my femininity? Not to me. Out of frustration, I simply decided one day that because I was a female, that, in and of itself, made me feminine. If others, male or female, had a problem with their image of my femininity, it was their problem. Not mine. Since I've never had the desire to be anything but a female, it was a decision that saved my sanity.

I wasn't a man. I was not performing or behaving like a man. Rather, I was performing and behaving like a bank vice president in charge of a major loan and deposit portfolio.

Neither was I performing or behaving like a woman of the 1970s.

In fact, I was quite alone.

As a woman who took that first step into a man's world, I can tell you what universities and research facilities have spent millions upon millions of dollars to investigate. Women are different from men. In fact, the female principle is 180 degrees the opposite of the male principle.

The biggest lesson I learned from my experiences is how to face my fears. It gives you a wonderful sense of freedom. It makes you into a very positive person who is not afraid to have hopes and dreams or to pursue them with energetic vigor. It is an experience almost all Active conservatives share.

I also learned that the biggest mistake women can make in their attempts to declare themselves equal with men is to lose their unique sense of being male opposites.

Feminists of the new millennium appear to me to imitate male behavior. It became very noticeable as I traveled around the country during the 1980s, consulting for banks. From New York to San Francisco, from Seattle to Miami, women in banking dressed like men. They talked like men. It was feminist macho to emulate men.

Since their achievements occur in a traditionally male domain, it seems logical to think that is what they should be doing.

I disagree. In my world, women have very strong traits uniquely their own. They should be highly valued by society and the business community. They would be if women started acting like their very strong, valuable feminine traits have value.

> *A MacGruder Axiom: What do you want to do? Be a parent? A professional? Success requires personal commitment and a sense of purpose. Find your purpose, commit to it.*

Because women have emulated men rather than exhibit feminine strengths in the world of business, their potential lays dormant. It is difficult to earn respect for female strengths when women, by emulating males, compete from a position of weakness rather than strength. What comes naturally to anyone – what has been handed down from generation to generation for more than a thousand years – is a strength with which no one who has not had that experience can compete. Existing business standards are filled with black and white arrows pointing to male strengths as representing the road to success. It would be pretty stupid for women to paint a new sign, right?

What can women bring to the business world that it currently lacks?

How about true compassion? Men tend to intellectualize it. Women feel it in their hearts and souls. How about intuition? How about gentility? Or common sense? How about an inbred-by-nature security drive? Security is a long-term thing, not something one achieves today that will come back and bite one in the ass a year from now -- like manufacturing faulty tires that kill people, then denying it even when the evidence is overwhelming.

"But," you might say, "business isn't compassionate. It doesn't function on intuition. It isn't gentle ... and, often it uses little common sense. And you've said business is about managing risk, not eliminating it."

You'd be right on all counts. Regarding the last point, managing risk does not mean ignoring it. Ideally it means pitting a totally competitive and high-risk nature against its totally security-driven opposite. It provides intelligent balance. It is called Yin and Yang by the Chinese.

If men and women functioned in the world of business as true equals, a sense of risk management skills that come naturally to men would be offset by the security drives that come naturally to women. Balance would result. Actives would function compatibly with Passives – just as nature intended.

Companies would be properly competitive. Attention would be paid to short-term profits. Security-conscious women would ensure a positive long-term profit future. You would not have a tire company denying that its tires kill people, then admitting that they do. You would not have a major U.S. auto manufacturer producing cars with gas tanks that explode, burning people to death. The feminine security-drive and sense of compassion would eliminate the need for costly corporate cover-ups. Tobacco companies would have admitted that nicotine is addictive far sooner than they did. Companies would not be cooking their books to falsely attract investor dollars to their stock offerings.

If the world of business gave equal respect to women's intuition as to men's ability to crunch numbers, the marketplace of ideas would be greatly broadened. It did not take a lot of intuitive skill to see the personal computer was going to revolutionize the information industry.

I sat next to an IBM executive on a flight into Palm Springs from Dallas in 1985. I asked why that company had, to that point in time, avoided becoming more aggressive in the personal computer market. The answer was that they had no intuitive sense of what was coming.

If businesses recognized the importance of intuitive skills, that would not have happened. IBM would not have lost billions of dollars to Microsoft and Apple Computers.

> **A MacGruder Axiom: Before you try walking in someone else's shoes, be sure your own are in a safe place.**

In other words, because business has always been male dominated, it reflects male strengths. Competitive business plans that harm consumers lack feminine compassion. It places short-term corporate good in opposition to long-term business survival. The CEO at United Airlines got taught this lesson very recently.

Risk management that succeeds in the short-term but fails in the long-term means the competitive drive is too strong. The feminine security need is lacking.

Spending too much in the short-term results in long-term cost cutting. Such stupidity is unnecessary when the common sense of most housewives is applied. No one understands cost efficiency better than women. Men understand cutting costs (cost effectiveness) as a means to achieve economic objectives. They sometimes spend irresponsibly until economics causes them to rein in their appetites. When companies are cost efficient (the female security drive makes women save for tomorrow), the need to constantly cut costs is eliminated ... along with all of the human pain caused by the jobs that are eliminated as costs are cut.

If the business world functioned at an optimum level, it would work in concert with the Laws of Nature. Women would be encouraged to bring to the corporate table their natural talents rather than feeling they must adopt male strengths to compete effectively. Female strengths would then be integrated with male strengths within the business environment.

Since the beginning of time, nature has created balance at the highest possible point of positive action by placing two equally strong forces in opposition to one another. In this case male and female.

In such an environment, women's femininity would be valued, not derided. Men would be encouraged to exercise their strengths (which are female weaknesses), and women would be encouraged to exercise their strengths (which are male weaknesses).

Instead, most women leave their female strengths outside the doors of their offices each day. They compete with men whose strengths set the standards for performance. It is logical that when one group competes from a position of weaknesses with a group using its strengths, the group using its weaknesses suffers a disadvantage. If feminists were a little less demanding and a little more open-minded, they might even begin to realize that the reason they earn less money for similar work is because they compete from positions of weakness, not strength.

Can women walk into the world of business and demand to have their as yet unrecognized strengths written into next year's corporate business plan? Of course not! They can, however, do what over one-third of America's business owners do: become independent, hire and utilize male strengths in concert with their own, and set a successful business example the giants of commerce cannot ignore.

Additionally, they can avoid falling into the trap of forgetting their feminine strengths.

When women avoid imitating men as the primary means of seeking equality, they will be on the true road to equality. Moreover, while avoiding the loss of their feminine identities, they can gain respect for their strengths.

How? By making the strengths work for the corporation. Gently... as is the way with feminine women. We created the concept of an iron fist in a velvet glove. Ask any mother.

A MacGruder Axiom: Carbon copies are always just that: Copies. Value is found in originality.

www.ingramcontent.com/pod-product-compliance
Lightning Source LLC
Chambersburg PA
CBHW030050100526
44591CB00008B/93